Toward Genuine
Global Governance

Toward Genuine Global Governance

Critical Reactions to "Our Global Neighborhood"

Edited by
Errol E. Harris and James A. Yunker

Westport, Connecticut
London

Library of Congress Cataloging-in-Publication Data

Toward genuine global governance : critical reactions to "our
    global neighborhood" / edited by Errol E. Harris and James A.
    Yunker.
        p.   cm.
    Includes bibliographical references and index.
    ISBN 0–275–96417–5 (alk. paper)
        1. International organization.   I. Harris, Errol E.   II. Yunker,
    James A.
    JZ5566.T69   1999
    327—dc21   98–47746

British Library Cataloguing in Publication Data is available.

Library of Congress Catalog Card Number: 98–47746
ISBN: 0–275–96417–5

First published in 1999

Praeger Publishers, 88 Post Road West, Westport, CT 06881
An imprint of Greenwood Publishing Group, Inc.
www.praeger.com

Printed in the United States of America

The paper used in this book complies with the
Permanent Paper Standard issued by the National
Information Standards Organization (Z39.48–1984).

10 9 8 7 6 5 4 3 2 1

Copyright Acknowledgments

The editors and publisher gratefully acknowledge permission to reprint the following materials:

A Call to Action, the summary of "Our Global Neighborhood" (Report of the Commission on Global Governance), Oxford University Press, 1995.

Richard Falk, "Liberalism at the Global Level: The Last of the Independent Commissions?" © *Millennium: Journal of International Studies*. This article first appeared in *Millennium*, Vol. 24, No. 3, 1995, and is reproduced with the permission of the publisher.

Philip Isely, "A Critique of 'Our Global Neighborhood' " and its appendix "A Bill of Particulars: Why the United Nations Must Be Replaced," World Constitution and Parliament Association, 8800 West 14th Ave., Lakewood, CO 80215.

Contents

Preface

It is a basic tenet among world federalists that the prospects of human civilization upon the planet Earth would be dramatically improved by the immediate formation of a genuine world government. At the present time, this judgment is shared by only a tiny fraction of the world's population. The predominant judgment remains that the establishment of a legitimate state entity superior to the national governments at the present point in human history could and would dangerously destabilize a delicate international equilibrium, leading either to totalitarian despotism or to devastating civil war. Therefore (in the predominant judgment), our hopes for peace and progress must necessarily continue to reside mainly with the balance of power—the stability of which is hopefully being augmented by the gradual strengthening of tolerant, cosmopolitan, and internationalist attitudes among both the general population and its political leadership.

Nevertheless, few of those who subscribe to this predominant judgment of the present day are completely happy with it. The peril of relying on the balance of power among sovereign nation-states has been amply demonstrated by the two world wars of the first half of the twentieth century. On top of that, most of the second half of the twentieth century was blighted by a nuclear arms race between the superpowers that might easily have resulted in a catastrophic nuclear world war. Although the Cold War has receded greatly during the 1990s, memories of it are still fresh. Modern history clearly demonstrates the strong propensity of the sovereign nation-state system to generate international confrontation and conflict, so that the very dangerous conditions created by the Cold War of the recent past might easily be replicated by new—and presently unanticipated—conflicts in the near future. At the same time, the marvelous technological advances of the contemporary era in communications and transportation have greatly reduced the practical relevance of distance as a barrier to world government.

The idea of a world government embracing the whole of humanity is, in fact, a potent idea with strong inherent appeal. Such a universalist government would serve both utilitarian and psychological purposes. The League of Nations, founded at the conclusion of World War I, represented a first effort at such a government. However, the League of Nations was thoroughly discredited by its inability to forestall World War II. At the end of World War II, a second effort was made to establish a universalist world government: the United Nations. Unfortunately, the United Nations was unable to forestall the perilous Cold War confrontation between the superpowers which threatened the very survival of humanity. The recedence of the Cold War threat to human survival in the 1990s must be attributed not to the United Nations, but rather mainly to internal political developments within the ex-Soviet Union.

The end of World War I in 1918 presented humanity with a precious opportunity to greatly advance the cause of international organization. The end of World War II in 1945 presented humanity with a second such opportunity. Similarly, the end of the Cold War in the early 1990s presented humanity with a third such opportunity. As the first opportunity resulted in the League of Nations, and the second opportunity resulted in the United Nations, both of which must be regarded—despite their shortcomings—as historic milestones in the development of international organization, it seems natural that the third opportunity might result in a further advance.

Thus, considerable interest and anticipation were aroused throughout the world by the 1991 Stockholm Initiative on Global Security and Governance, which resulted in the formation of the Commission on Global Governance. The Commission, consisting of 28 eminent individuals from many countries and all walks of life, received a high level of support from the United Nations, several national governments, and a host of private organizations. Its final Report, entitled *Our Global Neighborhood*, was published by Oxford University Press in 1995.

Even its admirers must concede that the Report of the Commission on Global Governance is a very cautious, conservative, and limited document. It endorses the basic structure and operations of the existing United Nations, explicitly rejects world government, and proposes that primary reliance toward the objective of enhanced international security and further human progress be placed on the gradual development of properly enlightened, tolerant, humanitarian, and cosmopolitan attitudes among both the general human population and its political leaders. A few small innovations are proposed in the Report, but they are too minor to arouse much interest or enthusiasm. Most likely these innovations will not be adopted, but even if they are adopted, their practical impact on international conditions is likely to be immeasurably small.

Among world federalists, disappointment with the Report has been especially intense. An opportunity was presented to the Commission to strike a powerful blow toward the cause of world government—and the opportunity was wasted. Apparently, the members of the Commission did not themselves possess those precious qualities of vision and leadership that are strongly and repeatedly urged upon the readers of the Commission's Report. It is particularly galling to world federalists that the Report does not discuss or even take notice of the abundant literature in favor of world government produced over the course of the twentieth century by numerous proponents of world federalism. Even the mere possibility of world government is dismissed categorically and summarily by the Commission. In a volume which purportedly deals comprehensively with "global governance," this blanket dismissal is veritably insulting to the many talented and dedicated men and women, past and present, who have argued the case for world government.

This volume collects several critical essays on *Our Global Neighborhood* by individuals associated with world federalism. With the single exception of Richard Falk, all of the contributors have published books and/or articles in the past that explicitly endorse some type of world government qualitatively beyond the United Nations of the present day. (Prof. Falk, while not a "card-carrying world federalist," clearly represents the most sympathetic attitude toward world federalism to be found among mainstream authorities on international organization.)

Although all of the essays have in common a highly negative viewpoint on the Report of the Commission on Global Governance, aside from that they are quite diverse. The approaches range from the general philosophical background to world federalism of Glen T. Martin ("A Planetary Paradigm for Global Government"), to the specific institutional proposal for a Federal Union of Democratic Nations of James A. Yunker ("A Pragmatic Route to Genuine Global Governance"). Richard Falk ("Liberalism at the Global Level") skeptically examines the notion of the independent commission as a route to significant innovation in international organization and questions the implicit judgment of the Commission, an apparent product of the laissez-faire zeitgeist of the current moment, that governments are inherently untrustworthy and that human progress must be achieved mainly through independent, voluntary action by individuals and small groups. Several of the contributors, especially John C. de V. Roberts ("Governance—An Opportunity?"), Ronald J. Glossop ("Global Governance Requires Global Government"), Errol E. Harris ("Global Governance or World Government?"), and Philip Isely ("Critique of Our Global Neighborhood"), focus on the remarkable—and to a world federalist veritably mind-boggling—inconsistency of the Commission in simultaneously preaching the cause of "global govenance," while explicitly ruling out, with virtually no discussion, any sort of "global government." David Ray Griffin ("Global Government: Objections Considered") responds to the various objections to world government implicitly and uncritically accepted by the Commission on Global Governance. Jean-Marie Breton delivers a "line-by-line" indictment of the Report from the point of view of a "world citizen." Finally, Errol E. Harris, co-editor of the anthology, provides brief descriptions and comments on the included essays in a final chapter entitled "Summary and Conclusion."

Some of the contributors to this volume have been active in various world federalist organizations. Philip Isely is the founder and secretary-general of the World Constitution and Parliament Association, while Jean-Marie Breton is the Secretary-General of the International Registry of Citizens of the World. Ronald J. Glossop is a vice-president of the World Federalist Association. Most of the contributors are university professors, either currently or emeritus. Glossop, Griffin, Harris, and Martin are philosophers, Roberts is an historian, Falk is a political scientist, and Yunker is an economist.

Although the initial impetus to each of these essays has been a negative reaction by the respective essay's author to *Our Global Neighborhood*, it should not be concluded that this anthology is merely destructive criticism and offers nothing of a positive nature to the literature on international organization and world peace. To the contrary, this volume represents *constructive* criticism. The authors put forward a clearly defined alternative to the unimaginative approach of the Commission on Global Governance. That alternative is world government: *genuine global governance through the instrumentality of a global government*. Beyond this basic alternative, the authors provide considerable specific discussion of the precise whys and hows of world government. It is *destructive* criticism when the critic merely dismisses a certain approach without offering any sensible alternative to it. None of the contributors to this volume are guilty of destructive criticism.

While the Report of the Commission on Global Governance is obviously a deep disappointment to world federalists, some solace must be found in the fact that the Commission was indeed established, was authorized to study and recommend on the subject of "global governance," and was given substantial support by both government and private organizations. This in itself is evidence of an increasing level of interest in the subject of international organization in general and world government in particular. Perhaps the discussions generated by the appearance of the Commission Report, including this one, will contribute to the degree of education and enlightenment necessary for humanity to recognize that world government, despite the current consensus to the contrary, is in fact both feasible and desirable. It is to be hoped that this recognition will dawn upon humanity before human civilization is engulfed in a terrible and irretrievable calamity brought on by the sovereign nation-state system of today.

The nature and flavor of the Commission Report published in 1995 is clearly suggested by the numerous quotations from it provided by the authors of the critical essays included in this volume. But for those readers who desire more extended exposure to the Report, and who may not have convenient access to it, the final chapter of the Report is published herein as Appendix I ("A Call to Action: Summary of Our 'Global Neighborhood'"). Our deep appreciation is expressed to the Commission on Global Governance and to Oxford University Press for permission to reprint this material.

James A. Yunker

Chapter 1

A Planetary Paradigm
for Global Government
Glen T. Martin

The unleashed power of the atom has changed everything except our way of thinking. Thus we are drifting towards a catastrophe beyond comparison. We shall require a substantially new manner of thinking if mankind is to survive.

—Albert Einstein

THE LIMITED ASSUMPTIONS OF MODERNITY

A common theme in textbooks on the history of Western civilization is the idea that reason was emancipated from "blind faith" during the Middle Ages, an emancipation that made possible the rise of modern science and technology, the spirit of free inquiry, the growth of democratic theory with its ideas of equal rights for all persons, the development of free enterprise, and other important features of "the modern spirit."[1] Indeed, these significant developments have spread worldwide in the twentieth century and to a great many appear to hold tremendous promise, the promise of a free, decent, secure, and humane life for all or most inhabitants of our planet. Yet many of the twentieth century's most significant thinkers have raised profound questions about this seeming promise. Thinkers from otherwise differing philosophical orientations have recognized that the appalling history of the twentieth century reflects a very deep failing at the heart of our modern world. Works by such thinkers as Masao Abe, Nicolas Berdyaev, Martin Buber, Eric Fromm, Jürgen Habermas, Martin Heidegger, Karl Jaspers, Nishitani Keiji, Gabriel Marcel, Herbert Marcuse, Max Picard, and Ludwig Wittgenstein have seen the promise of the modern world twisted into a sort of human nightmare that has characterized much of the present century.

After nearly 500 years of modernity, instead of science and technology giving us a world of health, adequate food, and material abundance, we have a world where one fifth of its population face starvation, sickness, and death. Instead of a world of democracy, freedom, and respect for human rights, the twentieth century has given us mass murder, torture, and genocide beyond all comprehension. Instead of a world of peace and security, our century is one of militarism and perpetual war. Apparently, the common view of the promise of reason emancipated from dogma, authority, and blind faith of the Middle Ages is a vast oversimplification concerning modernity. What deeper assumptions lie at the heart of the modern spirit that complicate the so-called promise of an emancipated reason?

In addition to development of science and technology and largely Newtonian assumptions about the nature of the physical universe, the modern era has been characterized by several other developments that have become dominant features of our twentieth-century "world system." First, modernity has seen the rise of sovereign nation-states with the attendant phenomenon of nationalism. The present world system is structured around assumptions about "sovereign territory" of each nation, "sovereign authority" over the internal affairs of each nation, and "sovereign independence" in the relations between more than 180 autonomous units of this system. Nearly all the major events of the twentieth century have revolved around this international structure of competing and conflicting nation-states. A second fundamental development of the modern era has been the rise of capitalism with its gigantic institutions devoted to private profit. At present, there are very few places on the planet not yet integrated into the global system of capital and finance, a system of transnational corporations often quite independent of the particular nations within which they do business. If some American Indian tribes follow the "rule of seven," in which decisions made today should reflect the needs of seven generations into the future, many modern corporations tend to follow the rule of "quarterly profits" in which even the immediate future is sacrificed to the current needs of investors and owners. If profits, with the financial and industrial institutions that serve them, require only so many jobs and consumers, then, in the words of Noam Chomsky, "most of the species becomes superfluous."[2]

If thinkers such as Martin Heidegger have some insight, in addition to these phenomena the modern era has been characterized by a metaphysic focused even more completely on the will (rather than reason) as ultimate reality, giving rise to philosophies (such as those of Schopenhauer and Nietzsche) and movements (such as fascism) focused on will, will to power, and domination.[3] Are these deep currents of modernity linked together in ways that undercut the democratic promise of an emancipated reason? Is there a drive based on sheer will, will to power, and domination, which has characterized the nationalism, ethnocentrism, and capitalism of the modern era, and which has flooded and all but drowned the voices of democracy, equality, and human dignity that have struggled for recognition? One recalls the unspeakable brutality of the conquistadors, the European conquests of large areas of the world, the era of slavery, the period of colonialism with its oppression and exploitation of non-European peoples, which devolved into the brutalities of neocolonial imperialism that persist even today. To compound these power-based drives, the modern world has continued to experience the virulent forces of perpetual war, racism, male domination of women, and cultural and religious hatreds that have proven so destructive right up to the final decade of the twentieth century. Is there a way of understanding the modern spirit that draws together all these negative forces in opposition to the hope for a more democratic, global world order?

A number of contemporary thinkers have pointed to the problem of the "self" as at the heart of our deep internal contradictions and seemingly uncontrollable passions on both personal and social levels. A growing philosophical literature, including several of the authors previously mentioned, has pointed to a flawed human self-understanding based on the mistaken premise of a real, substantial self, somehow existing prior to its relations with others. This assumption that we exist as independent egos over and against one another has as a corollary our definition of ourselves as *not being the other*, a phenomenon that also generates our larger tendency toward collective egos: entire groups or nations, defining themselves over and against one another. Selves defined in this atomistic fashion find themselves trapped in relations of fear (and often hatred) of the others whom they necessarily define as the "other," as not what we are. Our very self-understanding requires egoistic assertion over and against what is defined as "not self."

The corresponding impulse of such isolated and fearful selves is a drive for power and domination to engulf the other as conquered, colonial, slave, or inferior. The isolated and unrelated modern self is riddled with disease and discontent, a compulsive longing never satisfied. It compulsively seeks to appropriate what is not self (in the forms of property, consumption, conquest, or spiritual devaluation of the other). The fundamental characteristics of modernity outlined earlier may all be rooted, one way or another, in such false assumptions about the human self. During the Middle Ages, for all their brutality, the fearful egoistic self was restrained within a larger framework of seemingly universal faith, and an apparently objective moral outlook. But with the collapse of medieval civilization and this restraining framework, it was not only reason that was unleashed to create modernity; it was the individual and collective ego emerging into an ever more pluralistic world, lacking any framework to control or restrain its collective or individual egoistic self-assertions.

At the onset of the modern era science and technology were soon born, but rather than being used to create housing, health, and well-being for civilization, these were put in the service of individual and collective egos acting on the assumption of an autonomous will with its nearly inevitable desire for power, self-promotion, and domination of self and others. Modern capitalism soon evolved, premised, as Adam Smith and John Stuart Mill argued, on the notion of independent, autonomous, individual egos, acting out of rational self-interest and competing in an open marketplace that would generate an "invisible hand" from which would result "the greatest good of the greatest number." Instead, we have discovered a tendency toward huge concentrations of wealth which are institutionalized to create further wealth via exploitative relationships, together with massive accumulations of poverty and misery that today, in terms of the category of "absolute poverty" alone, comprise over one billion of the earth's citizens. The autonomous, sovereign nation-state was also born, soon evolving the idea of a "social contract" in which the government and rulers were responsible for the security and wellbeing of their citizens. Instead, we have frequently experienced brutal oppression of citizens within nations and the rise of virulent nationalism in external relations: collective identities exacerbating war, hatred, and the internecine will to power of rival nation-states.

The modern era born during the Renaissance has given us an increasingly anarchic world lacking any framework for restraining egoistic will to power as this is manifested through the scientific and technical drive for domination, the institutionalized greed of the capitalist pursuit of profit, or the nationalist imperative for the economic and political self-promotion of nation-states over and against all other citizens of the planet. When Einstein wrote that "the unleashed power of the atom has changed everything except our way of thinking," he was not referring only to the idea that we must learn to deal with nuclear weapons. He was speaking of the deep assumptions of creatures who have so much scientific and technological power in their hands, yet so little wisdom. He was speaking of a "substantially new manner of thinking," a new paradigm for human life that is required if we are to survive on this planet.

The seemingly insurmountable problems of the modern world are functions of assumptions we make about ourselves that remain largely unquestioned and unexamined: the assumption of an inevitable "progress" corresponding with scientific and technical research, the assumption of the sovereign nation-state as the only legitimate form of governance, the assumption of the legitimacy of unrestrained private accumulation of wealth at the expense of others. Yet at the root of each of these are assumptions about the human self that remain unexamined and hidden from view. In a world of ever-increasing multiplicity of power centers, voices, languages, cultures, religions, philosophies, and customs, we can no longer afford to let the assumption of an individual or collective ego-self remain unquestioned. Indeed, several of the thinkers noted earlier have focused on the problem of the self as part of the growing consensus of philosophical voices that see the question of the self as absolutely basic. Let me mention here just one of these thinkers. The contemporary German philosopher Jürgen Habermas has been building on the work of Immanuel Kant, Ludwig Wittgenstein, Karl Marx, and the social pragmatist George Herbert Mead, toward an understanding of the basic presuppositions of all human language and forms of communication.[4] These presuppositions of all possible human communication, for Habermas, reveal *the human self as fundamentally relational.* Philosophical study of the roots of communication seems to reveal the self as arising in and through a matrix of culture and language, not as autonomously existing prior to culture and language.

If the human self is indeed fundamentally relational, our tendency to define ourselves over and against the other *as other* is cut off at the very start. Our tendency to see differences as hostile and foreign to ourselves, to cling to our self-identities as being what we are and *not* what they are, and to promote our own interests and desires in opposition to theirs is understood to involve a fallacious understanding of being human. Is it possible that human beings might understand and ultimately experience themselves in new ways that could deal with the global crises that we face in the late twentieth century? Is it possible to create concrete institutions that promote a relational self whose identity and destiny are inextricably linked to the identity and destiny of all others on the planet, and whose destiny is understood as fully interdependent with the destiny of the fragile ecostructure of our planetary environment? How might such a new understanding of the human self help provide a framework for thinking about the problem of global governance within a world facing planetary crises on a scale that calls into question the very probability of human survival beyond the next century?

A PLANETARY PARADIGM

The many-sided global crises facing our world have moved us to a planetary scale regardless of our intentions or assumptions. The population explosion, projecting an earthly population of some 9 or more billion by the year 2025, is utterly beyond the scope of any existing earthly institutions to deal with. Massive poverty and starvation, encompassing one-fifth of the earth's population and steadily growing, seem out of control of the best intentioned efforts of the United Nations and others. Widespread destruction of forests and phytoplankton in the oceans, occurring on a massive scale, could mean the disappearance of those very ecosystems that produce the oxygen we breathe and bond the carbon dioxide that we produce. Soil erosion from unsustainable agricultural practices amounts to hundreds of billions of tons per year, pointing forward to a future Earth that will be largely desert, unable to grow food for its inhabitants. Depletion of the ozone layer, which filters the sun's lethal ultra-violet radiation and protects all living creatures on the planet, is already at an advanced stage. These are but a few of the crises that exist on a planetary scale, while none of our institutions are truly planetary in scope, predicated as they are on the limited assumptions of modernity. Finally, global militarism, with the production and distribution of weapons worldwide amounting to $1 trillion per year, is intimately linked to the structure of autonomous nation-states, to global poverty, to global economic systems, and to global environmental destruction. All these crises are interdependent and interrelated, part of a system that we clearly cannot control and that many currently have little desire to change.

Yet the possibilities for reconceptualizing our planetary framework have been widely recognized only since the early 1960s, when the first space vehicles began to transmit pictures of the planet back to Earth. For the first time in human history we had witness of a tiny, fragile jewel of a planet floating in the blackness of empty space, a planet that is home to billions of human and other forms, struggling, in the words of the philosopher Nolan Pliny Jacobson, "to become successfully interdependent."[5] For the first time, ordinary citizens of the planet could begin to see themselves as such, understanding that *the Earth is our primary home*, not the community, the city, or the nation (all partial and divisive categories when separated from the whole). Together with the emergent eco-environmental sciences, we could begin to understand this tiny third planet from the sun as having evolved over approximately 5 billion years to form the fragile, interconnected planetary habitat that supports all life on Earth. Indeed, this has led to a growing community of men and women from all nations and walks of life who see themselves as "global citizens," and who work tirelessly, within the United Nations or international nongovernmental organizations, for the betterment of the human condition or the preservation of the environment. Yet, in the absence of a reconceptualization of the dominant institutions and assumptions of the modern era, the best efforts of these global citizens have not been able to reverse a growing sense of planetary failure and despair.

The concept of "democracy," with all that this implies, is an important pointer toward a truly planetary framework. When the US Declaration of Independence of 1776 declared that "we hold these truths to be self-evident, that all persons are created equal, and are endowed by their Creator with certain inalienable rights," it was making a universal, planetary claim which was perhaps incapable of being realized before the twenty-first century. It was a planetary claim made by a small group of wealthy white men, many of them slaveowners, all of them with nearly absolute, nondemocratic control over their wives and daughters, a group by and large totally ignoring the non-property-owning poor and illiterate masses of their own society. (As John Jay wrote at the time: "The people who own the country ought to govern it."[6]) The subsequent century and a half saw the development of democratic thought to the point where this vision of the dignity and equality of all persons was embodied more completely in the 1948 UN Declaration of Human Rights. This includes an elaborated, concrete extension of the democratic vision of planetary equality and dignity, including so-called second generation rights, that identify absolute poverty and starvation as violations of human equality and dignity. For example, Article 25 reads, "Everyone has the right to a standard of living adequate for health and well-being of himself and his family, including food, clothing, housing and medical care and necessary social services, and the right to security in the event of unemployment, sickness, disability, widowhood, old age or other lack of livelihood in circumstances beyond his control." Yet the present "world order" is clearly in massive contradiction with this most elemental of our human rights.

Today it is becoming ever more clear that the universal human rights recognized by the United Nations declaration are incapable of realization within the current world system, where one-fifth of the world's population is in a condition of semistarvation and where war, genocide, and repression of civilian subjects by governments are commonplace. Not only are many nations not democratic, but racism, nationalism, patriarchy, militarism, and many aspects of world economics militate against the realization of this planetary vision of the dignity and equality of all persons. The United Nations itself is a profoundly nondemocratic organization, controlled by the powerful nations which have frequently used their veto to nullify nearly unanimous decisions of the General Assembly. Its Charter is a treaty between sovereign nation-states; it is anything but a world federation. Even if the nations within the General Assembly were to achieve some real voice through having restrictions placed on the veto (unlikely as this is), many of these nations themselves are not internally democratic, and their ambassadors to the UN thus do not represent their people as a whole. In addition, nations are not represented at the UN on the basis of population, so even a majority vote in the General Assembly is profoundly undemocratic in terms of representation of the world's people. The UN is not a planetary organization, but one predicated on the nondemocratic institutions of the modern era. The only viable alternative for actualizing democratic ideals on our planet is a nonmilitary world federation in which the nation-states give over their sovereignty to the people of the Earth, who then elect a government that operates in terms of a truly planetary framework.

The conceptual basis for this democratic vision is not, whatever the US Declaration of Independence seemed to imply, any claim to metaphysical knowledge or the truth of a certain point of view. The religious, cultural, and metaphysical "certainties" of the past are gone forever and cannot be replaced. There is no going back to ontological claims to knowledge about the ultimate reality of things, whether religious or philosophical. The limits of human knowledge are too narrow to countenance metaphysical frameworks, and knowledge itself is too contextual, flexible, pragmatic, and open to revision to serve as a firm basis for a new planetary framework. The rise of religious and cultural fundamentalism and dogmatic ideologies in our day may well be a last historical reaction to the seemingly trackless sea of relativism into which our modern assumptions have led us. The new framework to which I am pointing is not a revitalization of the dead options of the past. Wholeness will become apparent only after we have moved to a genuinely new level of existence and taken our stand upon the relational self and its possibilities for communicative action. The new framework involves moving into relationship, into the dynamic of unity in diversity, not new knowledge claims or metaphysical certainties. This requires only dropping the false assumptions of the past. Within dynamic relationship is where we have been all along (contextual, interdependent, and mutually defining), although we have repeatedly failed to recognize the fact.

Within a planetary framework, the more voices we allow to speak, the more the unity of the whole becomes apparent. The more we let diversity express itself, the more we find the universal forms of discourse being actualized. The whole and the part, unity and multiplicity, arise together within language, and language itself is more and more being recognized as our defining human ability, serving us not as a defining essence but as a myriad of possibilities for community and self-realization. Within the fragmented assumptions of the past—atomistic and individualistic selves, incommensurate ethical and cultural identities, sovereign and absolutistic nation-states, and vast, autonomous, profit-making institutions—there can be no unity in diversity. Fragmentation threatens to overwhelm us, and power becomes the criterion of action regardless of what voices are allowed to speak. Decent men and women tend to become cynical and exhausted about ever realizing democracy, freedom, human dignity, or equality, since these pointers toward unity cannot be adequately realized within the limited assumptions of modernity. Only a planetary framework, giving voice to all human participants within a recognized sovereignty of the whole of humankind, can make possible the realization of respect for the dignity and autonomy of individual differences. As Habermas puts it, "morality... cannot protect the rights of the individual without also protecting the well-being of the community to which he belongs."[7]

It is significant that we see an ever-growing literature concerning inter-religious and intercultural dialogue. The roots of human unity are in dialogue, as Martin Buber made clear in *I and Thou* a half century ago.[8] Selves in authentic dialogue and intent upon communication are open to one another and to the realization that these very selves with their respective identities are realized and continually transformed through the communication process.[9] Such selves are also open to the natural world with which they are deeply interconnected. Interreligious dialogue and intercultural exchange are positive developments that need to be complemented by the development of democratic institutions facilitating and protecting such intercourse. This *communicative action* is fundamentally different from the parasitic modes of discourse that feed upon it and that are often dominant in current institutions: deceptive, strategic, mani-pulative, commercial, or propagandistic uses of language. Just as Kant pointed out that a lie is parasitic (and only possible) on the expectation that people normally tell the truth, so strategic uses of language are parasitic upon the more fundamental dialogical and communicative possibilities of language.

Democracy, in terms of this planetary framework of the relational self and its possibilities for communication, will no longer be the imposition of abstract laws on citizens without recognition of differences; rather, it will involve the genuine realization of freedom and equality through all voices being heard within a communicative context.[10] It will involve the understanding that unity and diversity mutually imply one another, that these arise together in our experience of the world and of human relationships. In contrast to this, the ideological conflict called the Cold War involved in part, an overemphasis on one or the other of these poles. The former Soviet Union emphasized the whole (unity and community) at the expense of the parts (diversity and individual rights). The United States has overemphasized the parts (individual rights and self-interest) at the expense of the whole (the common good). But the mutual interrelationship of the whole and the part can be embodied within well formed human institutions. For example, the "Constitution for the Federation of Earth" proposed by the World Constitution and Parliament Association, in several locations explicitly affirms the mutual entailment of unity and diversity.[11] Even in its Preamble, the proposed Constitution includes the following as a motivation for the establishment of world government: "Conscious that Humanity is One despite the existence of diverse nations, races, creeds, ideologies and cultures, and that the principle of unity in diversity is the basis for a new age when war shall be outlawed and peace prevail; when the Earth's total resources shall be equitably used for human welfare; and when basic human rights and responsibilities shall be shared by all without discrimination; ..."[12]

The notion here that "humanity is one," which involves the "principle of unity in diversity," includes an awareness that the human self is participatory and relational, that rights *and* responsibilities go together, and that our institutions must be premised not only on individual self-interest and diversity but on the principle of equitable use for general "human welfare." Authentic world democracy, like all planetary institutions, must be based on the relational character of human beings and the planetary environment. Whole and part, freedom and responsibility should imply one another on all levels: political, economic, social, cultural, environmental, and spiritual.

Similarly, in his essay "Sovereignty Rests with Mankind," the Japanese Buddhist thinker Masao Abe affirms a sovereignty of humanity in which "the age of nation states as the bearers of history must proclaim its end, and the age of mankind must begin."[13] For Abe, such sovereignty of humankind can arise only with the insight into the "original nature of the Self" in which the individual ego-self, like the "national egoism" that is its collective expression, is transformed into a truly relational self "wherein both self and other are fulfilled."[14] The egoistic assumptions of the modern age, he writes, involve "an age wherein the power of the nation-state alienates the individual from mankind and does not truly enliven either the individual or mankind."[15] In our age "individual, race, class, and nation—endless conflicts that have at their base ego and power," serve to define our inability to transform our assumptions on the basis of "self-negation" in which the whole of mankind is at last recognized as inseparable from individual fulfillment and well-being. The atomistic ego-self, for Abe, like the nation-state that is its collective expression, is at the root of our current global crisis.

By contrast, Abe writes that the sovereignty of humankind (which is established through this "self-negation" of our current divisive institutions of nation-state and ego-self) "encompasses all races and all peoples in their respective particularity. For the human community as a self-aware entity, races and peoples are no longer basic political entities linked by power, but rather are cultural and ethical existences that give life to the individual and that, through the actions of individuals, are harmonized with mankind."[16] We are at the end of a brutal history of partial institutions and limited assumptions, and are ready to move to a new level of existence wherein the whole and the parts arise together, in mutual recognition and fulfillment. It is my thesis that Abe's vision is incorporated in a preliminary way within the proposed Constitution for the Federation of Earth, and that only by moving to a new planetary paradigm, which would include a nonmilitary democratic world government, can human beings survive for long on this planet.

We have seen that the assumptions that provide a framework for action and discussion within any particular era are interdependent and mutually rein- forcing. For this reason we can speak of "the ancient world" or "the medieval world" and discuss the worldview of each with some intelligibility. Similarly, we have discussed the modern world's development of a paradigm involving a number of interrelated assumptions, of which I here review five central ones in order to compare them easily with the larger assumptions of a new planetary paradigm. (1) Beginning with thinkers like Descartes and Galileo and cul- minating in the work of Newton, modern physics was framed around the assumption that the universe involved discrete bodies (matter) in motion within independent spatial and temporal dimensions and governed by the laws of universal gravitation. (2) Science and technology were born under the Baconian idea that "knowledge is power" and were directed, from the Industrial Revolu- tion through to the contemporary electronics revolution, to the technological control and mastery of nature and of people (the latter through military and other applications). (3) Part of this matrix of ideas involved the development of modern economics predicated on individual and corporate self-interest and primarily leaving the general welfare to the operations of uncontrolled market forces (Adam Smith's "invisible hand"). (4) With the birth of the modern world there emerged the principle of independent, territorially autonomous, sovereign nation-states within a competitive and conflictive international situation involv- ing many other sovereign nation-states. (5) Integrally with all of these, we have seen, has been the modern notion of an autonomous ego-self, which, assumed to be independent like the Newtonian atom, promotes its self-interest through its economic activities and the mastery of nature and expresses itself collectively in the forms of nationalism and ethnocentrism.

By contrast, the twentieth century has seen the emergence of many thinkers and scholars pointing to a new paradigm, which I am calling a "planetary paradigm," fundamentally different from the assumptions behind modernity. As with the modern paradigm, the assumptions of the emerging planetary paradigm are interdependent and mutually imply one another. (1) At the level of physics, the new paradigm involves Einsteinian relativity physics, which understands space, time, matter, and energy to be aspects of an interrelated whole, com- prehensible in terms of "fields," rather than as atomistic "bodies in motion." (2) Rather than technological mastery of nature, the emerging paradigm centers on the science of ecology, which understands the interdependence and inter- relationships of fragile living organisms within equally fragile environments and ecosystems, including the planet Earth as itself an encompassing ecosystem. (3) At the level of economics, the planetary paradigm focuses on sustainable development and the responsibility of economic systems to consider the welfare of all the citizens of the planet as well as the welfare of future generations. Rather than relying on an "invisible hand" to deal with the welfare of all, sustainable development requires careful consideration of the impact of techno-logical innovation, careful understanding of the environment and the effects of human economic activity, and a significant degree of democratically guided, socially responsible planning to maximize economic benefits and minimize damage for all concerned. (4) Finally, at the level of political organization, the planetary paradigm requires responsible, nonmilitary, democratic federal world government to replace the fragmented and divisive system of sovereign nation-states in mutual competition and military defensiveness against one another. (5) Involved with all these notions is the relational understanding of the human self: relational like Einstein's field theory, like the ecological model of inter-dependent living things, and like a sustainable economics of cooperation and mutual benefit rather than one of unbridled competition resulting in absolute winners and losers. At the level of political organization, the relational self requires the mutual recognition, participation, and communication among the citizens of the planet possible only on the level of democratic world federation.

THE REPORT OF THE COMMISSION ON GLOBAL GOVERNANCE

The only alternative to adopting a planetary framework is modification of the limited and partial arrangements of the modern era: incremental modifications of those present political, economic, and international institutions that were never conceived or evolved to operate on a truly planetary scale. The United Nations, for example, is explicitly predicated on the assumption of sovereign nation-states, with the corollary assumption of military force to keep order and with the clear and explicit recognition that all treaties and agreements (including membership in the UN itself) are strictly voluntary. The book *Our Global Neighborhood: The Report of the Commission on Global Governance* is an attempt to confront the global crisis of the late twentieth century on precisely these limited assumptions of modernity.[17] This Report is the collective response of twenty-eight diverse world leaders to our global situation and is a synthesis of extensive studies and reports on militarism, poverty, the environment, the situation of women, the UN system, the population explosion, and international law that their Commission has investigated in preparing this Report. As such, the Report is full of valuable information about the present world situation in all these areas and gives the reader insight into how some respected, mainstream world leaders are attempting to deal with the situation. The Commission calls for a new generation of emerging world leadership to take up their vision and confront our global crisis. "The world needs leaders," they tell us, "made strong by vision, sustained by ethics, and revealed by political courage that looks beyond the next election."[18] Yet the "vision" they promote is not a planetary vision, but the limited and utterly failed "vision" based on the outmoded assumptions and institutions of the modern era.

After laying out a picture of the world situation in Chapter 1, this Report continues to fill out the details of the major world problems in its subsequent chapters while arguing for specific proposals on how governments, the UN, NGOs, and world citizens can take action to deal with these problems. Chapter 2 argues for "a global civil ethic" centering on democratic rights and responsibilities and the "neighborhood values" of "respect for life, liberty, justice and equality, mutual respect, caring, and integrity." Despite its many practical proposals, these value recommendations constitute the central theme of the Commission Report. These world leaders are urging governments, multinational corporations, and citizens of the Earth to adopt a new attitude before it is too late. They continually reiterate the need for change, for example, by quoting Vaclav Havel's address to the US Congress in 1990, in which he affirmed that "without a global revolution in the sphere of human consciousness, nothing will change for the better in our being as humans, and the catastrophe towards which our world is headed will become unavoidable."[19]

Chapter 3 is concerned with "promoting security" for people and the planet. The Commission proposes revision of the UN Charter enabling the Security Council to authorize military action within countries, on extreme humanitarian grounds, when a people's security is violated. They propose a permanent rapid deployment force under the authority of the Security Council, the cost of which would be integrated into the annual budget of the UN. They also propose the progressive elimination of all nuclear weapons and ratification of existing biological and chemical weapons conventions. Chapter 4 (by far the longest) concerns "global economic governance." Among its several proposals, the central ones include (1) establishing an Economic Security Council within the UN not larger than the Security Council, but including the "world's largest economies," to oversee trade and sustainable development worldwide (one wonders how the world's largest economies can promote "sustainable" development); (2) establishing new rules through the World Trade Organization to "strengthen global competition"; (3) making some reforms in the International Monetary Fund and World Bank to make them "more democratic"; and (4) creating an international tax and other charges for the use of global commons in order "to provide money for global purposes."

Chapters 5 and 6 concern reforming the UN and strengthening the rule of law worldwide. The Commission recommends enlarging the number of nonpermanent members on the Security Council and *voluntary restraint* by the permanent members in using the veto—with a view to phasing out the veto after ten years of this practice. They urge greater funding for the UN and recommend that all nations pay their assessed dues on time. They recommend that it be made mandatory to refer disputes over international law to the World Court, and the establishment of an International Criminal Court. To "enforce international law," the Commission recommends working to establish respect for "universally recognized norms and values" and, failing this, economic sanctions and/or military enforcement by the Security Council. Chapter 7 reviews their main proposals and calls for the new world leaders referred to before who are to have the "vision" to move the world and its institutions forward in confronting the global crisis.

The Commission's Report adduces the facts, alluded to above, that show a rapidly deteriorating global environment, rampant world militarism, a condition of absolute poverty for a large portion of the world's citizens, massive violations of human rights amounting to near genocide in some places, and an unchecked population explosion. They tell us that "the new generation knows how close they stand to cataclysms" and that without immediate drastic action "the alternative is too frightening to contemplate."[20] Yet their agony and concern over the world situation take the form merely of urging people to change their ways, to "care," as the Commissioners themselves apparently do, and to act with responsibility and integrity.

In this Report there are no causal roots of the world crisis. Massive poverty just happens; no one is responsible for it. Massive destruction of the environment is just a fact to be described. No institutional arrangements or systems need be blamed for the ongoing destruction of the Earth. Genocide and massive torture and murder of citizens by governments seem to happen simply because all people have not yet adopted the recommended ethic of care and concern. The Report is very circumspect about assigning responsibility to any of the major power players on today's world stage. Multinational corporations, global financial institutions, and the ruling nation-states in the world system come across as actors that have occasionally made some mistakes but, with adoption of the recommended "global civil ethic" of care and concern, would basically be on the right course for dealing with the multifaceted planetary crisis. Worse yet, the Report of the Commission on Global Governance is utterly unhistorical. The Commissioners carefully avoid understanding our present world system in terms of the historical development of modernity, from the conquistadors and world conquests of the European nations and the institutionalization of slavery, to the giant colonial systems designed and operated to exploit the resources and people of conquered nations, to the neocolonial political, economic, and military relationships that today contribute so deeply to our global situation.

It is apparently unthinkable to these Commissioners that world militarism, widespread poverty and misery, massive violations of human rights, and destruction of the environment might be institutionalized within the framework itself in terms of the principles of technological domination of nature, sovereign territorial autonomy of nations in a posture of mutual hostility and economic competition toward all other nations, and worldwide economic institutions based on the principle of individual and corporate self-interest. Yet in fact, according to the World Health Organization, there was a $50 billion net transfer of wealth worldwide from the "poor" to the "rich" nations between 1984 and 1994, as well as *$10 trillion* in military expenditures during the same period. To the Commissioners, such facts seem to be simply an accidental feature of otherwise beneficial institutions. In this Report, which refuses to examine or to challenge the dominant assumptions or established institutions of the modern world, there is little or no "vision." Vision is impossible for people who refuse to confront the issues of history, causality, or responsibility. An intelligent vision for the future is impossible for people who will not attempt to understand the past.

Indeed, their vision of the future is so limited that their book explicitly denies that a democratic, nonmilitary world government is needed where the rule of law would be enforceable and where human rights and the environment would be legally protected by the democratic sovereignty of the people of the Earth. While urging change in our spiritual attitude, their specific proposals affirm precisely those institutions that have often been criticized as being at the center of the world crisis: the principle of the sovereignty of nations in military and economic competition with one another, the license of transnational corporations to roam the world in search of resources to exploit and profits to be made, the World Bank and IMF with their regressive notions of "development," and the ineffectual UN system with its domination by the rich and powerful nations over all others.

The Commissioners urge "more democratic" forms of global governance as these are embodied in their suggested modifications of the UN Charter. They define this as governance by "not only governments and intergovernmental institutions but also nongovernmental organizations (NGOs), citizens' movements, transnational corporations, academia, and the mass media."[21] Like international law, environmental treaties, and UN principles, all compliance under this "system" is voluntary (which the Commission calls "consensual"). It seems clear that what they call "governance" is a modification of the present world anarchy of no governance. For the present writer, to call this proposal "more democratic" evokes the same sense of the word as that used in 1985, when the US government called the repressive, near-genocidal military regime in El Salvador a "fledgling democracy." "Democracy" without the slightest legal empowerment or protection of citizens (as would be reflected, e.g., in the principle of one person one vote, or the rule of enforceable law) is simply a sham.

Within the present world structure, how can "citizens' movements" or NGOs possibly participate with superpower nation-states or multinational corporations (with assets larger than those of some governments) in something called "consensual democratic global governance"? Such recommendations amount to an ideological cover-up of a profoundly antidemocratic world situation. In our day, many reputable thinkers have named this so-called "system" the rule of international chaos, the law of might makes right, or war of the strong against the weak.[22] In the view of the present writer, the Commission on Global Governance has refused to confront our global crisis and has affirmed continuation of the present world anarchy, that will ultimately mean the massive destruction of even more human beings and the global environment of the planet.

The Commissioners seem well intentioned, but their flawed notion of "common sense" leads them to believe human beings can deal with a *global crisis* by incremental modifications of the very set of institutions that have produced the crisis. True "common sense" in the context of the present limit-situation (where we are facing the limits of the Earth's capacity to sustain this modern madness of the pursuit of power, profit, and false autonomy) means *moving to a new level of existence.* It means embracing a new planetary paradigm, operating in a larger framework, within which we can deal with the crisis on a new, global, and more fully human level. Every fact reported in this Report calls out for genuine, democratic world government. The very portrayal of the world situation on which the book is based shows that without real global governance, without a nonmilitary, democratic Constitution for the Federation of Earth, the planet will not survive. There is no way to avoid a future total collapse without *moving to the entirely new level of planetary existence.* Yet the Report of the Commission on Global Governance, well intentioned as it is, does not point to anything resembling a planetary framework.

CONCLUSION

The key issue for the realization of democratic world government is "legitimation." All political power, all authority, all ideas of sovereignty rest on a general recognition that certain people (those in power) have legitimate authority to issue laws or commands. If the present writer were to begin issuing laws regulating international shipping, no one would pay attention. Legitimacy is directly dependent on general recognition. In the face of the present planetary crisis, the traditional institutionalized forms of power (nation-states, multi-national corporations, and, in certain areas, the UN) are rapidly becoming "delegitimated." They have shown themselves in the last half century as simply not capable of addressing the global destruction of the environment, growing desperation of world poverty, the population explosion, or world militarism. If citizens begin to withdraw recognition of the legitimacy of these institutions, their seemingly invincible power will evaporate like steam in the wind, just as the power of the Philippine dictator Ferdinand Marcos evaporated in 1986, when the majority of the citizens of his country nonviolently refused to recognize his fraudulent reelection, and just as the former Soviet Union, once considered a monolith of unassailable power, dissolved almost nonviolently within a few years of the widespread questioning of its legitimacy. In terms of this insight, military institutions, nation-states, and the current global financial system might be more or less rapidly delegitimated if the peoples of the world begin to transfer their recognition of legitimacy from these planetary fragments to the whole, as embodied in the proposed federal world government set forth in the above-mentioned World Constitution.

It is not necessarily a lack of good intentions or good leaders that has caused the present global crisis but rather the fact that modern institutions are premised on those limited assumptions discussed above that gained ascendancy centuries ago. But only in the last fifty years have the central problems of the world been widely recognized as genuinely global crises—not as national, regional, or local problems. Within this dawning awareness, what were once considered common-sense procedures, the patient working within existing institutions to reform them in the direction of a better world, have now become a prescription for suicide. The framework has changed and with it the meaning of common sense directed toward a better world. The only true and authentic common sense remedy for the threatened extinction of a viable earthly environment is for human beings to reorder their thinking within a new planetary paradigm.

"Democracy," we have seen, is a concept that points toward this new planetary framework and the possibility of human beings transforming their assumptions about themselves and their institutions. When the Report of the Commission on Global Governance speaks of making governance of the world "more democratic," it is presenting a meaningless slogan insofar as it refuses to challenge the antidemocratic structures of the modern world system: the autonomous nation-state over against all other nation-states, the near totalitarian working of global concentrations of private capital institutionalized for profit of the few at the expense of the many, the assumption of the private self- (or group-) identity in competition with all other selves or groups, and the use of science and technology by these antidemocratic forces for power and mastery over the Earth and other people, rather than for human welfare. Democracy is predicated on the assumption of the equality of all: that, for example, each person should have only one vote and hence a general equality of communi-cative voice and political influence with others. It is based on the assumption that government functions with the consent of the governed, and that a democratically based government will act for the welfare of all. The present modern world system has institutionalized the antithesis of these principles, and its dominant world institutions are antidemocratic to their very core.

The only hope of addressing our planetary crisis is to transform our thinking from the modern paradigm to the truly relational, interdependent, and democratic paradigm being expressed by the most advanced thinkers of the twentieth century. A truly relational human species requires relational (not partial and atomistic) institutions, institutions that will make possible the per-petual realization of human potentialities. True cultural, ethnic, racial, political, and religious diversity can flourish only if they are protected by an authentic democratic framework that embraces and legitimates that diversity. True inalienable equality and dignity of individual citizens of the Earth can flourish only if it is protected and promoted by a *planetary framework* that embraces and legitimates equality and dignity. The numerous local ecosystems that help constitute the global environment can be protected and interrelated with the whole only through a framework of *planetary* planning and concern. This is not pious idealism. Pious idealism is reflected in the urgings of the Commission on Global Governance for a very unlikely "spiritual transformation" that must take place in the face of the Commission's own affirmation of those institutions of power and conflict that militate against such a transformation.

By contrast with this unwitting prescription for planetary suicide, there are immediate common sense steps that we can take that can, at the very least, *make it possible* for human beings to begin to see and think differently about their situation. To change the institutional framework is to *make it possible* for people to see and think differently. Modern communications, transportation, and computerization have brought us to the point where democracy for all citizens of the Earth is possible for the first time. This technology can be used, not for power, exploitation, and militarism, but for communication, equality, and human dignity. Within a democratic planetary framework, people can begin for the first time to think of themselves as *truly relational*, in a dialogue with the other citizens of the planet. They can begin to think of the human *relationship with our planet* as a whole as one of fragile interdependence, requiring caring, sustainable, and carefully designed institutions for human planetary well-being. At the present moment, as we approach the symbolically significant year 2000, by far the most concrete, practical, and immediately realizable act by which we can begin to deal with our planetary crisis is to ratify a constitution for a nonmilitary, democratic world government.

NOTES

1. For example, see Stewart C. Easton, *The Western Heritage* (New York: Holt, Rinehart, and Winston, 1966), Chs. 12-16.

2. Noam Chomsky, *What Uncle Sam Really Wants* (Berkeley, CA: Odonian Press, 1993), p. 73.

3. Martin Heidegger, *Nietzsche*, vol. 1: *The Will to Power as Art*, trans. David Farrell Krell (New York: Harper and Row, 1979), Sections 6-10.

4. Jürgen Habermas, *The Theory of Communicative Action,* vol. 1: *Reason and the Rationalization of Society*, trans. Thomas McCarthy (Boston: Beacon Press, 1984), and vol. 2: *Lifeworld and System: A Critique of Functionalist Reason*, trans. Thomas McCarthy (Boston: Beacon Press, 1987).

5. Nolan Pliny Jacobson, "A Buddhistic-Christian Probe of the Endangered Future," *The Eastern Buddhist*, Spring 1982, p. 38.

6. Quoted by Noam Chomsky, *World Orders Old and New* (New York: Columbia University Press, 1994), p. 189.

7. Jürgen Habermas, *Moral Consciousness and Communicative Action*, trans. Christian Lenhardt and Shierry Weber Nicholsen (Cambridge: MIT Press, 1991), p. 200.

8. Martin Buber, *I and Thou*, trans. Ronald Gregor Smith (New York: Charles Scribner, 1958).

9. See Remy C. Kwant, *Phenomenology of Language*, trans. Henry J. Koren

(Pittsburgh: Duquesne University Press, 1965), pp. 22-27.

10. See Habermas' essay, "Struggles for Recognition in the Democratic Constitutional State," in Charles Taylor et al., *Multiculturalism* (Princeton, NJ: Princeton University Press, 1994), pp. 107-148.

11. This can be obtained from the World Constitution and Parliament Association, 8800 West 14th Avenue, Lakewood, CO 80215. The proposed constitution is also found as the Appendix to Errol Harris, *One World or None: A Prescription for Survival* (Atlantic Highlands, NJ: Humanities Press, 1993).

12. Harris, *One World or None*, p. 122.

13. Masao Abe, *Zen and Western Thought* (Honolulu: University of Hawaii Press, 1985), p. 250.

14. Ibid., p. 249.

15. Ibid., p. 257.

16. Ibid., p. 256.

17. *Our Global Neighborhood: The Report of the Commission on Global Governance* (Oxford: Oxford University Press, 1995).

18. Ibid., p. 353.

19. Ibid., p. 354.

20. Ibid., pp. 356-357.

21. Ibid., p. 335.

22. See, for example, Noam Chomsky, *Year 501: The Conquest Continues* (Boston: South End Press, 1993); Ramsey Clark, *The Fire This Time: U.S. War Crimes in the Gulf* (New York: Thunder Mouth Press, 1994); Richard Falk, *Explorations at the Edge of Time: The Prospects for World Order* (Philadelphia: Temple University Press, 1992); or Cynthia Peters, ed., *Collateral Damage: The New World Order at Home and Abroad* (Boston: South End Press, 1992).

Chapter 2

Liberalism at the Global Level
Richard Falk

LIBERALISM IN AN ILLIBERAL WORLD

Our Global Neighborhood embodies two complementary traditions of liberal internationalism: first, a Wilsonian championship of political democracy and the possibility of a more peaceful world by way of international institutions, and second, a Kantian commitment to the organization of a cooperative league of constitutional democracies—a zone of peace—which could ultimately be enlarged to encompass the whole planet.[1] However, because of its historical setting, the Report also stresses the sanctity of private ownership of property and a general reliance upon the market to produce a brighter human future for humanity. This ambiguity reflects a broader tension between the dynamics of economic globalization, on the one hand, and democratic political orientation of liberal internationalism on the other.

The Commission on Global Governance self-consciously based itself on the opportunities to create a more cooperative world order in the aftermath of the Cold War, and the practical necessity in doing so to handle the complexities and interdependencies that are increasingly characteristic of international life. Such rationalist faith underpins a wide-ranging and coherent set of proposals that generally move in the direction of institutionalizing and democratizing international life, including extensions of the rule of law in a variety of reformist directions. So long as many leading governments were led by American-style liberals and social democrats, these sorts of reformist ideas related to decency, fairness, and sustainability, were likely to exert some influence.[2]

But what about the closing years of the twentieth century? On one side, liberal internationalism is severely challenged by "the neoliberal consensus," that disavows governmental responsibility for social goals and entrusts the future to the dynamics of the market, including priorities set by the flow of capital.[3] As such, liberals of the sort that make up the Commission on Global Governance would seem to have little to say in a political climate that is increasingly distrustful of the role of governments in improving the quality of national or international life. This perception is reinforced by three additional influential considerations: the discrediting of utopianism and all forms of social engineering in reaction to the collapse of the Soviet Union; the profound postmodern distrust of metanarratives, including universalizing programs of reform; and the mood of disillusionment associated with the United Nations in relation to global security and wellbeing, which is accentuated by the rightward drift of foreign policy in the United States. This negative atmosphere makes the core emphasis of *Our Global Neighborhood* on strengthening the UN seem out of sync with the manner in which, for better or for worse, the world is currently drifting.

Despite this unfavorable situation, this Report deserves serious appraisal for several reasons. First, the current illiberal atmosphere in world politics is likely to be episodic and ephemeral, and could be displaced within the decade by the emergence of more constructive attitudes that include a revived sense of social responsibility. Second, and more fundamentally, the combination of complexity and fragility of contemporary international life is likely to generate a series of politically relevant demands for a variety of institutional steps amounting to the creation of global governance even if the language used denies such wider implications.[4] To this end, *Our Global Neighborhood* offers informed and persuasive arguments for a more comprehensive regulation of international economic and political activity than is now available, and a helpful, even mobilizing, basis for engaging in political conversations about the future. Finally, the publication of this Report at this time provides a provisional test as to whether the liberal internationalist orientation retains its earlier attractiveness as a practical, yet nonthreatening type of idealism, which recognizes the need and possibility of a better world order, while still believing in evolutionary and procedural, not revolutionary and structural, reforms. Thus, the importance of *Our Global Neighborhood* persists *despite* the obsolescence of its liberal lineage, the unresponsiveness of the policy community, and the likely future irrelevance of the international commission format.

My assessment first seeks to locate the Commission on Global Governance within the framework of liberal internationalism, and then moves on to an inquiry into the substance of its recommendations for coping with the main challenges in international life. A third section briefly discusses the imagery of the world as "neighborhood," questioning the ethical and functional viability of such a metaphor at this time.

THE IDIOM OF THE INDEPENDENT GLOBAL COMMISSION

A distinctive, if minor, feature of recent decades has been the formation of independent commissions of eminent persons, almost all of social democratic persuasion, drawn from a range of elite backgrounds, gathered together for a series of meetings that eventuates in a report on some sector of international public policy. The process was initially associated with the former West German chancellor Willy Brandt, whose commission was established in 1980 to provide an improved approach to international development policy, a means to encourage a renewed commitment to North/South economic assistance. The impulse to form these commissions is quintessentially liberal in the American sense of the term: that is, wise and respected leaders incrementally promoting the capacity of the state system to meet more successfully such primary challenges as the management of North/South relations on development, security, environment.[5] The fact that the likely period of existence for such liberally constituted commissions is the short interval between 1980 and 1995 suggests a particular moment in the history of international relations, a period during which leading governments were seen to be insufficiently responsive to the world order challenges of the day, while the viewpoints of distinguished liberal statesmen were thought to be still capable of exerting a galvanizing influence on both leaders and their publics.

The most prominent attempts following the Brandt Commission were the Independent Commission on Disarmament and Security (the Palme Commission), the World Commission on Environment and Development (the Bruntland Commission), and the South Commission (chaired by Julius Nyerere).[6] These commissions have certain generic traits: their report is associated by informal name with a past, present, and future head of state, their recommendations and findings are supported by research and consultancies with known experts ("the usual suspects") supervised by a small professional secretariat, their prose style is such as to limit their real readership to a tiny band of devoted followers, and their main intended audience are the policymakers of states and international institutions. Their influence, and the extent that it exists, have derived from a combination of public respect for their membership, which helps achieve some media attention, and governmental access, which at least ensures that the report will be seen, if not read, by sympathetic national and international bureaucracies. By and large, aside from their usefulness as competent, substantive summaries to academic specialists and graduate students, the influence of these reports has had to do with conceptual clarification rather than policy results.

Against this background the Commission on Global Governance was formed in 1992, its Report being published in 1995 under the deliberately enticing title of *Our Global Neighborhood*, presumably an effort to reach as wide a literate, yet nontechnical, audience as possible. Ingvar Carlson, the Swedish prime minister was cochair along with Shridath Ramphal, a long-prominent Third World statesman from Guiana who had served as the secretary-general of the

British Commonwealth from 1975 to 1990. Each commission has its own particular background, and this one on global governance originated in a meeting convened by Willy Brandt in 1990 at Konigswinter, Germany, bringing together members from the earlier commissions to assess the world situation as the Cold War was ending, with the assembled bigwigs agreeing that the stage was now set for moves designed to strengthen multilateral institutions, especially improving capacities for coordinated action among states. The first step encouraged by the Brandt initiative was a formal gathering of selected eminent persons brought together at Stockholm at the invitation of Carlson, Ramphal, and the then minister of development and cooperation in the Netherlands, Jan Pronk.[7]

The Commission on Global Governance was the recommended sequel to the work done in Stockholm. Its efforts were to be completed in ample time to inform discussions that were expected to accompany various meetings planned to celebrate the 50th anniversary of the United Nations, the Commissioners, in their more grandiose moments, hoping to do for the next half century what the framers of the UN Charter had done at San Francisco in 1945.[8] The authors of *Our Global Neighborhood* fortunately widened the focus to encompass the whole governance process in international society, and although the United Nations system remained the institutional centerpiece of its proposals, the underlying analysis and policy perspective were far broader and richer, responding especially both to the challenges of economic globalization and to the emergence of a rudimentary global civil society in the form of transnational social forces agitating for democratizing change on matters ranging from the rights of women and indigenous peoples to the protection of the environment and the empowerment of the poor. Intellectually and politically, this more encompassing understanding of global governance helps to keep the Report relevant to the concerns of the 1990s, and avoids the utter embarrassment of glorifying the security functions of the United Nations at a time when its stature, through little fault of its own, is at an historic low. In this respect, the contrast in global mood between April 1991, immediately following the seemingly successful UN response to Iraqi aggression against Kuwait, when the Report of the Stockholm Initiative was issued, and the release of *Our Global Neighborhood* (hereinafter OGN) in early 1995, is stark. At this latter time, the humiliating inability of UN peacekeepers to protect several urban areas in Bosnia designed as safe havens by the UN from vicious Serb attacks was most discrediting, as was the brazen bypassing of the UN in the form of military actions of NATO and independent diplomatic initiatives by the US government. A recent skepticism about all forms of internationalism has probably further muted the media impact of the Report.

LIBERAL INTERNATIONALISM IN THE MID-1990S

OGN can be read in several different ways. Its manifest intention is to exert substantive influence in official policy circles relating to governments and international institutions, especially by setting forth concrete proposals for reform; these proposals are well considered, do not challenge existing geopolitical or geoeconomic structures, and offer sensible ways to reach goals that have been previously widely endorsed by influential sectors of public opinion. On this level, unfortunately in part, OGN has descended upon the world as a lead balloon. It is an unpleasant reality that liberal reformism cannot find receptive audiences these days either in relation to global institutional structure or with respect to the functioning of the world economy. Neither elites nor publics are receptive, and what visionary voices exist (for instance, Nelson Mandela, Auug San Suu Kyi, Vaclav Havel) are domestically, or at best, regionally preoccupied, although, interestingly, both Mandela and Havel appear on the cover of OGN with glowing endorsements, more likely confirming the statist and social democratic linkages of the Commission than any genuine enthusiasm for the programmatic aspects of OGN.

OGN may most usefully be read as an informed and comprehensive portrayal of world order, a snapshot of the world as of 1995. If this understanding is chosen as the basis of approval, then OGN is an impressive achievement. It presents information accurately and elegantly, often relying on simple tables that summarize data on trends. Because it advocates reforms based on ethical principles, OGN also offers a kind of gentle critique of the ways in which international political life is interpreted by the realist orthodoxy. As a critique, OGN is not penetrating enough to be illuminating, because it avoids any real questioning of either structural features of world order or of the ideological consensus that prevails among Western elites. As would be expected, the Report is thoroughly secular, rejects extremism in all forms, while assuming that the modernist momentum will persist, but that with the proper attunements it will remain possible to reconcile globalization with humanist values.

There are three further achievements of OGN. First of all, the Report goes beyond the usual liberal, pragmatic tendency to refrain from any general assessment for fear of being labeled "ideological." The point of departure for the Report is so articulated: "The world needs a new vision that can galvanize people everywhere to achieve higher levels of co-operation in areas of common concern and shared destiny."[9]

The Report acknowledges that "ethnic cleansing in the Balkans, brutal violence in Somalia, the genocide in Rwanda" have undermined the confidence that existed three years earlier when the Stockholm Initiative was endorsed. The unifying call for "global governance" is put forward, then, in the Report despite "deepening disquiet" about any immediate receptivity on the part of either governments or the United Nations. This notion of global governance is broadly identified with "The sum of the many ways individuals and institutions, public and private, manage their common affairs... It includes formal institutions and regimes empowered to enforce compliance, as well as informal arrangements that people and institutions either have agreed to, or perceive to be in their own interest."[10] That is, governance involves arrangements at all levels of social interaction from grassroots/local to those embodied in the UN system.

Second, the Report, unlike others in this genre that rest their policy claims exclusively on intellectual arguments amounting to an appeal to pure reason, acknowledges openly an adherence to certain values, as well as the importance of shaping governance on the basis of an ethical framework of universal scope that frames the role of policymakers: "We believe that all humanity could uphold core values of respect for life, liberty, justice and equity, mutual respect, caring and integrity. These provide a foundation for transforming a global neighborhood based on economic exchange and improved communications into a universal moral community in which people are bound together by more than proximity, interest, or identity."[11] These values are derived from a reliance on the encompassing metaphor of a "neighborhood," which is treated both as descriptive of an integrated global reality, and as prescriptive of how the people of the world should be connected for purposes of mutual wellbeing.[12]

The third normative contribution of OGN is to acknowledge the emergence and significance of global civic society ("a multitude of institutions, voluntary associations, and networks—women's groups, trade unions, chambers of commerce, farming or housing co-operatives, neighborhood watch associations, religion-based organizations, and so on").[13] The Report strongly recommends extending the notion of democracy to include global civil society, thus indirectly challenging the exclusivist, statist makeup of almost every international institution and also recognizing the need to facilitate new modes of political participation in light of the widespread popular "disenchantment with the performance of government."[14] Paradoxically, this disenchantment appears to be most pronounced in nations considered to be the most successful constitutional democracies at the present time.

The body of the Report sets out various ideas for realizing these three points of normative commitment without challenging too dramatically the neoliberal consensus. The most revealing, and in certain respects disappointing, proposals relate to the challenge of economic globalization. After usefully summarizing the phenomena of globalization the Report recommends the establishment of an Economic Security Council, intended to be a more representative body than either the G-7 or the Bretton Woods institutions, and more legitimate and effective than such UN bodies as ECOSOC or UNCTAD (both of which the Report recommends eliminating).[15] The primary role of the new body would be to coordinate economic activity and to promote "consensus" and "dialogue" "on the evolution of the international economic system." The Economic Security Council "would work closely with the Bretton Woods institutions, not in opposition to them."[16] According to the proposal the membership would be drawn from the five largest economies together with an allocation of seats based on principles of regional representation.

It seems extremely unlikely that an Economic Security Council could be established in this period, especially if its explicit mandate included the protection of vulnerable societies and peoples from various economic security threats. The language of the Report makes it clear that it is not questioning the basic premises of neoliberalism, whether it be privatization or market-guided approaches to social and environmental policy, but adapting them to fit more acceptably into a world of increasing complexity. Yet not quite, as the ethical concerns of the global neighborhood are somehow also to be taken seriously, but to realize these valued ends would appear to place a premium on regulating the activities of corporations, banks, and financial markets at least partly on the basis of social criteria, which would be at variance with neoliberal precepts. The Report stops short of prescribing policy implications, and even fails to identify the sorts of societal disruption being caused by corporate wrongdoing (as in Bhopal), currency manipulations, and banking operations that routinely launder and offer secret accounts for money stolen by corrupt leaders from their own peoples. In this respect the liberal orientation of OGN is disappointing, but predictably so: formulating an attractive ethical framework, yet exempting from criticism the very social and economic forces that obstruct the values at stake and proposing machinery that lacks the capacity to overcome the political challenge posed by globalization, which is to impose on governments, regardless of their preferences, an iron discipline of global capital which has given consistent priority to market-driven concerns whenever these conflict with people-oriented concerns.

The same tantalizing combination of forward-looking proposals and ideological capitulation to the status quo is associated with the other main policy recommendations put forward. OGN impressively calls for the elimination of nuclear weapons as being "[w]eapons of mass destruction" that "are not legitimate instruments of defence,"[17] through a process extending over a period of 10 to 15 years.[18] At the same time the Report does not specifically challenge the nuclearism of nuclear weapons states, or their hostility to any move that is designed to achieve the elimination of nuclear weaponry, or even question the legality of its retention. For instance, no mention is made in the Report of the World Court Project, of the historic effort of civil society in collaboration with several governments to test the legality of threat or use of nuclear weaponry, by stimulating a General Assembly resolution that requested the World Court to issue an advisory opinion this year, and resulted in an advisory opinion that undermines claims of legality and unanimously insists on the legal duty of all nuclear weapons states to pursue nuclear disarmament in good faith.[19] The avoidance of such concreteness gives the Report a tone of blandness associated with UN documents, and is the clearest indication that its eminent authors do not intend to offend the powers that be. In this crucial respect, OGN takes a position that is quite the opposite of what one would expect from the most representative transnational forces that make up global civil society, namely, a clear indictment, identification of culprits, far-reaching regulatory mechanisms, resource allocations needed to reach goals, and, most especially, endorsement of civil initiatives that challenge statist imperatives. In this respect, global civil society, to the extent that it is an actual participatory presence, tends to be confrontational, whether it be Greenpeace organizing a campaign in mid-1995 to resist the resumption of French nuclear testing in the Pacific, or the efforts of the 30,000 women drawn from NGO ranks to make the occasion of the UN Conference on Women and Development a milestone in shaping a global agenda for women and building a transnational implementation network.

The same ambivalence pervades virtually all aspects of the Report. A call is made for strengthening the rule of law in international life, but nothing is said about the failure by large constitutional states to constrain their own uses of force by reference to independent judicial assessments of the relevance of international law.[20] Familiar, yet still welcome, suggestions are made in some detail to extend the role of the World Court, and to support the establishment of an International Criminal Court. There is also a notable specific criticism of the United States government and France for their respective failures to respect the authority of the Court in the Nicaragua and nuclear testing cases.[21] Again, these recommendations, which exhort governments to accept more law-oriented approaches, are unlikely to be acted upon in the foreseeable future, and give the Report a slightly preachy tone of policy irrelevance. A more engaging focus would have been on the extent to which transnational civil initiatives are managing to appropriate and extend the rule of law without awaiting the approval of governments. In this regard the Permanent Peoples Tribunal operating out of Rome for almost two decades is exemplary, as are efforts at law enforcement by way of citizen boycotts, but these developments are not even mentioned. Such civil initiatives and innovations currently give more promise for actualizing the Rule of Law in international life than do efforts to persuade large governments to change their ways.[22]

The substantive material organized around reform proposals is highly professional in its careful formulation and presentation. What it lacks is political bite. Although there is much that is constructively reformist and useful in the Report, the overall impression is one of old hat, the familiar kind of liberal internationalist agenda set forth at a time when the policy pendulum is swinging in a particularly illiberal direction in most countries.

The most honest response to these kinds of criticisms of the Report is the simple question: "But what could you expect?"—given the composition of the Commission, the problems of funding such an operation, and the implicit sense that the most significant dialogue is still necessarily with the representatives of the established order.[23]

THE SEARCH FOR A MOBILIZING METAPHOR

OGN will definitely be associated in policy circles with the metaphor of global neighborhood. Like such predecessor metaphors as "spaceship earth" and "global village," the idea of global neighborhood is intended to stress the implication of interdependence, but to do so in a manner that is less technocratic and more communitarian. In the words of the Commission: "The changes of the last half-century have brought the global neighborhood nearer to reality—a world in which citizens are increasingly dependent on one another and need to cooperate. Matters calling for global neighborhood action keep multiplying. What happens far away matters much more now."[24]

In an important sense, the global neighborhood metaphor creatively emphasizes the centrality of people at a time when markets and capital seem dominant, affirming, as well, the solidarity of humanity and the ethical need to promote fairness and caring. This frame of reference has no specific political implications, and does not imply a liberal program of reform. The Report also lauds the beneficial effects of democracy, commerce, and human rights, and thus embodies a kind of Kantian view that a peaceful world can be constructed out of these sorts of ideas provided they are widely adopted.

But the particular policy focus is less on fundamentals than on the practical benefits of cooperation for mutual benefit, an orientation that seeks small steps forward in contexts in which basic structures of wealth and power are treated as stable and acceptable. To be sure, the outbreak of ethnic conflict and political fragmentation is acknowledged, but in a manner that requires only small adjustments in what the Report calls "old norms," namely, "sovereignty" and "self-determination."[25] The strict territorial postulates of sovereignty are to be relaxed in favor of protecting the fundamental rights of peoples and nations, but operational hard cases are not discussed; the situation is similar with self-determination. Vague support is given to moderate approaches to self-determination that do not involve shattering existing states or subjecting minorities to threatening state formations, but what to do about contradictory nationalisms struggling for primacy within the same territorial space is not addressed.

The implication of the word "neighborhood," as employed in the Report, is friendliness, a shared concern for the wellbeing of neighbors, a willingness to help out in times of need. But the modern world exhibits other, far more sinister, conceptions of neighborhood—gang struggles for exclusive control, interethnic hostility, class differentiation. Some of the worst instances of genocidal violence have been between those intimately linked by bonds of proximity and shared traditions, including language.

Perhaps more devastatingly, the premises of economic globalization involve indifference to those sectors of societies, regions, and the world that are perceived by markets as not being currently productive for capital. Africa has been neglected in recent years. During the Cold War, geopolitical rivalry led both superpowers to compete for influence in Africa by bestowals of economic assistance, as well as destructively by lavish arms transfers and recourse to devastating covert and overt intervention.[26] This tension between the ethical imperative of the global neighborhood and the operative dynamics of economic globalization is evaded, an evasion which has been characteristic of all post-Wilsonian variants of liberal internationalism. This evasion is all the more damaging in the contemporary setting, because globalization-from-above has been so successful in subordinating the state to its goals.[27]

This evasion is particularly damaging to OGN's refreshing receptivity to the relevance of transnational social forces, i.e., globalization-from-below, that constitutes the operational reality of global civil society. The ethical stress on neighborliness suggests a people-oriented globalism, yet the Report's strong endorsement of Bretton Woods institutions and approaches as well as its acceptance of the dynamics of economic globalization imply a market-oriented globalism. Such incoherence arises from a credibility compulsion to avoid, at all costs, displeasing the established order. This blend of qualities erodes the seriousness of several proposals intended to democratize the United Nations, such as calling for the establishment of a Forum of Civil Society that would meet prior to the General Assembly in the same facilities used by governmental representatives, and a Right of Petition for aggrieved individuals and groups that will be reviewed by an independent Council of Petitions, recommending a referral, if appropriate, to the Security Council, the General Assembly, and the Secretary-General. These initiatives are not likely to be accepted, but even if they were, there is not much prospect that the statism of the United Nations could be challenged by these means. At most, such innovations would provide global civil society with entry points and mobilizing occasions, not for neighborly discussion but to posit demands and convey to wider audiences the depth and intensity of cleavages and perceived grievances. Finally, I would be quite surprised if the phrase "global neighborhood" catches on at all, because it appears to fly directly in the face of recent political realities and is thus unlike such phrases as "common security" or "sustainable development," which clearly struck a responsive chord at the time of their utterance.

IS THE INDEPENDENT COMMISSION ON GLOBAL GOVERNANCE A LAST HURRAH?

In the end, OGN falls somewhat clumsily between two stools, while endeavoring to sit astraddle both. Its proposals and orientation are too reformist, humanist, and populist to be acceptable to either leading states or the new elites of globalization. Yet these proposals are insufficiently radical to excite, or even satisfy, the most influential orientations in global civil society: the embrace of economic globalization by the Report especially invites suspicion, given the critical consensus among transnational activists, especially in the South, that such a market-driven world accentuates the suffering of the vulnerable and disadvantaged. Perhaps, in the end, liberal internationalism (that is, social democracy globalized through the agency of an enlightened, energetic sector of the leadership cadre in the established order) is always better off avoiding the big picture, concentrating its efforts on well-constructed specific proposals of incremental benefit, which, at their most successful, can build bridges of joint support that link elites and moderate activists in common endeavor. As might be expected, the best thinking in the Report involves the presentation of carefully nuanced specific reform possibilities, and the worst parts are devoted to generalities about promoting economic equity or strengthening the rule of law that ignore the presence of towering structural obstacles.

It is probably a bad sign that eminent persons of liberal internationalist persuasion are currently out of fashion, and that our political future is being primarily shaped by interactions among the many varieties of technocratic globalist, social reactionary, and mean-spirited pseudotraditionalists. We can, perhaps, best comprehend this new failure of liberal internationalism mainly through its inability to come sufficiently to terms with the advent of an era of globalization, with the class origins and short-term horizons of most eminent liberals, disabling them from taking a leap of faith by casting their lot more directly with transnational social forces.[28] Instead of taking such a plunge, OGN continues the commission tradition of being sufficiently ingratiating to the established order so as not to provoke an explicit rejection at high levels of officialdom.

To some extent this Commission, more than its predecessors, tried hard to be receptive to the global civil society perspective that is at odds with both statist antecedents and economic/cybernetic globalization. Its orientation was less conventionally an expression of establishment thinking than any previous commission, and arguably went as far as any fundable project of this sort could go. Herein lies the dilemma. This Commission on Global Governance went as far as it is possible to go within such a format, and yet it is not nearly far enough. More radical perspectives tend to be underfunded, neglected by the media and policy elites, and thus to the extent that they exist, they are lost in the background noise of a global civilization overwhelmed by information, with only the richest providers normally able to present their ideas in a manner that exerts an influential impact. Perhaps, in time, new modalities of electronic empowerment for visionary outlooks by way of computer networks will generate influence that can have a positive, galvanizing effect on the political imagination of agents of change situated throughout the world.[29]

In my judgment, this Commission is the last such effort by this ideologically compact perspective that is, at bottom, a legacy and extension of the Enlightenment faith in reason, persuasion, humanistic values, and social learning. It is, as such, too Western and too remote from the new, amoral coalitions between global market forces and leading states to exert significant influence either on the social agenda of states or to facilitate an understanding of intercivilizational antagonisms and synergies. There will be commissions or transnational bodies in the future, with prestige and a high-profile, but I would expect their makeup and mandate to be far more heterodox, and their recommendations much less easily classifiable as social democratic or liberal in character.

Is this farewell party an occasion for regret? This Commission effectively articulated the moderate case for a humanistic approach to global governance, but without seriously questioning the structural assumptions of the established (statist, geopolitically unipolar) and emergent (globalized economy and communications frame) world order. Is such a humane voice to be interpreted as a politically irrelevant and wasteful indulgence, or does such a Commission provide at least some encouragement for transnational social forces, the most credible current vehicle of hope and struggle, to gain influence and legitimation? It is difficult to say, and neither alternative can be convincingly selected.

Despite my pessimism about the work and worldview of this Commission, the substantive goals it champions are not outmoded, nor is their political potency permanently lost. The temporary eclipse of socialist values is partly a result of a distorted, yet prevailing, line of interpreting the Soviet collapse and partly a consequence of the increasing weakness and co-option of organized labor, but the goals of social accountability and the relief of human suffering are almost certain to be revived as part of new political projects, although in all likelihood with a fresh political language, a new construction of history, and a different take on the opportunities for drastic reform. In some respects the surge of support for green parties and politics in the 1980s prefigures such a rebirth of a socially and ecologically sensitive, people-oriented politics, and in its own often harsh ways, several variants of Islamic militancy have based their populist appeal less on specifically religious messages than on their dedication to the delivery of social services to the poor in national settings where decades of secular incompetence and corruption had generated massive grassroots despair. Such gropings are, at most, anticipations of new varieties of politics. Let us sincerely hope, at the dawn of a new millennium, that the owl of Minerva will be restless enough to take flight before the dusk descends.

NOTES

1. See Anne-Marie Slaughter, "International Law in a World of Liberal States," *European Journal of International Law*, especially p. 6; Andrew Moravscik, "Liberalism and International Relations Theory," Center for International Affairs, Harvard University, Working Paper, No. 92-6, 1992. Kantian ideas have been influentially presented and assessed by Michael W. Doyle, "Liberalism and World Politics," *American Political Science Review*, 80, 1986, pp. 1151-1169, at 1155-1162. For a general survey see Hidemi Suganami, *The Domestic Analogy and World Order Proposals* (New York: Cambridge University Press, 1989).

2. Of course, in the security domain of war/peace relations, realism always provided the underpinning for liberal internationalism. Also, as Henry Kissinger has been fond of

pointing out, the United States alone was susceptible to liberal internationalist posturing, often, he argues, at the expense of a clearheaded pursuit of national interests. See, for example, Henry Kissinger, *Diplomacy* (New York: Simon and Schuster, 1994), especially pp. 804-835.

3. The terminology of "liberal" and "neoliberalism" invites confusion. "Liberal" as used in the United States is roughly equivalent to "social democratic" in the European context, while the European use of "liberal" refers generally to a diminished reliance on the state, and a greater confidence in the private economic sector. "Neoliberalism" has been recently employed to denote an ideological confidence in market-oriented public policy to resolve economic and political, as well as social problems, and is identified with the rejection of an activist state, including a Keynesian approach to monetary policy and the general perspective of welfare economics.

4. For example, the ambitious moves toward regional and global institutionalization in the Maastricht arrangements for Europe, and through the creation of the World Trade Organization as a sequel to GATT, definitely move toward global economic governance, but such labels are avoided; also the normative implications of such governance schemes may tilt the distribution of benefits even further in the direction of the rich and privileged. It is important to appreciate that global governance can be either beneficial or detrimental to the achievement of human wellbeing, and, in this crucial respect, its appraisal resembles the appraisal of the strong territorial sovereign state.

5. These commissions should be distinguished from global conferences under UN auspices on similar issues that provide arenas for governments and for transnational social forces; also distinct, yet related, was the Trilateral Commission that brought together private sector elites in Japan, Europe, and North America, exerting a significant influence in the 1970s, but losing influence as their neoliberal orientation became operative policy.

6. For a brief overview of these Commission activities, see "Common Responsibility in the 1990s," *The Stockholm Initiative on Global Security and Governance*, April 22, 1991 (hereinafter referred to as "the Stockholm Initiative"), pp. 6-9; *Our Global Neighborhood*, pp. xiv, xvi, and 359.

7. See OGN, pp. 361-386, for description of formation, working plan, and makeup of the Commission.

8. A similar undertaking to that of the independent commission, with a comparable make-up, mandate, and result, is the Report of the Independent Working Group on the Future of the United Nations, entitled *The United Nations in its Second Half-Century* (New Haven, CT: Yale University Press, 1995), with Moeen Qureshi and Richard von Weisacker as co-chairs, and Paul M. Kennedy and Bruce Russett as co-directors of the Yale University Secretariat.

9. OGN, p. 1.

10. Both quotations, OGN, p. 2.

11. OGN, p. 49.

12. The penultimate section will consider whether "neighborhood" is actually a helpful metaphor at this time when the encounters of modernism, traditionalism, and postmodernism are so intense.

13. OGN, p. 32.

14. OGN, p. 33.

15. OGN, pp. 155-162.

16. Both quotations, OGN, p. 156.

17. OGN, p. 338.

18. OGN, pp. 340-341.

19. This decision has now been handed down and falls far short of what was hoped.

20. See Falk, "The Extension of Law to Foreign Policy: The Next Constitutional Challenge," in Alan S. Rosenbaum, ed., *Constitutionalism: The Philosophical Dimension* (Westport, CT: Greenwood Press, 1986), pp. 205-221.

21. OGN, p. 312.

22. On the theorizing underlying the establishment of the Permanent Peoples Tribunal, see the essays collected in Antonio Cassese and Edmond Jouve, eds., *Pour un droit des peuples* (Paris: Berger Levrault, 1978).

23. In fact, as earlier argued, the most receptive audience is likely to be moderate segments of global civil society, despite the failure of the Report to represent their views and methods with accuracy. Is the need for respectability so great as to explain this mismatch between the content of the Report and its real audience?

24. OGN, p. 336. Is this last assertion generally convincing? Why did Somalia seem to count for more during the Cold War than since 1989? Why has so little been done in Bosnia, Rwanda, even Chechnya and Kosovo, in the face of genocidal outbursts? The neighborly ethos seems weak, indeed, especially at the intergovernmental level of action.

25. OGN, pp. 67-75.

26. For a vivid, informed account of the impact of intervention, see Victoria Brittain, *Hidden Lives, Hidden Deaths* (London: Faber, 1986).

27. See Jeremy Brecher and Tim Costello, *Global Village or Global Pillage: Economic Reconstruction from the Bottom Up* (Boston: South End Press, 1994); and Smitu Kotharti, "Where Are the People? The United Nations Global Economic Institutions and Governance," paper given at the UN 50th Anniversary Conference, The United Nations: Between Sovereignty and Global Governance? (Melbourne: Latrobe University, July 1995), pp. 2-6.

28. For efforts to do this from a similar ethical perspective, see Falk, *Explorations at the Edge of Time: The Prospects for World Order* (Philadelphia: Temple University Press, 1992), *On Humane Governance: Toward a New Global Politics* (University Park, PA: Pennsylvania State University Press, 1995).

29. For fascinating explorations of such visionary possibilities, see recent issues of *Wired Magazine.*

Chapter 3

Governance—An Opportunity?
John C. de V. Roberts

CHALLENGES FOR HUMANKIND

The Report of the Commission on Global Governance, *Our Global Neighborhood*, is the result of a growing awareness of the scale of the problems confronting the human race. We are now meeting head-on a series of different challenges for humankind. Their particular impact has been multiplied by their coming together. Most are not new; indeed they have been growing in gravity and significance for a century or more, but they have become more pressing and urgent with the increasing power of human science and technology.

The writing on the wall has been evident, if only to a few, for a long time, from the days of the knitting together of the world in the sixteenth, seventeenth, and eighteenth centuries, with the development of European empires that spanned the globe. The warning signs could first be seen in the way that the nation-states Britain, France, and Holland began to carry their continental quarrels into other hemispheres. But even in the eighteenth century their capacity to harm the environment and to affect the planet was minimal. Not until the nineteenth century was there a serious risk that human activity would do lasting damage to the natural world.

Previous generations had often been less destructive. In the British Isles, for example, millennia of human activity had produced a tamed landscape, but one where the efforts of farmers and cultivators had usually been in harmony with the natural world. This had generally been to the benefit of both, although savage animals such as bears and wolves were killed off. Marshes drained and rivers dredged meant more production, but did not usually lead to the mass extermination of whole species of plants or insects. Wresting a living from nature was best accomplished where cooperation, and not simply control, was achieved.

The rise of technology began to change all that, as industrialization put more and more raw power into people's hands, and evidence of their capacity to change the world became clear. Animals like the dodo followed the long-gone mammoths and saber-toothed tigers as victims of human hunting skills. But the losses were on a small scale, although complete extermination of millions upon millions of passenger pigeons in North America might have been noted as a harbinger of the newfound propensity for destruction.

Also, capacity for plunder—the search for wealth and minerals, above all, gold—led to serious havoc wreaked upon areas of wilderness; but these were usually capable of recovery when left alone after the first successful creaming-off of profits. But the relentless demands for oil during the past century and the need to feed an ever-growing population have led to changes that may never be reparable. We are now, having hunted several species of whales to extinction, on the point of wiping out fish stocks that will be unable to recover.

The twentieth century has brought new threats; it has also brought clearly and into startling relief the new powers to destroy and annihilate with which science has equipped our technology. The speed and thoughtlessness with which we can now sweep away the habitat of animals and plants present a totally new scale of danger to all forms of life on the planet; and human beings, as the beneficiaries of a balanced and harmonious global ecology, are threatened along with all their victims.

By the 1920s and 1930s, some writers and thinkers, such as Lewis Mumford, foresaw these dangers and began warning of them. They were almost totally ignored, and instead the nation-states embarked on their second vast orgy of destruction from 1939 to 1945 and, in their heedless, frantic haste to secure or preserve political and economic supremacy, subsequently hastened most of the destructive trends that were already threatening the global environment. When the blood-letting eased, the rulers of humankind turned their attention to urgent attempts to export their quarrels into space, while their "reconstruction" was generally carried on oblivious to the devastating implications of industrial development and urbanization.

GOVERNMENT AND WAR

War is a peculiar danger; not only does it exacerbate all the other harmful effects of uncontrolled plunder, but it contains more serious threats of its own. Apart from the wholesale devastation caused by weapons of mass destruction, war is corrosive of human values. In place of heedlessness leading to the careless and destructive use of natural resources, the pressing needs for self-preservation that war brings about, whether they have prompted it or not, cause deliberate devastation and inhumanity. Social instincts and refusal to act against the common good are inhibited, and the social conscience is perverted in order to make murder and spoliation not merely accidental but central, deliberate, and premeditated. War is evil not only because it brings out immoral behavior but, even more, because it calls forth the best in human beings in the service of the worst and most immoral purposes. It is, in fact, "the lie in the soul" because it twists whole societies and sends them down the wrong paths of action.

Government is what, above all, should prevent war. The maintenance of "the King's peace" has always been the primary function of government. Only in our international affairs, because national governments are sovereign, does this primary function become perverted into the corruption that is war. People, however, while they cling to government for internal order, subconsciously realize the perversion of its function in the pursuit of external security; so they distrust government when suggested in international relations, and we must see the relevance of this fact to the use of the term "governance" by and in reference to the Commission on Global Governance.

As the Chinese proverb has it: "Man can fly in the air like the birds and swim in the water like the fishes, but how to live on the earth he knows not." Only in the past twenty-five years has the dawning realization of what the degradation of our environment threatens begun to sink into the public consciousness; and it is already too late to save a good deal of what our planet has offered for a balanced and good life for human beings. Thus, our problems—of the environment, of overpopulation, of war, of poverty, of disease, and of ignorance, allied and interacting as they are—together constitute what has been summed up as "the superproblem" for humankind. But they are compounded by the fact that "everybody's business is nobody's business," and there is no one in the world with the responsibility of attempting to tackle this greatest of all challenges to the human race, except an ineffectual "United Nations" crippled by its own Charter, which obliges it to respect and uphold the sovereign independence of its members. It is this final complex situation that prompted the setting up of the Commission on Global Governance.

GOVERNANCE AND GOVERNMENT

To begin with, we need to consider definitions of the term "global governance," for governance is an English word said not to be found in other languages. This may seem to be something of a disadvantage, but, in fact, it leaves us with an opportunity to make the word mean something worthwhile in our vocabulary. We can benefit from its use, if we know why and how. Those seeking global unity will be wise to reflect, therefore, on the various possibilities that the word "governance" can offer us.

There was a writing, once celebrated in its time, by an English judge of the fifteenth century. Sir John Fortescue composed an account of "The Governance of England"—perhaps the start of that long love affair of the English ruling class with their own creation—in which he discusses various advantages of the English Constitution. Thereafter, the word appeared in different guises, never being easily pinned down or compelled to serve any very precise definition. Dictionary explanations may be inadequate, but usually they offer clues to understanding. The *New English Dictionary* gives some choice. It states: "the action or manner of governing," "controlling, directing or regulating influence, control, sway, mastery," or "the state of being governed." Further, it suggests: "the manner in which something is governed or regulated," "conduct of life or business; mode of living," and finally, "discreet or virtuous behavior; wise self-command," the last giving a tone of approval to the word that is less clear in earlier uses.

Thus, governance has had, as yet has, no precise meaning. It is a term now being brought into current use partly to recognize a reality—that the complexity of our world has required and led to a whole complex of new arrangements to deal with it. In the nation-states that grew up in Europe and colonized the world in successive centuries of the modern age, our classic forms of "government" evolved after the Middle Ages. In turn, these have developed during the twentieth century into "welfare" states and "national-security states." Yet these forms neither are suitable for, nor do they closely approximate to, the emerging patterns of global organization that are becoming visible.

But this term "governance" is also, not surprisingly, employed as a way of escape from crunch notions of law, enforcement, and responsibility that have accompanied the evolution of the nation-state. This evasion of hard political terminology presents us with a need to disentangle the more reputable from the less reputable uses of the word, and to make sure what really is what, in relation to that hard political fact of ruling in the modern state. The example before us of the Commission on Global Governance is one in which the term has not been satisfactorily analyzed before the facts of global power are discussed.

Nevertheless, there is no way to engineer a semantic escape from the hard realities of our present world, and, in fact, the word "governance" is rapidly gaining a new meaning as a consequence of association with the term "global." Probably, it will come to be seen as the equivalent of upholding world law to enable global management in order to ensure protection of the environment and further ensure that no other threats to human survival succeed in destroying the race. But that must imply certain other things that have, until now, been associated with the cognate term "government."

Thus, Mike Gravel, a former American senator, declared: "Governance is what government does. Our planet is [a] living organism, subject to human technology now powerful enough to destroy it. That power coupled with basic human sovereignty requires some degree of governance at all levels of human activity, from the individual human being to the entire world society. Lack of governance at any level impairs the effectiveness of governance at all other levels. As long as we lack effective global governance we will continue to suffer gridlocked governments at local, state and national levels. We need a world governed by law." In framing this statement he laid down criteria by which the use of the word "governance" should be measured, and he challenged, among others, the Commission to face its responsibilities.

Today our planet has a need for effective action, perhaps requiring "the smack of firm government," but in the minds of most people the word "government" is most closely associated with nation-state sovereignty. For them government has many tasks, but its coercive function is the most characteristic and it culminates in the final and primary power to defend itself—a power that (most people believe) must be kept intact above all others. Nation-states are power structures that live in a world of sovereign states and have to be competitive. Because they exist in that world of sovereign, independent nations, their first imperative is to retain armed forces in order, ultimately, to uphold their own sovereignty. But since this imperative is intimately linked to the widespread corruptive force of militarism, many, perhaps most, people see government as dangerous, dictatorial, and potentially oppressive.

Federalists need to recognize this view, often a fear, of government, widely held among the public. It comes to the fore in the minds of many people when they hear the term "world government," which, groundlessly or irrationally, they then associate with tyranny. Not so long ago, I had occasion to take issue with the chairman of the World Association of World Federalists, the late Father Gerry Grant, when he declared that world federalists were working for world federation, not a world government, "which would be world tyranny." If so eminent and knowledgeable a federalist spokesman can get it wrong, is it surprising that the general public can be easily roused to fears and apprehensions by the term "government"?

As a consequence, the word "governance" is often chosen as an alternative term, something that is nonpolitical, or at least less political than government. This is partly due to distaste for the frequent, even normal aura of shady or dubious deals that seem inseparable from the practice of politics. Partly it is due to the hope that there can be some way to evade hard, even impossible choices that government forces upon its practitioners and subjects alike. It is significant that human beings have long suggested that the only certainties are "death and taxes," and government has always had the lion's share in providing both of these twin evils.

Thus, many people coming fresh to the problem of world unity are reluctant to tackle the usual messy business of politics but prefer instead to see themselves as participating in a form of "management" of global economics or environment, carried on often by semi- or nonpolitical entities, which can be termed "governance" rather than "government." But politics is concerned with the fact of power in societies: dealing with people always involves the use of power; and sometimes, men and women being as they are, the reality is that there will, at times, be abuses of power. Most important, politics must take account of the risks of that happening. This cannot occur if those responsible for the management of affairs are unaware of, or determined to ignore, that reality.

Here it is vital to emphasize the crucial difference between the past world, the one that is still the world in which we live, and the future world when war and international violence must have been abolished. One may regard the situation in Bosnia today, where a supposed "police-force" sent in by the NATO allies had to be armed to fight, if necessary, one, two, or three armies of the Bosnians, Croats, and Serbs. There one sees the raw, even crude aspect of government—military power—on display. This is what inevitably must happen in a world of nation-states. However, when the human race becomes united politically, it will be necessary to eliminate that particular function of government, since there can then no longer be competition between sovereign states.

Thus, there is a highly important reason to see a future global authority as differing significantly from our present nation-state governments. It will not be equipped with the coercive power, for example, of nuclear weapons, nor, indeed, should it have more than the minimum of military power. Instead of being a sovereign state government with the need to uphold national independence against 200 or so other systems of national government, it will have the function of upholding the one world law against any individual or group that wishes to break it. Nor will it be able to be instituted until nation-states have determined to disarm.

Thus, global governance can be a useful term if it enables us to emphasize that a world authority would have to be significantly different from our familiar, presentday, nation-state governments. These, living under a system of power politics, have evolved into their present form in opposition to their neighbors. The raison d'être of a nation-state is its capacity to survive in a world of other more or less hostile states. The emergence of any system of world governance will stem from very different origins, since it will be a response to international anarchy and must base itself fundamentally, not upon power, but upon law and the acceptance by public opinion of its authority.

Governance would, in fact, be both more and less than government as we usually think of it, embracing a far wider sphere territorially, while its claims would be infinitely greater, since it would be intended to bring the entire planet into peace under law. Yet it would not claim to intrude into affairs that are exclusively local, regional, or national. It would be debarred from interfering in a whole slew of matters that families, towns, counties, provinces, and nationalities consider to be their own concerns and no one else's.

THE COMMISSION REPORT

The Report of the Commission on Global Governance has good things in it, but it is weakened and even rendered nugatory by a continuing failure to define its terms, particularly the central term, governance. Because the Commission did not do this, it was severely handicapped in its main task, to offer answers to the immediate need of our time—how the world can be equipped with institutions capable of dealing successfully with the challenges of the coming century. No one could expect such a group of well-meaning world citizens to come up with an adequate program for human survival and regeneration of the environment. That will have to await a properly representative body from all countries. What these good folk could—and should—have done, given the title of their brief, was to tackle that immediate need, for no one else in a similar situation has ever done it.

Perusal of *Our Global Neighborhood* reveals a full tally of good intentions, some clear statements of the pressing needs of our time, and an understanding of the problems; but the Report does not finally emerge as an adequate answer to the needs of the time nor to our planetary predicament. It has not enough grip. The Report is on the side of the angels, but inevitably, in view of its nature and credentials, it fails to be as severe as it should be upon the devils.

The glaring need for some global remedies leads the Commission to worry away at the problem. Its members know the world needs a firm hand: clearly something must be done, but what? This leads to the statement of impeccable sentiments, such as: "Global security must be broadened from its traditional focus on the security of states to include the security of people and the planet." Fine words, but the institutions to ensure results are insufficiently spelled out (or are entirely absent). The implications may be there, but their necessary consequences are not recognized; and when tackled afterward on public platforms, members of the Commission have shied away from endorsing the need for power in the hands of a global authority, what in other contexts would have to be called "government."

This is partly a political consideration. The Commission members are afraid to impugn the sacred cow of national sovereignty, for fear that their whole Report will be junked. Instead, they feel it necessary to use circumlocutions and evasions. They trust that people will get the message, even if it is not spelled out but only hinted at. This, unfortunately, is just not good enough. The world will not be saved by mealymouthed evasions of the truth.

MISSED OPPORTUNITIES

Nor, even more unfortunately, will the world be saved by blunt statements from the federalists and mundialists, who perceive the need for global institutions. They have been uttering these statements in season and out for fifty years. They have been regularly and comprehensively rubbished or ignored, and there is no sign that this is changing. For several years in the 1950s and 1960s the Sunday *Observer* in England used to offer an editorial advocating world government—about once a quarter. Yet regular readers of that newspaper could still turn round and declare to federalists that they had never heard of the notion.

Much more recently, Strobe Talbott, an American civil servant who is now an assistant secretary of state, before he was in that position, published a full page in *Time* on the need for a world government. It was not rubbished but sank almost without trace, and not even federalists seem ever to refer to it. People and their rulers have an immense capacity for "stumbling over the truth and going on again as if nothing has happened."

This is where a closer study of the term "governance" and the use of it in the way here suggested may be of real value. There is a rooted reluctance to face the needs of the time and to examine the realities of power in the modern world. Some of this reluctance may be due to stupidity or shortsightedness, but some may be caused by real fears and experience of the shortcomings of government and its practitioners in national and local affairs. We must recognize valid concerns and not brush them aside thoughtlessly. So federalists would be well advised to consider the advantages, as well as the disadvantages, offered by a term too often misused by those who oppose world federation or who, like the Commission, reject it out of hand.

But the Report does not examine the significance of the term at all, except to dismiss all thought of world government. Under the guise of governance, it promises more than it can deliver, best epitomized in the title of one chapter: "Rule of Law Worldwide," which sounds good. It makes very good, even ideal statements, but fails, in the end, to analyze the problems in depth. "Acceptance of the compulsory jurisdiction of the ICJ [International Court of Justice] should surely be a basic condition of membership in the United Nations," it says. Surely! Surely?—what's that weasel word there for? Perhaps, confident that in this case at least, world opinion is overwhelmingly favorable, it comes down strongly in support of the need for an international criminal court. But there is no mention of how the compulsory jurisdiction is to be enforced.

There is also a serious matter of omission: what the Report does not say is at times more revealing than what it does say. It is surprising to find so responsible a group of notables failing in this way; and yet it may well be that such an attitude is an almost inevitable result of a failure to come to grips with the key problem of our time, indeed, of all international affairs since the time when organized political units began to come into regular contact with each other. The nub, of course, is national sovereignty, and it is essential to notice what the Report says, or rather fails to say, on that score. So, does the semantic question loom large? Is it significant that the Commission fails to grapple with the definition of this word "governance" that is the limit of their brief? Yes, it is! Because it betrays their failure also to grapple with that problem at the heart of all our international ills—national sovereignty.

A further missed opportunity is what the Commission fails to say about world citizenship. There is no doubt that sooner or later there will be an enormous response to the need for human unity. There is no reason why the same patriotic emotions that have inspired nations—or such non-national states as the Roman empire—should not also do the same for the whole of humankind. Indeed, quite the reverse. The ideals of human solidarity and brotherhood will be evoked in order to build a new civilization. Even Ronald Reagan glimpsed this fact when he suggested that global unity would come if there were an invasion from outer space. Were that to occur, there would not be any further need for nation-state governments to dragoon their populations. "Governance" would occur naturally and inevitably. It is remarkable that the mortal dangers already threatening the survival of the human race do not yet seem to be having the same effect.

Chapter 4

Global Governance Requires Global Government

Ronald J. Glossop

The Report of the Commission on Global Governance called *Our Global Neighborhood*[1] addresses the grave issue of how our rapidly evolving global community should be governed. We must be grateful that people of such stature have addressed themselves to this issue in this comprehensive way. At the same time, the publication of such a Report merits a critical response by those who have difficulty with some of its fundamental assumptions and recommendations.

On the positive side, one cannot but admire the general thrust of this Report. It presents an optimistic and morally sensitive vision of what our world community should and could become. It covers in a very knowledgeable way a wide range of issues and concerns which the world community must address. The amount of factual information about what is already being done with regard to global issues is impressive. Some of the proposals such as those for the creation of a permanent International Criminal Court where individuals would be held accountable for violations of international law (pp. 323-25 and 348) and for the institution of a Right of Petition "within the UN system for individuals and organizations to petition for action to redress wrongs" (pp. 253-54, 301, 345-46) are significant suggestions for moving beyond the current international system designed for national governments, toward a new system which would involve interaction with individual members of the global community.

On the other hand, there are some important problems and omissions which a critic is obliged to note. The most important difficulties revolve around a statement in the Report which the Report as a whole unfortunately ignores. The crucial statement is: *"Good governance requires good government"* (p. 61). This principle that we cannot have good governance on the *national* level unless we have appropriate governmental structures as well as good individuals and groups in the top positions of that government also applies at the *world* level. Again and again the Report makes mention of the need to extend "the rule of law" to the global sphere, but it never succeeds in showing how we can have effective world law without establishing a democratic world government which could make and enforce law against individual violators. In fact, the Report itself observes that "the weaknesses in the international legal system today are largely a reflection of the weaknesses in the overall international system" (p. 331). Yet on several occasions when the flow of the argument is leading the reader to infer that creating a global government is the ideal way to deal with the problem being discussed, the Report inexplicably and defensively goes out of its way to tell the reader not to conclude that world government or world federation is being advocated (pp. xvi, 4, 336). Such defensiveness is not only completely unwarranted by anything in the Report itself, but also quite contrary to the Report's overall emphasis on the need to move beyond internationalism to globalism.

Also there is an extremely important issue for the global neighborhood which needs to be addressed but which is totally ignored in this Report: namely, the issue of what common language members of the world community should use. Despite repeated references to the desirability of democratic institutions at the world level and the evolution of a global civil society, no mention is made of the need for a common language that everyone in this global neighborhood could use in order to communicate with one another. How can democracy function if people do not have a common language for communication? How can NGOs be global in their membership if some potential members don't know the one or two languages used by that NGO? Perhaps it is just assumed that everyone in the world community will have the service of translators and interpreters whenever desired, as is the case for the top officials in governments and multi-national corporations. (I searched in vain for some kind of indication of how the Commission itself handled the language problem. Quite possibly they all used English.) Maybe the Commission just assumed that everyone in the world community will have to use English, but in that case the issue of equity for those whose native language is not English needs to be addressed. If all of us are living in a democratic global neighborhood, the problem of which language(s) we *all* can use in communicating with each other cannot be ignored.

GESTALT SHIFT FROM INTER-NATIONALISM TO GLOBALISM

One of the heartening aspects of *Our Global Neighborhood* is the awareness on the part of those responsible for the Report of the magnitude and nature of the changes currently taking place in our world. But one of the more disappointing aspects is their failure to be sufficiently careful about key concepts at the very center of their concerns.

It is not only the authors of this Report but also a substantial proportion of those addressing the issues confronting our world community who use "inter-national" and "global" as completely synonymous terms. In some situations those terms may, in fact, be interchangeable, but to think clearly about what is happening and what should be happening in the world today, it is essential to make a clear distinction between them.

The changes occurring in the world society are so great that they require a Gestalt shift in the way we view that world.[2] As is noted in the Report: "Even in 1945, few could envision the world as one neighborhood" (p. 41). We are experiencing a momentous shift from "inter-nationalism" to "globalism." The usual map of the world with the various countries in different colors is illustrative of "inter-nationalism." This paradigm sees the world as composed of a collection of sovereign nation-states with definite boundaries. It is this *inter-nationalistic view* of the world which is the basis of the United Nations, an organization composed not of the "peoples" of the world, as the opening words of its founding Charter might suggest, but rather of the sovereign nation-state governments, as the rest of the Charter makes clear and as the history of the organization has repeatedly demonstrated.[3] On the other hand, the *globalistic view* of the world is that conveyed by the familiar photo of the Earth from space. In that photo our world is seen as a single planet suspended in space with no national boundaries and with a great portion of its surface covered by oceans. This globalistic way of viewing our world represents a significant shift that should influence our attitudes and ideas about what kinds of institutions are appropriate for the planetary community. The title of the Report, *Our Global Neighborhood*, suggests that this new, globalistic view has been adopted as a basis for everything that is being discussed and recommended, but most of the contents of the Report show that the inter-nationalistic perspective is still exer-cising a predominant influence.

Let me cite a few instances where the Report fails to distinguish adequately between the old inter-national paradigm and the new global perspective. In the Co-chairmen's Foreword we read about "the growth of *international* [should it not be global?] civil society" (p. xiv), about "the [non-governmental] organiza-tions of *international* [shouldn't it be global?] civil society" (p. xvii), that "a sense of *internationalism* [shouldn't it be globalism?] has become a necessary ingredient of sound national policies" (p. xviii), and that "the right way requires the assertion of the values of *internationalism* [shouldn't it be globalism?]" (p. xix).

The failure to distinguish clearly between inter-nationalism, on the one hand, and globalism, on the other, is also found in the concluding "call to action":

Global governance, once viewed primarily as concerned with inter-governmental rela-tionships now involves not only governments and inter-governmental institutions but also non-governmental organizations (NGOs), citizens' movements, transnational corpor-ations, academia, and the mass media. The emergence of a global civil society, with many movements reinforcing a sense of human solidarity, reflects a large increase in the capacity and will of people to take control of their own lives. (p. 335)

In this paragraph the global perspective is clearly presented. But in the very next paragraph we read:

States remain primary actors but have to work with others. The United Nations must play a vital role, but it cannot do all the work. Global governance does not imply world government or world federalism. (p. 336)

So now it seems that we aren't really going to move beyond internationalism after all. The sovereign nation-states are still going to be the main actors with a complete monopoly on political and military power. They will continue to work through the inter-nationalistic United Nations, and there will be absolutely no transfer of any sovereignty whatsoever to a global federal government. But in the next paragraph we are back to globalism!

The changes of the last half-century have brought the global neighborhood nearer to reality—a world in which citizens are increasingly dependent on one another and need to cooperate. Those matters calling for global neighborhood action keep multiplying. What happens far away matters much more now. (p. 336)

So the national governments which were so prominent in the inter-nationalistic perspective of the previous paragraph are once again ignored when the focus is shifted to this global outlook.

The tension between these two attitudes becomes even more obvious in the subsequent discussion of national sovereignty:

Sovereignty has been the cornerstone of the inter-state system. In an increasingly interdependent world, however, the notions of territoriality, independence, and non-intervention have lost some of their meaning. In certain areas, sovereignty must be exercised collectively, particularly in relation to the global commons... The principles of sovereignty and non-intervention must be adapted in ways that recognize the need to balance the rights of states with the rights of people, and the interests of nations with the interests of the global neighborhood. It is time also to think about self-determination in the emerging context of a global neighborhood rather than the traditional context of a world of separate states. (p. 337)

And on the next page we read:

The concept of global security must be broadened from the traditional focus on the security of states to include the security of people and the security of the planet. (p. 338)

So it seems that the unconstrained national sovereignty of inter-nationalism should be cut back to accommodate the realities of globalism. Furthermore, we are told that the sovereign national governments working through the United Nations should do this. But the Report timidly asserts that they need not go so far as to change the system itself into a democratic world federation. Clearly the Commission feels the tidal undertow toward globalism, but cannot adjust its thinking to accommodate the new paradigm.

WHY THE UNITED NATIONS IS NOT MORE EFFECTIVE

A view expressed both in the Commission Report and by others is that the real blame for the failure of the United Nations to deal more effectively with global problems should not be placed on the organization itself but rather on the member nations. After all, the United Nations is not an entity that can do things on its own; it is only an organization through which its member states can take collective action. The Report notes:

The UN is a complex collectivity, but in essence it is formed and maintained by its members. Worthwhile reforms of UN structures ought to be pursued, and we propose several in this report, but the greatest failings of the UN have not been structural, they have been collective failings of the member-states. (p. 227)

The national governments at the United Nations, however, are not operating in a vacuum. They are operating in a context, and that context is *global anarchy*. There is no higher political and judicial authority than the national governments, so national governments are required to look out for their own national interests as best they can. It is therefore disingenuous to criticize national governments for being so focused on their own national interest, for trying to acquire the most powerful weapons they can, for not surrendering their veto power in the Security Council, and so on, while totally ignoring the context in which they must operate. The biggest problem is *not* the governments themselves, but rather the *anarchic framework* in which they must operate—and the United Nations has not changed that. A lawmaking world government would eliminate the anarchy, but the UN cannot because its Charter requires it to respect and uphold the sovereign independence of its members, so it is not a world government.

Why not, then, create a democratic world federation for the global community? It has already been noted that the Report reminds us on several occasions that no world government or world federation is being advocated, but I was able to find only one location where any attempt was made to say why a world government would be a *bad* thing, and this attempt occurs in the Co-Chairmen's Foreword:

We are not proposing movement towards world government, for were we to travel in that direction we could find ourselves in an even less democratic world than we have—one more accommodating to power, more hospitable to hegemonic ambition, and more reinforcing of the roles of states and governments rather than the rights of people. (p. xvi)

But the assumptions that are being made here about *any* world government are totally unwarranted. Why couldn't a world federation be democratic? As far as I know, that is the only kind of world federation that has ever been seriously proposed by anyone. Furthermore, the Report is very critical of the absence of democratic decisionmaking in the present inter-national arena, especially with regard to economic matters (pp. 149-156). Even the enthusiasm throughout the

Report for relying on NGOs has to be somewhat tempered when it is noted that "fewer than 15 percent of NGOs registered with the UN Economic and Social Council (ECOSOC) are from developing countries" (p. 153). What is so democratic about relying (as this Report wants to do) on NGOs based, for the most part, in the richer countries? Is it likely that a specified system of representation in a democratic world parliament would be less democratic than the existing system?

What about the suggestion in the cited paragraph that a democratic world federation would be "more hospitable to hegemonic ambition"? Part of the Report deals with the existing hegemonic control of global decisionmaking, especially in the economic area, by G-7 countries (pp. 147-49 and 154-55). Why suggest that a democratic world federation would be any "more hospitable to hegemonic ambition" than the existing system? The same kind of response could be made to the suggestions that a world government would yield a world "more reinforcing of the roles of states and governments rather than the rights of people." It is precisely the current inter-national system based on national sovereignty that overemphasizes the roles of states and governments and tends to ignore the rights of individual people, whereas a world federation would do the exact opposite. These almost parenthetical negative comments in the Report about the possible consequences of world government are unsubstantiated and totally without merit.

We could at this point push the argument even further to support the view that a democratic world federation is the appropriate kind of government for the global community. The Commission suggests that national governments should spend less on their own armed forces and contribute more to UN peacekeeping (p. 113). It is also suggested that all nuclear weapons should be eliminated (pp. 115-116). It is further suggested that we should have mechanisms of global financing independent of national governments in order to support specific UN operations (pp. 217-221). These are nice ideas, but why expect that national governments would agree to do anything of this kind until the existing inter-national anarchy is replaced by some system in which conflicts are resolved by reliable political and judicial means? What is required is a world parliament with the power to make laws, plus a world court and a designated executive with the authority to enforce the laws against individual violators regardless of their rank in their own countries.[4]

THE RULE OF LAW AND INTERNATIONAL LAW

One of the Commission's main emphases is "the need for extending on the global stage the rule of law which has been so great a civilizing influence in national societies" (p. xvii, and also Chapter 6, pp. 303-334). But the frequent mentioning of the rule of law provides just one more case of failure to pay enough attention to the distinction between an inter-nationalistic perspective and a global one. The Commission's focus is totally on inter-national law: the kind of law that typically comes into being as a result of the signing and ratifying of treaties by national governments, and which, even in theory, is binding only on those specific national governments which have signed and ratified the treaty in question. The possibility of global law for the global community is not even contemplated.

As already noted, one impressive recommendation of the Commission is the creation of a permanent International Criminal Court (ICC) which could try individuals for violating international law (pp. 323-325, 328). This is not a new idea. It was introduced in the UN General Assembly under the leadership of A.N.R. Robinson, Prime Minister of Trinidad and Tobago, in 1989.[5] A treaty to create an ICC was approved in Rome on July 17, 1998, and it will go into effect after being ratified by 60 countries. The creation of a permanent international court before which individuals could be charged with violations of international law would represent a significant move beyond an inter-nationalism which permits only national governments to be involved in legal proceedings at the world level. It would move us a bit toward a global outlook holding individual members of the world community accountable as individuals.

At the same time, even when and if the treaty initiating the ICC gets enough ratifications that the court can be established, we will still be very far from the kind of legal situation which now exists within national states. The law would be applicable only in those countries that decide in favor of the treaty. Since the arrangements for this court have been established by sovereign national govern-ments, we could have expected that the provisions would be more helpful to national governments interested in convicting persons who are a nuisance to them than useful in bringing to book any individuals accused of violating global law. A provision in the treaty says that an inidividual can be taken before the court only in those cases where permission to proceed is granted by the suspect's home state or by the state where the crime occurred. This stipulation means that national governments can protect their residents from the court's jurisdiction unless the state where the crime occurred wants the case to go to the ICC. Restrictions like this are the natural result of the common tendency among sovereign states to give precedence to their own national interests, and they are bound to arouse cynicism about what can be accomplished under international law as opposed to world law.

Another praiseworthy idea proposed by the Commission, which would move us beyond the kind of international law that recognizes only national govern-ments, is the proposal to institute a way for individuals and organizations to submit petitions to bring to the UN's attention situations in which the security of groups of people could be endangered (pp. 260-263, 301, 345-6). This provision would allow NGOs and others to call attention to grave situations that national governments might well prefer to conceal from the rest of the world. Such an arrangement seems to be a very small step, but nevertheless it has the very large consequence of seeking to prevent national governments from blocking efforts to provide humanitarian help to their own citizenry. But the actual impact of this suggestion, even if implemented, could well be negligible in view of the fact that no means are proposed for obligating either the General Assembly or the governments concerned to take the action requested in the petitions.

With regard to the use of international law to govern the behavior of nation-states in relation to other nation-states, even the Report, which is generally very optimistic about what can be accomplished by international law, points out that two Western nations "that claim leadership in international affairs" (p. 312), namely, France and the United States, have refused to abide by various decisions of the International Court of Justice in the past 25 years. Nevertheless, the Commission recommends that

some appropriate body should be mandated to explore ways in which international law-making can be expedited—without, of course, calling into question the consensual nature of international law itself. (p. 330)

But it is just this consensual nature of international law that displays the carryover from an inter-nationalistic world and represents a main obstacle to the making of effective and meaningful law to serve the global community.

When the Commission talks about "the rule of law that has been so great a civilizing influence in national societies," it seems that it should pay more attention to the manner in which that law within national societies is made, applied, and enforced. National law can operate as it does only because, being part of a system of government, it can be effectually enforced. The Report says:

Scholars once argued that international law was not law in the true sense, as there was no international police force to enforce it, no sanctions if it were disobeyed, and no international legislature. But with the growth in use of international law, these arguments are heard less often today. (p. 304)

The arguments may be heard less often, but that does not mean that they are no longer fully valid and relevant. Perhaps there can be some rules that most countries can agree to follow most of the time in their relations with each other (as long as they do not conflict with their national interests), and everyone can agree with the Commission that it would be helpful if national governments would adopt more such rules. Nevertheless, such international law remains quite different from the municipal law that has been so important in the advancement of civilized life within our several countries. Municipal law is enforceable upon individuals, but international law generally admits only sovereign states as its subjects, and upon sovereign states no law can be enforced except by military action, which national governments are unwilling to take except in extremis, and resort to which in any event contradicts the very purpose of the rule of law. Not to recognize or draw attention to this difference is misleading in the highest degree.

THE LANGUAGE ISSUE

In an inter-nationalistic world, nations and nation-states have their own national languages, and communication between different language groups is accomplished by using interpreters or translators. This arrangement is feasible when there are relatively few persons interacting across relatively few national borders. Educated persons, adapting to the idea of multilingualism, can often learn two or three languages and thus travel and interact with other people in several other countries.

Currently, our inter-nationalistic world is still organized in accord with these principles. Even international bodies such as the United Nations and the European Union operate by adopting some limited number of national languages as the "official" languages of the organization. All participants will convert what has been said or written into the other official languages. If you are from an important country, you will probably be able to use your native language. If not, you will be expected to learn one of the other "major" languages. At the UN, where 185 countries are members, there are six official languages (English, French, Mandarin Chinese, Russian, Spanish, and Arabic). In the European Union, which seeks to be more democratic and thus allows each member nation-state to choose one "official" language, there are now 15 member states and 11 official languages (Danish, Dutch, English, French, German, Greek, Finnish, Italian, Portuguese, Spanish, and Swedish). As you can imagine, there are many well-paid interpreters and translators working for the European Union as well as the UN.

But the Europeans are running into problems (not only financial) as they seek to develop a single European society. How can children be expected to learn ten languages in addition to their native language so that they will be able to travel, or go to school, or work, anywhere in the community? And what will happen as new countries such as Poland, Hungary, and the Czech Republic become part of the Community? If only some languages are selected to be used in the whole European community, which ones will they be? Won't there be unfair discrimination against those who use other languages? And on the world level, how can such multilingualism possibly work? In the world community there are now 13 national languages with more than 100 million speakers each, plus another 14 with 50 million or more speakers.[6]

In our global neighborhood, it is going to be necessary for people to communicate with one another. There is a limit to the number of languages anyone can be expected to learn. The most obvious solution to the problem of allowing free communication throughout the neighborhood without sacrificing linguistic diversity is to have everyone learn the same second language; but the difficulty will then be to decide what that common second language should be. Another difficult issue will be determining how that decision will be made. In the absence of a world parliament, how should the decision be made? Here we have a real test for the principle of democratic global decisionmaking. If we were to have a worldwide referendum with all persons simply voting for their own language, the choice would be Mandarin Chinese. If voting were done by the delegates to the UN General Assembly, the decision might be for English or French or Spanish. If it were decided, on grounds of fairness, to rule out each voter's native language, the decision might be for Esperanto. People who had studied the issue also might opt for Esperanto because it has been deliberately designed to be learned rapidly (completely phonetic, no exceptions to rules, rule-guided prefixes and suffixes for rapid vocabulary expansion, and so on).[7]

This matter of which common language(s) the global neighborhood should use is not a minor matter. If communication is to be two-way and not just from the rich to the poor, the language issue will have to be addressed on a global level. If NGOs are going to be truly global and not limited to those who speak English (or French or German), the language issue will have to be addressed at the global level. If there is going to be democracy on that level, this is unavoidable. It is an indispensable condition for any real global neighborhood; yet it is not addressed by the Report at all.

GLOBAL GOVERNANCE AND GLOBAL GOVERNMENT

One important theme of *Our Global Neighborhood* is that "global *governance* is *not global government.*" (p. xvi) But what *is* "governance"? And what role does government play in governance?

Here is the Report's attempt to answer the first question:

Governance is the sum of the many ways individuals and institutions, public and private, manage their common affairs. It is a continuing process through which conflicting or diverse interests may be accommodated and co-operative action may be taken. It includes formal institutions and regimes empowered to enforce compliance, as well as informal arrangements that people and institutions either have agreed to or perceive to be in their interests... Examples of governance at the local level might include a neighborhood co-operative formed to install and maintain a standing water-pipe, a town council operating a waste recycling scheme, a multi-urban body developing an integrated transport plan together with user groups, a stock exchange regulating itself with national government oversight, and a regional initiative of state agencies, industrial groups, and residents to control deforestation. At the global level, governance has been viewed primarily as intergovernmental relationships, but it must now be understood as also involving non-governmental organizations (NGOs), citizens' movements, multinational corporations, and the global capital market. Interacting with these are global mass media of dramatically enlarged influence. (pp. 2-3)

So what does "governance" involve? It seems that in any community there are many activities by various groups which are *helpful* in solving communal problems. The Commission rightly encourages all groups (national governments, international organizations, non-governmental organizations, citizens' movements, multinational corporations, and those who control global capital) to devote themselves to helping the global community to solve its problems, seeming to identify global governance with their mutual cooperation. But is it still "global governance" if these same groups engage in activities which *hinder* the solution of global problems? For example, if a multinational corporation promotes the cutting of trees in the rain forest of the Amazon, is this part of global governance or is it not? Another example: if some NGOs oppose family planning programs in poor countries with rapid population growth, is this part of global governance?

The Commission seems to focus on all the helpful things that different groups in the global community might do to deal with various global predicaments and then to call this "global governance." But when these very same groups do things that are harmful to the process of solving global problems, then the term "global governance" is no longer applied. If terminology is used in this way, "global governance" is bound to be seen as desirable. But can we rely on such verbal tricks as a way of dealing with the substantive issues?

We need to look more closely at the kinds of institutions that might enable us to solve global problems and then assess their strengths and weaknesses to judge whether we should rely on them to deal with the difficulties we have to face. Let us consider the situation of (1) national governments, (2) international organizations (composed of representatives appointed by national governments), (3) citizen organizations (NGOs) devoted to the solution of particular problems or to advancing particular viewpoints, and (4) multinational corporations.[8] Afterwards, for comparison, we consider the proposal of a democratic world federation.

National governments, especially of the larger nations, have substantial financial and other resources at their command. That is their main strength. If they decide to do something to deal with some global problem, they may have a noticeable impact. Their great weakness is that the goal of each nation-state is always simply to advance its own national interest. If the national interest coincides with the global interest, much can be accomplished. For example, if it truly is in the national interest of China to control the rate of its population growth, the government of China can offer various incentives to reduce the number of births in the territory it governs, or it can impose penalties on families of more than a specified size. This action will also help to curtail the rate of population growth in the world at large, so the national government of China is helping to solve a world problem. But this assistance is merely fortuitous. Some other national government may decide that it should adopt a pronatalist policy and enact measures to increase the number of births in its domain. This certainly would not help solve the global population problem. Apparently, the authors of *Our Global Neighborhood* would regard the former case as a success for "global governance"; but in the latter case we are witnessing something other than global governance. If we are to call it "global governance" when national policies happen to coincide with the interests of the global community, what are we to say when no such coincidence exists, as is often the case?

What is the situation with regard to international governmental organizations such as the United Nations, the World Health Organization, the Universal Postal Union, and the International Atomic Energy Agency? These generally have much more limited resources at their disposal than the bigger governments. They also are inhibited from carrying out programs opposed by any of the larger national governments, since their funding depends on what is contributed by these governments. The United Nations is hardly likely to do anything contrary to the wishes of any of the permanent members of the Security Council. Organizations such as UNESCO and the International Labor Organization have already discovered that they lose about one-fourth of their financial resources if they do anything opposed by the United States. Such subservience to the larger national powers is one of the great weaknesses of international organizations. On the other hand, what is in their favor is that they are generally addressing global problems from a global point of view rather than pursuing a policy dictated by the interests of one or a few national governments.

Let us consider the position of the NGOs, the heroes of global governance in the Report. Certainly, one of their major strengths is that most of these organizations focus on solving global problems. Nobody doubts the sincerity or desirability of organizations such as Amnesty International or the International Red Cross. On the other hand, there are also various non-governmental organizations promoting views or action that not everyone finds desirable. But even when the goals of the NGOs are worthy of universal support, there is the problem that, almost all being dependent for the most part on voluntary contributions from individuals, they do not have adequate resources to accomplish their aims. Moreover, if they come into conflict with the national interests of any of the great powers, they cannot hope to compete. The great weakness, even of the more benign NGOs, is their lack of financial resources compared with the national governments and multinational corporations.

In contrast, multinational corporations have tremendous financial resources at their command. That is their strength. Their weakness is that their goal is simply to make a profit. Sometimes their efforts to do so will coincide with what is good for the global community, as, for example, when Dupont developed a new kind of refrigerant to replace the older ozone-depleting chlorofluorocarbons. That development was very helpful to the global community even though Dupont's main goal was to make money. But, more often, the money-making activities of multinational corporations is extremely harmful, as when Nestle promoted the use of infant formula in parts of the world where sterilization of bottles was difficult and not customary, where people could not read the directions, and where the cost of proper usage (avoiding overdilution) was more than most of the population could afford. So the overall situation of multinational corporations with regard to solving global problems is somewhat parallel to that of national governments. When making money happens to coincide with the needs of the global community, we (or the Commission) can call it "global governance." But more often the two do not coincide. Then is it still "global governance"? If not, why and how should "global governance" be related to it?

By contrast, what would be the situation for a democratic world federation when it comes to dealing with global problems? It would possess power and authority, as any government does, to raise taxes to gain funds for attacking the collective problems of the community. From the first, use of this power should be strictly limited, and people would need to observe whether the government was putting the resources so acquired to good use. As to the adoption of policies aiming at the successful solution of the problems confronting the global community, the situation would be comparable to what we find in any democratic government: that is, if the elected leaders are not getting the problems solved, they will be replaced at the next election by those who seem to have better ideas about dealing with the difficulties. There would be public discussion and debate about the best courses to pursue. Laws would be passed to promote helpful behavior on the part of individuals, local governments, civil organizations, and commercial enterprises, and to punish behavior harmful to the interests of the world community, as the elected representatives would determine them. We would then have "global governance" by an elected global government rather than a situation in which we simply lump together, under the name of global governance, all the helpful things done by various organizations (whether deliberately for the good of humanity in general, or coincidentally with other aims, such as maximizing profit), while just ignoring all the harmful things done by these same organizations.

Of course, governments are not always good. Sometimes they come under the control of groups who aim at their own limited welfare rather than at the welfare of the community as a whole.[9] When a democratic world federation is designed, it will be necessary to plan well to avoid such a development. We have many national governments which can serve as models of how to do this. They can show us proven techniques for avoiding pitfalls, methods such as adopting constitutional safeguards to prevent corruption or undesirable control by vested interests.

In the end, then, we are led back to the statement on page 61 of the Report: *"Good governance requires good government,"* with reference to developing the appropriate governmental structures and of making sure that able and well-motivated individuals and groups occupy the top positions in that government. We cannot afford to adopt the superficial view that some individuals will be doing many things helpful to the global community that can be grouped under the name "good governance," while we simply ignore everything that other individuals and groups—some of them very powerful—are doing for their own benefit and contrary to the general welfare. We also need to recognize that with governance in that weak, nongovernmental sense, some problems of the global community (such as the huge disparity between rich and poor) may not get addressed at all, simply because there is no particular group of legislators or executives who will be held responsible for dealing with the whole range of problems that the global community must handle. Without a world government, the world community lacks the global institutions which will give priority to and have the obligation to care for the universal interest.[10]

NOTES

1. *Our Global Neighborhood: The Report of the Commission on Global Governance* (Oxford and New York: Oxford University Press, 1995).

2. For a comprehensive discussion of the nature of a paradigm shift and its role in the history of science and changes of world view, see Thomas S. Kuhn, *The Structure of Scientific Revolutions*, 2nd ed. enlarged (Chicago: University of Chicago Press, 1970).

3. This same point is made in the Report on pages 67-68 and again on pages 225-226.

4. One has to wonder whether the Commission took any account whatsoever of the arguments for the need for a democratic world federation as might be found in recent books such as Errol E. Harris, *One World or None: A Prescription for Survival* (Atlantic Highlands, NJ: Humanities Press, 1993), or Ronald J. Glossop, *World Federation? A Critical Analysis of Federal World Government* (Jefferson, NC: McFarland, 1993), or James A. Yunker, *World Union on the Horizon: The Case for Supranational Federation* (Lanham, MD: University Press of America, 1993).

5. Cf. Bryan F. McPherson, *An International Criminal Court: Applying World Law to Individuals* (Monograph #10 published by the Center for United Nations Reform Education, Washington DC, 1992), p. 7.

6. *The World Almanac and Book of Facts, 1998* (Mahwah, NJ: World Almanac Books), pp. 444-445.

7. See Ronald J. Glossop, "Language Policy and a Just World Order," *Alternatives*, Vol. XIII (1988), pp. 395-409, and John Roberts, *A World Language for One World* (London: Association of World Federalists, 1993).

8. For a longer discussion of the various kinds of institutions which have a role in addressing global problems, see Barry B. Hughes, *World Futures: A Critical Analysis of Alternatives* (Baltimore: John Hopkins University Press, 1985), pp. 190-211.

9. Aristotle in his *Politics* (Book III, Ch. vii) noted that the difference between good governments and bad is that the former aim for the welfare of the whole community, while the latter aim for the welfare only of the rulers. See Ernest Barker, ed. and trans., *The Politics of Aristotle* (Oxford and New York: Oxford University Press, 1962), pp. 113-114.

10. See Ronald J. Glossop, "Why Global Governance Is Not Enough: Beyond International Governance to World Federation," in Philip Isely, ed., *Global Governance or Federal World Government* (Lakewood CO: Emergency Earth Rescue Administration, 1995), esp. pp. 6-8.

Chapter 5

Global Government:
Objections Considered
David Ray Griffin

The title of the Report of the Commission on Global Governance suggests that the world today is a global neighborhood in which everybody lives in friendly, cooperative relationships, and the Commissioners make recommendations professing to indicate the best way "our global neighborhood" should be administered. But when we look about us at the international scene, we observe a very different panorama, with wars and rumors of wars (civil and international), terrorism and famine, whole countries sown with land mines, huge flights of refugees, and destruction of the planetary environment. The Commission is acutely aware of all (or most) of these evils, and proposes improved "global governance" as the remedial way forward.

Contrary to the views of those who maintain that the only effective remedy would be a world federation, the Commission sets its face against any such solution of world problems, rejecting it as harmful and implying that it is not really possible. This twofold objection is more presupposed than argued in *Our Global Neighborhood*. We can assume, however, that the authors accept the standard arguments to the effect that that the creation of a global government would be both undesirable and impossible. Let us consider each of these two objections in turn.

THE CHARGE OF UNDESIRABILITY

The most common reason for considering the idea of a global government undesirable is the fear that such a government would likely turn into a world tyranny. The very idea seems to conjure up in many people demonic images, such as that of a Joseph Stalin armed with a worldwide KGB and a monopoly on nuclear weapons. However, to refuse even to consider the idea because of such images, is hardly rational.

That a global government could be dangerous can readily be admitted. *Any* government nowadays can be dangerous, and the same is even more true of any global order. But the essential question is: Would the creation of a global government be *more* or *less* dangerous than continuing with the presentday anarchical lack of order among sovereign states? International relations are conducted between nation-states whose primary national interest is inevitably security—the defense of their national independence against ever-present risks of aggression. In consequence, the threat of war constantly prevails, with results that have been all too evident, and still are, throughout this century.[1] Einstein, in response to a correspondent who raised this objection said: "I agree with you with respect to the dangers which would be involved in the creation of a world government. But I believe that these dangers are less significant than the dangers of international anarchy which, in fact, involves the perpetual threat of war. It seems to me that the latter is the most effective means by which government can keep the people in some sort of slavery."[2] Einstein's response, in other words, was that the present system is more dangerous in two respects: besides allowing war, it is also more conducive to tyranny.

The objection that a central government would probably lead to tyranny was raised by those opposed to the plan to create a federal government for the United States of America; and yet the framers of the Constitution did quite well in setting up a form of government that could avoid becoming tyrannical, especially when the Bill of Rights was added to the checks and balances built into the separation of the executive, legislative, and judicial branches. The major failure of the framers was to make no provisions that would have excluded the inordinate influence of money and, thereby, *de facto* rule by the wealthy. In any case, framers of a global government today could surely do as well as those gentlemen did 200 years ago and, assuming that we have learned something in the intervening two centuries, even better, especially with regard to insulating global government from the corrupting influence of money.

The idea, finally, that the global government's monopoly of military power would be too dangerous, because it could be taken over by some faction, should not be a serious concern. The troops, including their commanders, would be drawn from people of all nations, and would be stationed in all parts of the globe. Also, the main sources of present conflict, instead of leading to the threat of international war, would, under a global government, be settled by legal judgments between individuals; and the enforcement of these judgments would (at most) involve police, not military, action. In sum, the specter of tyranny is largely illusory and is no good reason to dismiss global government without further thought.

A second reason for thinking the idea of global government undesirable is that it conjures up the image of a bureaucratic nightmare, a US governmental bureaucracy writ large, with its tentacles reaching into every aspect of human life around the globe. The proponents of global government, however, have almost always spoken of a *strictly limited government* whose authority would be restricted to specified areas. Some proposals, to be sure, specify more areas than others, but they are almost all very limited, with nothing like the range of responsibilities, such as health, welfare assistance, education, housing and transportation, borne by national governments. In short, a global administration would be limited to those departments of government that deal with matters of common concern to all nations alike, such as the planetary ecology, which, in any case, fall outside the jurisdiction of every national government.

It might be maintained that "governance" would be a better term than "government" because it would less readily conjure up these tyrannical and bureaucratic images. I have used the term "government," however, to indicate that, if effective global governance is to be exercised in those areas in which governance is needed, there must be an organization with both the constitutional mandate and the power to exercise such governance.

Yet a third reason for rejecting the idea of global government as undesirable is that, whereas what we need today is more political and economic decentralization, global government would be the ultimate form of political and economic centralization. The first part of the answer to this objection is that, whereas many issues that have been controlled at national levels should indeed be put under more local control, especially in large countries such as the United States, legislation and enforcement with regard to other important issues, such as global environmental protection, security from outside attack, and guidance of the overall direction of the global economic system (for example, reduction of the inequality between rich nations and poor), can be effectively carried out only at the supranational level.

The second part of the answer is that political and economic decentralization of the type that is desired can occur only in tandem with a type of centralization. Herman E. Daly and John B. Cobb, Jr., in *For the Common Good: Redirecting the Economy toward Community, the Environment, and a Sustainable Future* (Boston: Beacon Press, 1989), have argued convincingly that *political* decentralization, for which so many have called, cannot be had without *economic* decentralization, because, unless a community can control its economic life, it can have no real control over its political life. To their argument I am adding the further point that, apart from a global government that determines the general direction of the global economy, the kind of economic decentralization for which they call will almost certainly not come about. One can hardly expect economic decentralization on a global scale unless, for instance, the multinational corporations can be regulated by some supranational authority.

As Richard Falk has argued, global governance of one sort or another is going to come about willy-nilly if not by choice. If we continue in the direction we have been going, this governance will be effectively exercised by the international banks and multinational corporations. Political decisions will increasingly be guided and even dictated by the global economic market, so that even the remnant of morality that still exists in politics will be obliterated. If we reject political global government, we will, in effect, be choosing this amoral form of governance, in which decisions are increasingly made without respect to equity, rights, preservation of local communities, or ecological sustainability. The other possibility is to make a deliberate choice for *political* global governance. I, like Falk, am saying that this should be a *democratic* form of political government, in which all the peoples of the world, including the advocates of ecological sustainability, would have a voice. I am adding the argument that, for this sort of governance actually to be effective, so that it could indeed change the direction of the global economy, it would have to be exercised by an organization with the constitutional authority to pass legislation and the judicial, financial, and police power to enforce it.

With regard to the Daly-Cobb vision of economic decentralization, in which each community becomes as self-sufficient as possible so that trade is minimized rather than maximized, this total reversal of the course we have been on for the past several hundred years, is veritably inconceivable apart from a global government that would mandate and provide policy guidelines for such a change. The kind of centralization involved in the form of global government envisaged here is, then, not the antithesis of the desirable kind of economic and political decentralization, but its precondition.

A fourth reason for thinking a global government undesirable is the belief that it would lead to a further homogenization of the planet, accelerating a process already under way through which the diversity of cultures is being destroyed. This belief might be somewhat true if global government were understood as a US federal government writ large. Even within the United States of America, however, considerable diversity in terms of beliefs, values, traditions, and even practices is possible and persists; commonality is required only with regard to some basic values, such as respect for the Constitution (especially the Bill of Rights), tolerance of diverse beliefs and values, and acceptance of democratic principles. All the more would diversity be compatible with the kind of limited world government proposed here, according to which the nations would retain their autonomy in many respects, having much more actual autonomy vis-à-vis the global government than the individual states have vis-à-vis the US federal government at the present time.[3]

The main point to be made, however, is that global government, far from being an instrument of further uniformity, could (and should) serve as a means to protect humanity's cultural diversity. The homogenization that has already occurred has been due not to political unification, but to the global reach of Western-based (mainly US-based) mass media and multinational corporations. The development of a global political organization would (as I suggest later) serve as an *alternative* to, and thereby a possible restraint upon, a globalization driven purely by economic motives, which if left unchecked will surely lead to an increasingly homogenized, and thereby greatly impoverished, human race.

THE CHARGE OF IMPOSSIBILITY

The charge that a global government would be undesirable is usually made only in passing (as, for instance, in Kenneth Waltz, *Man, the State, and War: A Theoretical Analysis* [New York: Columbia University Press, 1959], pp. 15 and 228), apparently to make a virtue out of the necessity of remaining in the state of international anarchy in perpetuity (or until doomsday). The main charge is actually that the creation of such a government would be impossible. Waltz, for example, says that the call for world government to solve the disease of war is a "utopian prescription," by which he means that it is "unattainable in practice" (pp. 228 and 238). His one-line explanation for this unattainability is that "the amount of force needed to hold a society together varies with the heterogeneity of the elements composing it" (p. 228). He thereby seems to be taking the same position as Hans Morgenthau, who had argued that, although world government is indeed the only way to prevent war, such a government could not possibly be created in our time. The precondition, he maintained, was a global society with much more uniformity in terms of beliefs and values than we have today, a degree of uniformity that would not emerge for perhaps another two centuries.[4] This objection seems to be based on the idea that a global government would preside over a United Nations of the World understood by analogy with the United States of America. In the kind of global government envisaged here, however, the kinds of agreement on basic values needed would be even more minimal than is needed among the peoples of the United States for us to have a functioning US government.

Furthermore, the required consensus among the peoples of the world on basic values arguably already exists. For evidence, I point to Dorothy V. Jones' essay "The Declaratory Tradition in Modern International Law" (*Traditions of International Ethics*, eds. Terry Nardin and David R. Mapel [New York: Cambridge University Press, 1992]). With reference to various public documents endorsed by the nations of the world, she lists nine principles that have been widely accepted: (1) the equality of states; (2) the integrity of states; (3) the equality of all peoples with regard to rights, including that of self-determination; (4) non-intervention; (5) peaceful settlement of disputes; (6) no use, or even threat, of force; (7) fulfillment of international obligations; (8) cooperation; and (9) respect for individual human rights.

Her point is not, of course, that most nations live by these principles in practice. Rather, it is that they have officially agreed that living by these principles would be desirable, so that the principles sketch a picture of the way "the states think the world ought to be" (pp. 43f). This is precisely the kind of consensus on values that is needed for a global democratic government to work (my point, not hers). She adds, furthermore, two more principles that have attained considerable acceptance, although not to the same degree as the other nine: (10) the protection of the natural environment, and (11) the creation of an equitable world economic order. The eleventh principle, of course, is the most controversial. Any global discussion of this principle would begin with very different notions of what kind of order would be "equitable." In any case, even if Morgenthau's claim about lack of consensus on values was true in the early part of this century (when his opinions were shaped), that claim can certainly now be disputed.

Part of the Morgenthau-Waltz claim, reflected in Waltz's statement that "the amount of force needed to hold a society together varies with the heterogeneity of the elements composing it," reflects a somewhat different issue than simply that of a consensus on basic values in general. The issue here is a loyalty to, even a sense of reverence for, a central government, especially the constitution and its offices. The United States is able to endure without too much internal coercion because, however much Americans may personally dislike the current Chief Justice of the Supreme Court or the current President, they generally have considerable reverence for the Constitution, the office of the Presidency, and the Supreme Court (and therewith its rulings).

If the argument proposed is that we cannot have a global government that would command the respect of the various peoples of the world until they all develop a loyalty to the global community, this would be to demand that the cart pull the horse. People in the states of Virginia or Massachusetts could not have had any reverence for the government of the United States prior to its existence. And there was, except in a few exceptional individuals, probably little concern for the common good of all the states—certainly no concern rivaling people's concern for their own states—prior to the creation of the federal government. Even after the Union was created, loyalty and reverence for it was not, it is safe to assume, generated overnight.

Accordingly, insofar as the "values" that do not yet exist are reverence for, and loyalty to, a global government, these values must, as a matter of fact, be developed after, not before, the establishment of world federation. To be sure, the creation of such a government will depend upon the prior existence of a sufficient number of "citizen pilgrims" (in Richard Falk's phrase) who already have a sense of loyalty to the embryonic global community. For most people, however, this loyalty, which will enable the world federal enactments to be carried out without undue coercion, will be more a product than a precursor of the actual creation of a global government. This is one reason why global governance will require a global government with powers of enforcement.

Having said all of this, I hasten to add that I do not at all minimize the importance of beliefs and values. To the contrary, it is to worldviews and their ethical implications that most of my professional time is devoted. Our efforts toward global governance must be two-pronged: at the same time as the case is being made for the necessity and possibility of global government, people in various religious and philosophical traditions need to be interpreting those traditions, probably through a combination of retrieval and reformation, so as to reveal and emphasize their support for this transition to world unity (which, after all, would be arguably the greatest transformation of human civilization since its inception).

My major project at present is, in fact, to develop a theology for a new world order, which will incorporate a greatly expanded version of this essay's central argument. In it I will distinguish those aspects of the Christian tradition which seem to reflect genuine divine revelation from those that are better explained as contributing to the ideological component of Schmookler's "parable of the tribes."[5] Whereas these latter elements support attitudes of superiority, exclusiveness, belligerence, and competition, the former aspects, which better reflect genuine revelation of divine values, provide support for those attitudes—such as justice, compassion, and concern for the general good, including that of all forms of life—that would lead to the advocacy of global governance in our time. Besides hoping that this kind of "postanarchistic hermeneutic" will catch on in our Western Christian circles, I hope that analogous efforts will be undertaken in other traditions.

In any case, although the effort to cultivate beliefs and values supportive of global government has to be part of the effort to bring such a government into being, we should not think of this more philosophical-religious-ethical aspect of the task as something to be completed prior to the actual establishment of world union. We should recognize that, whereas it is important to emphasize the extent to which we already have a consensus on basic values and the need to cultivate as much more as we can, most of this global sentiment will necessarily be developed after a world federation has been set up. This, incidentally, is not in conflict with the point made earlier about global government as a means to promote cultural diversity (as opposed to uniformity), because of the difference in level of abstractness between the different values in question. To argue the case for this point here would lead us too far afield, but the direction of the argument can be indicated by pointing out that one of the relatively abstract values upon which we need consensus is tolerance of, and indeed respect for, diversity with regard to concrete values and traditions.

One might agree with my response to the first objection against the possibility of global government, based on the need for a consensus about basic values, and still contend that the governments of the nations would never agree, even in principle, to enter into discussions about creating the kind of world federation envisaged here. The argument might be that the poor countries would reject such a proposal out of hand as one more scheme by the rich to exploit them even more effectively. This objection, however, could be forestalled if, from the very beginning, proposals for global union were worked out by representatives from nations all over the world, including the poorest. It is also relevant that the poorer nations are *at present* excluded from most of the decisions made about international order. By definition they are excluded from the economic decisions made by the G-8 nations. And in the United Nations the recent demotion of the General Assembly in favor of the Security Council has deprived the poorer nations of most of what little influence they had acquired over global political decisions. Accordingly, these countries would have much

to gain, and little (if anything) to lose, in the kind of global government envisaged here, in which political, environmental, and economic policies affecting
common interests would be decided on a democratic basis, by a popularly
elected parliament, with no nations having veto powers, and no inner circle with
permanent (as opposed to temporary) membership.

A more serious argument, especially given what I have just said, is that the
rich countries would never agree to enter into discussion about a global government based on democratic principles. It was, after all, the United States that
refused to ratify the Covenant of the League of Nations, which would, among
other things, have limited the right of the US to intervene in Latin America. And
it was the United States and the other wealthy nations that gave themselves
permanent membership—with a veto power—in the Security Council and, in
general, made sure that the United Nations would not have the means to curb
their own desires. Given this history and our more general knowledge of human
nature, as well as of the way sovereign nations commonly behave, how do we
suppose that the rich nations of the world would ever seriously consider a
proposal for a global government that would not only set a restriction upon their
sovereignty (meaning their right to go to war whenever they believe that their
vital interests are at stake), but also commit them to begin overcoming the huge
economic disparity between themselves and the poorest nations?

To be more specific, we may pose this question in terms of the United States.
Einstein declared in 1947: "If the US does not take the initiative, no one will."[6]
But given its status as the world's sole remaining military and economic superpower, should we not suppose that it would be the most reluctant of the wealthy
nations to change the present rules of international relations? We might also
suppose, in contrast, that, if the United States *would* accept the idea of democratic global government and take the lead in promoting it, the other wealthy
nations would be likely to follow suit. There are, however, very good reasons to
assume that the United States, at least in the near future, would not contemplate
going along with any proposal for world democratic government, let alone lead
the way.

Although this clearly seems the most formidable of all the difficulties, I do
not believe that we can, even here, speak of impossibility. The main reason for
thinking that the United States might consent, and even take the initiative, is the
perilous situation in which the human race finds itself at the present time. The
case that global government is necessary if human civilization is to survive
much longer, at least without suffering unimaginable devastation, can be made
in a compelling way, once the various dimensions of the crisis in which we find
ourselves are examined together, and without wishful thinking: the risk of
nuclear proliferation, the possibility of nuclear terrorism, and the outbreak of
nuclear war; the accelerating deterioration and willful destruction of the natural
environment, including global warming and the resulting climate change, with
the devastating consequences that may ensue; the population explosion; and the
steady exhaustion of vital resources with resulting increase in the incidence and

ferocity of resource wars (as predicted in *Tapped Out* [Welcome Rain Publishing, 1998], by former Senator Paul Simon). Once this case is made and sufficiently publicized, the people of the United States from reasonably enlightened self-interest—by which I mean a concern for the world as it will be for their own children, grandchildren, and great-grandchildren, reinforced by a modicum of genuine concern for the future of humanity, and perhaps even for life as a whole on this planet—could well come to demand a transition to global government. This would, at least, be possible if they can be convinced of the truth, by the testimony of history and current affairs, that the chief obstacle to the solution of contemporary world problems is the inevitable pursuit by sovereign nations of their own national interests at the expense of the common good.

Another force that can be tapped for this result is the special sense of mission that has been an ingredient in the American psyche from the beginning. This sense of mission has, of course, sometimes had extremely undesirable consequences, as exemplified in some of the more extravagant notions of America's "manifest destiny," and it can still be a very dangerous notion. But there is also a positive side, as Richard Falk has pointed out, to this sense that the US has a special mission.[7] My suggestion is that, given America's self-understanding as "redeemer nation" (to use the title of Ernest Tuveson's book), it might in the ensuing decades come to see its task to be that of saving the world by leading the movement toward global government, through which our otherwise terminal crises can be overcome. Furthermore, given the Jewish and Christian roots of our understanding of the nature of a "redeemer," the fact that tremendous self-sacrifice might be involved in this transition might come to be regarded as a plus rather than a minus.

Of course, contemporary international theorists, given their generally Hobbesian-Darwinian view of human nature, will smile knowingly at such a suggestion. But, as Falk has pointed out, this completely egoistic psychology is one of the obstacles that need to be overcome if we are to have a truly realistic appraisal of human nature and its possibilities.[8] There really is an idealistic side to human nature. Whether it can be shaped so as to favor this kind of short-term sacrifice for the sake of altruism and enlightened long-term self-interest remains to be seen. What I am suggesting is that this idealistic dimension of human nature in general, plus the American sense of a special redeeming mission in particular, offers a basis for thinking that America, if properly educated and challenged, might rise to the occasion. If we see that global government is necessary for survival, we should not allow any of these largely specious objections to prevent us from making an effort to bring it about.

Another argument against the possibility of global government is that, even if we could get all the nations, rich and poor alike, to consider the idea seriously enough to try to work out a proposal that would be acceptable to all concerned, it would still be impossible actually to reach agreement on the constitutional details. For example, although agreement might be easily forthcoming on a separation of powers between judicial, executive and legislative branches, what principle would be used for representation in the legislature? On the one hand, the principle of one voting representative per nation would never be acceptable to the more populous nations, because it would allow the world's future to be charted by representatives of only a tiny percentage of the human race. Besides, it would encourage the fragmentation of all nations into smaller and smaller units. On the other hand, the principle of one voting representative for every so many million people would never be acceptable to the less populous nations, because it would allow the world's future to be determined by a tiny percentage of the nations of the world. One possible solution to this problem might be some form of bicameral legislature.

Another controversial issue would be whether the representatives, instead of being chosen by their governments, should be elected directly by popular vote, so that they would, in principle, be independent of their administrations back home and could vote according to their consciences. As Einstein perceived, the second alternative would, in principle, be far better, but to adopt it, of course, would make most governments more reluctant to ratify the proposal.[9] In any case, there would be many difficult issues of this sort in trying to write a formal constitution that would be acceptable to nations of all types and sizes.

This problem of an acceptable constitution should, like the prior problem, be taken with extreme seriousness. Taking it seriously, however, should not lead us in the direction followed by Grenville Clark and Louis Sohn in *World Peace through Law* (Chapel Hill: University of North Carolina Press, 1944). Thinking that these constitutional matters would prove to be a major obstacle to world government, they sought to work out a detailed proposal in advance. The result was, in Falk's phrase, "premature specificity." It is premature in three senses. In the first place, for obvious reasons, a plan worked out by two white men from the United States would be doomed to failure, no matter how excellent it might otherwise be. In the second place, it is most unlikely that a plan conceived by two such persons, no matter how broad their sympathies, would in fact be considered "excellent" by representatives from most of the other nations of the world. In the third place, the basic problem is not that of working out the details, but rather getting the nations to the point where they would even be interested in thinking about the kind of constitution a global government should have.

In any case, the best answer to this particular argument against the possibility of global government is that, whereas there would surely be many extremely difficult issues to iron out, this ironing out should be left to the creativity of the process itself, once we have representatives from the various nations committed in principle to the idea of world government.

One of the more crucial questions to be settled, incidentally, would be whether the global government should be a modification of the United Nations (as constantly assumed by the authors of *Our Global Neighborhood*), or an entirely new organization. On this issue I am inclined toward Einstein's twofold opinion: "The transformation of the UN into a world government is... the most natural course to pursue. However, it would amount to a radical transformation which would hardly differ from the creation of an entirely new organization."[10]

One more point is relevant to this discussion about the possibility of global government. In the past—certainly in the time of Rousseau and Kant, and perhaps even in the time of Woodrow Wilson—a global government would not have been *technologically* possible. Even in Albert Einstein's day, it would have been much more difficult than it would be nowadays. Our information systems are now much more sophisticated, so that global institutions could keep track of what is going on around the world with regard to the various matters that would be under their purview, especially the various factors affecting the environmental crisis, such as population trends, biodiversity loss, and global climate change. We now have much more elaborate and widespread methods of communication, enabling people in all parts of the world to know almost instantly what is happening in other regions. These systems, in particular television, have already helped to create an inchoate sense of global community, which is one of the preconditions for supporting remedial action in cases of natural catastrophe, as well as of human rights abuse. They would also allow a global government to monitor crises in a way that would not have been possible in earlier times. Finally, our *transportation* systems would permit police and other representatives of a global administration to respond quickly to critical situations in any part of the world. These developments have their ominous sides, of course; but they can also be employed for good, and this would be more likely in the framework of a global democracy, in which we were trying to cooperate for the welfare of all.

There is, accordingly, no reason to conclude in advance that global government is impossible, so that, as some put it, a "mature anarchy" is the best we can hope for.[11] A world government perhaps was not a real possibility in the past, for both technical and psychological reasons. In our time, however, not only is it a real possibility, because modern technology makes it technically feasible, but, even more, because modern technology (on its dark side) has made it an indispensable necessity. The deleterious effects of contemporary technology are now so threatening (nuclear bombs, pollution of air and water, hazardous waste, and the like) that psychological barriers to global government must at all costs be overcome. Whether this occurs will depend to a great extent upon whether intellectuals take up what Einstein called "the most important and most fateful social task intellectuals have ever had to shoulder," namely, making clear the need to change our inherited way of thinking about international relations.[12]

In all of the above, I have made virtually no reference to the text of the Commissioners' Report on Global Governance; but much of what I have said reflects upon their summary dismissal of global government as undesirable. The tacit presupposition throughout the Report, furthermore, seems to be that global government is impossible as a remedy for world problems, or at least as a way forward. I have been at pains to demonstrate that this is not the case. The Commissioners, indeed, have made a valuable contribution by undertaking "the most important and most fateful task" of stressing the need to change our inherited way of thinking about international affairs, but they have fallen far short of the desired result. I have dealt here with the most important ingredient that is missing from their proposals, which is, moreover, the logical conclusion to which much of their own argument implicitly points.

NOTES

1. See Hedley Bull, *The Anarchical Society: A Study of Order in World Politics* (New York: Columbia University Press, 1977); and Errol E. Harris, *One World or None: A Prescription for Survival* (Atlantic Highlands, NJ: Humanities Press, 1993), Chapters 3 and 4, *The Survival of Political Man: A Study in the Principles of International Order* (Johannesburg: Witwatersrand University Press, 1950), Part I, and *Annihilation and Utopia: The Principles of International Politics* (G. Allen and Unwin, 1966), Part I.

2. Otto Nathan and Heinz Norden, eds., *Einstein on Peace* (New York: Simon and Schuster, 1960), p. 570.

3. In this regard, see the Constitution for the Federation of Earth (proposed by the World Constitution and Parliament Association), Article XIV, Section B.

4. Hans Morgenthau, *Politics among the Nations: The Struggle for Power and Peace*, 5th ed. (New York: Knopf, 1972).

5. Andrew Bard Schmookler, *The Parable of the Tribes* (Boston: Houghton Mifflin, 1984).

6. *Einstein on Peace*, p. 418.

7. Richard Falk, *The End of World Order: Essays on Normative International Relations* (New York and London: Holmes and Meier, 1983), p. 108.

8. Ibid., pp. 89 and 102.

9. *Einstein on Peace*, p. 606.

10. Ibid., p. 482.

11. B.V.A. Roling, "Are Grotius' Ideas Obsolete in an Expanded World," in *Hugo Grotius and International Relations*, edited by Hedley Bull, Benedict Kingsbury, and Adam Roberts (Oxford: Clarendon Press, 1992), pp. 281-299, at 294.

12. *Einstein on Peace*, p. 495.

Chapter 6

Global Governance
or World Government?

Errol E. Harris

THE DECEPTIVENESS OF "GLOBAL GOVERNANCE"

Thirty-seven eminent and distinguished persons of international standing participated in the Stockholm Initiative on Global Security and Governance, and 28 persons of similar distinction make up the Commission on Global Governance, whose Report, entitled *Our Global Neighborhood*, was published by Oxford University Press in 1995. The Report, of which so much had been expected, is a most disappointing document, because its recommendations fall far short of what is desperately needed to remedy the perilous anarchy persisting in international relations today. There is a fatal flaw in the thinking that pervades the Report, and as the eminence of the persons on the Commission will undoubtedly give it considerable influence with readers, it is, unfortunately, all the more dangerous and misleading, because the recommendations will appeal to many who are unaware of the error. So far from strengthening global governance and increasing global security, these recommendations can make no significant difference whatsoever to the present state of affairs, for the simple reason that they preserve intact the root cause of all the trouble—the national sovereign independence of the nations. The Commissioners are, apparently, completely unaware of the problem persistently presented by national sovereignty in the international community, and unless this problem is faced and given primary consideration, no progress can be made toward global governance of any kind.

The word "governance" is etymologically synonymous with "government," but in their Foreword to the Report, the Co-Chairmen, Ingvar Carlsson and Sir Shridath Ramphal, make a point of distinguishing the terms. "We are not proposing movement towards world government," they write, "for were we to travel in that direction we could find ourselves in an even less democratic world than we have now—one more accommodating to power, more hospitable to hegemonic ambition, and more reinforcing of the roles of states and governments rather than the rights of people." *Nothing could be further from the truth.*

In fact, hegemony is no form of world government at all, but is simply the domination of one superpower in a power-political structure such as exists at present. World government, if it is to be established at all, must either be by conquest, which today is no longer possible, because modern warfare is totally destructive and, on the scale necessary for world dominion, would destroy the victor equally with the vanquished. Or else it will be by universal consent. There is no other way. Accordingly, the only sort of world government that is viable and that would be accepted by the peoples of the globe would have to be federal in form, and federal government, as the United States has made evident for the past 200 years, is based on the preservation of states' rights and the protection of individual rights, by entrenchment in a Constitution recognized and legally upheld. Such a constitution guarantees the democratic election of the federal legislature and executive, and ensures that the ultimate power resides with the people. It provides the best assurance of universal democracy and is the only assured bulwark against arbitrary exercise of power and hegemonic ambition. As it abolishes state sovereignty, it also does away for all time with the roles of independent states in global affairs (as opposed to internal affairs).

It is astonishing that the Co-Chairmen of the Commission could have written what is quoted above, when they already had in their hands the Constitution for the Federation of Earth, drafted by a World Constituent Assembly over forty years in four separate meetings, by which democratic elections are prescribed, individual and national rights are explicitly protected, and a World Ombudsmus is established to prevent corrupt or arbitrary exercise of authority by individuals or organizations. This is the only way to ensure global governance, in the proper sense of that word—a word which ought not to be used, as it so commonly is, as a weasel-word to disguise a situation in which genuine governance is rendered impossible by the claim to, and exercise of, national sovereignty.

Accordingly, before considering in detail the analysis of the present state of international relations and the recommendations made by the Commissioners, we must examine the problem of sovereignty in international relations.

NATIONAL SOVEREIGNTY

The theory of sovereignty developed since the sixteenth century by many philosophers can be summed up briefly by saying that the supreme authority of the state has two essential aspects, which may be called respectively juridical and ethical. The first is indispensable to the maintenance of law and order and consists in a power, that no individual is able to defy, and beyond which no appeal can be made, to make and promulgate laws and compel obedience to them. The second is the inevitable fact that the right to exercise this power is conditional upon the consent of the people subject to it and their recognition that it serves their best interests—interests common to the whole community and the body politic.

The first aspect was emphasized by such thinkers as the philosophers Bodin, Hobbes, Spinoza, Bentham, and Hegel, and by jurists such as Blackstone and John Austin. The second was insisted upon by Locke, Montesquieu, Edmund Burke, and the authors of *The Federalist Papers*, Hamilton and Madison. That both aspects were equally essential and mutually reconcilable, however, was made apparent by Rousseau, although it is also evident in the work of Spinoza and Hegel.

That the common good of the society is attainable only through the ordered cooperation of its members has been clear ever since Plato set out its conditions in his *Republic*, and Aristotle declared that the state comes into being for the sake of the bare needs of life and continues in existence for the sake of the good life. And it is clearly apparent that coordinated action among a number of people is possible only if their conduct is governed by rules that everybody observes. If order is to be maintained, these rules must be enforceable upon any who, for selfish motives, attempt to violate them; and there must, therefore, be some authority with the requisite power to enforce the law. It is equally apparent that there can, in the last resort, be only one such power, and that it must be superior to any other if it is to be effective. This is the sovereign power of the state.

On the other hand, no one person (nor even a few persons) can exert enough force to compel the delinquent members of a society to obey the law. In the first book of the *Republic*, when Thrasymachus declares that justice is the will of the stronger, Socrates asks whether he means by "the stronger" such a person as Polydamus the pancriatist. This is no mere joke, for no one individual, however strong physically, can impose his or her will on an entire community against its consent. As Hobbes puts it: "For as to the strength of the body, the weakest has strength enough to kill the strongest either by secret machination, or by con-federacy with others..." (*Leviathan*, Ch. 13). Every regime, even the most tyrannical, can exercise power only if its rule is supported and approved (or at least tolerated) by a large number of its subjects; for in fact, the power of the state is ultimately derived from that of the people, who provide the means (the personnel, the equipment, and the weapons) by which it is exercised.

Further, if such power is exercised in the interests of any one section of the society to the detriment of others, the whole society will, to that extent, suffer harm, because the common good depends upon the concerted action of the whole body of the people, and what is disadvantageous to some will ultimately prove to be detrimental to everybody. Consequently, unjust or despotic use of sovereign power contradicts the reason for its existence, which is the pursuit of the common good, and undermines the only sound justification for its authority. The same is true if, for any other reason than the misuse of power, a national government ceases to be competent to ensure the common interests of the nation. Accordingly, when sovereign power ceases to promote the general good of its subjects, or becomes incapable of doing so, it ceases to be legitimate, and it is liable to be overthrown, whether by violent revolution or by bloodless revolution (as recently occurred in Eastern Europe).

The juristic aspect of sovereignty is the more evident in international relations, where the independence of a nation depends on the recognition by others of the supreme authority and power over its citizens of its existing government. But the ethical aspect ought not to be forgotten, and it has far-reaching implications at the present time.

By definition and in practice, sovereignty is the exercise of supreme power over a community, and it thus involves the claim to independence. Dr. H. Lauterpacht, a distinguished international jurist, defines the sovereign State as follows: "The sovereign State does not acknowledge a central executive above itself; it does not recognize a legislation above itself, it owes no obedience to a judge above itself."[2] In the judgment of the Palmas case (1928), the Court pronounced: "Sovereignty in the relations between states signifies independence. Independence in regard to a portion of the globe is the right to exercise therein, to the exclusion of any other State, the functions of a State..."

There is no question but that states up to the present time conduct themselves in accordance with these definitions. Recognition in international relations is precisely of this independence and capacity to exercise supreme power over a defined territory. Witness the claims of Israel with respect to its neighbors and its policy toward the Palestinians, of Iraq with respect to Kuwait and its Kurdish and Shiite populations, and of Russia with respect to Chechnya. The public statements of the British Prime Minister, in regard to Britain's membership in the European Union and relations with its other members, constantly stress the paramountcy of British sovereignty over its own affairs. Not even the European Economic Community limits the sovereign powers of its members, for all its activities are based upon the terms of the Treaty of Rome, to which its members adhere by their sovereign acts and could, if their governments chose, renounce at any time. We shall presently see that treaties in no way limit the sovereignty of their signatories. Nearly all the wars and disputes going on in the world today are in some way connected with the claims by various peoples to sovereignty and independence: by Bosnia, Croatia, Slovakia, the Baltic States, Chechnya, and others.

An independent, sovereign state of its nature gives precedence to its own national interests, of which security is necessarily paramount, because unless it can effectively defend its independence against all comers, it cannot remain sovereign. Other states are therefore all potential enemies, in varying degrees usually proportional to their proximity. India is hostile to Pakistan and China, Iran to Iraq, Israel to its Arab neighbors, and so on.

If it cannot maintain sufficient forces from its own resources for its defense, a state seeks to ally itself with some stronger power, whose interests most nearly accord with its own. Consequently, states tend to form opposing blocs between which they seek to maintain a balance of power (that is, of military capability). But this balance is always unstable, for nothing more than a breakthrough in technology is sufficient to upset it, and the nations are thus involved in a perpetual arms race. Today, since the end of the Cold War, the arms race may seem to have slackened; but actually it has not, for among the smaller nations it continues unabated (between Pakistan and India, between North and South Korea, between various nations of the Middle East, and so on). The upgrading of weaponry continues among the more powerful nations, what is scrapped is mainly what has become obsolete, and where armaments are being reduced, it is chiefly due to economic stress, not to pervasive pacification.

The effort to maintain a balance of power and the resulting arms race lead inevitably to tensions and recurrent crises, with the perpetual threat of an outbreak of hostilities, so that since the end of the Second World War in 1945 there have been over 150 comparatively minor wars, and there is not yet any sign of an effective means of ensuring world peace. The opinion commonly expressed that the possession by the superpowers of nuclear weapons has, for fifty years, deterred aggression and prevented a major war, is specious. A hundred years elapsed between the Napoleonic wars and the First World War (the "Great War"), although there were plenty of smaller conflicts during that period, just as there have been since 1945, and the threat of a major war, with the use of nuclear weapons, has not yet, by any means, been removed.

The conduct of states is supposed to be regulated by International Law, which lays down that its only "subjects" are sovereign states. But International Law itself defines sovereignty, as we have just seen, as subject to *no* higher law. So it is in contradiction with itself, and is not effective law, because it cannot be enforced. A sovereign state cannot be arrested by a policeman, tried in a court of law, and imprisoned or fined. Sovereign states can and frequently do refuse to recognize the jurisdiction of the International Court of Justice, and the only way a sovereign state can be coerced is by military might; so without warfare, in some form or other, there is no way of enforcing International Law. Economic sanctions, to be effective, must be backed by military threat, both on countries attempting to break them and on those against which they are imposed. Nor do they affect the offending government so much as cause hardship and suffering among its innocent subjects. We have had numerous recent examples of these facts, which can hardly be contested by any who keep abreast of current affairs: in Iraq, in Libya, in Haiti and in the former Yugoslavia, for example.

The same is true of treaties, which, according to International Law, ought to be kept (*pacta sunt servanda*). But they are kept only as long as they serve the national interests of their signatories. Even then the parties are free to interpret their terms as best suits their own concerns, and any state, when its national interests are threatened, can renounce a treaty, or simply ignore its obligations. There have been numerous examples in the course of history of states violating treaties whenever it suits them, and only the threat of military action can prevent them from doing so. The sole meaningful remedy for the breach of a treaty is outright warfare. Incidentally, International Law has no firmer basis, for it is itself founded on treaties—the Hague Conventions and the like.

It follows that disarmament treaties tend to contradict the only conditions under which their terms might be respected. They are ostensibly agreements to forgo the only means their signatories have of ensuring their observance: the threat of military force against any who might violate them. It is not surprising, therefore, that no agreements genuinely to disarm have ever been made. For example, the START treaties, not yet fully implemented in any event, are really no more than agreements to dispose of surplus and obsolete weapons.

The Charter of the United Nations is itself a treaty entered into by sovereign states, and so the Organization suffers from all the limitations and drawbacks resulting from the unenforceability of International Law. Its main function is, according to the Preamble and Article 1 of its Charter, to maintain world peace; but it cannot do so because by Article 2 of that same Charter the Organization is declared to be based on the principle of the sovereign equality of all its members, whose conduct in consequence it can never restrain without waging war. There is no other way of enforcing the resolutions of the Security Council, which have been defied often enough, by South Africa (under the apartheid regime), by Israel, by Iraq, by North Korea—and when the Council decides upon enforcement, its only effective resource is to wage war, as it did in the Persian Gulf, and has done on several other occasions. In the nature of the case, therefore, it cannot keep the peace, and all its so-called peacekeeping activities have been constantly frustrated by the claim to, and arrogation of, sovereign rights by those to whom they have been directed, in Somalia, Yugoslavia, Rwanda, Cambodia and Cyprus, to mention only these. The same acknowledgment of the sovereign independence of its members restrains the Organization from intervening in their internal affairs (so-called, for in cases of crisis, the "internal affairs" of one country may affect the interests and welfare of its neighbors and of many other countries, as continues to be the case with the former Yugoslavia). This restraint confuses the efforts at "peacekeeping" of the United Nations, and makes them ineffective and counterproductive, as when military forces are sent in which are unable to defend themselves adequately, and which are prohibited from engaging those who violate the peace, or when cease-fires are negotiated which cannot be enforced.

National sovereign independence has been called the evil genius in international relations, and the problem it presents must be squarely faced and resolutely tackled in any discussion of global "governance." This is what the Commission has signally failed to recognize. As long as national sovereign states exist, and their sovereign independence is preserved and upheld, any so-called global governance is a sham, and among independent sovereigns neither security nor the rule of law can be maintained.

As long as national states remain sovereign and independent, no rule of law among them can be maintained and peace can never be guaranteed. Under such conditions, any so-called global governance is just a sham and has rightly been described (e.g., by Georg Schwartzenberger) as "power politics in disguise." Today the common interests of humanity require the preservation of the life-giving ecosystem of the planet, as well as assurance of safety from a nuclear holocaust, but none of the desperate, crucial, world problems—the maintenance of peace, the preservation of the environment, the control of the population explosion, and everything that is entailed by them—can be solved by national sovereign governments, because these problems are global, and their solution requires concerted global action. The jurisdiction of no national government extends beyond its own borders, and nothing it can do within those limits is sufficient to deal with global problems, inasmuch as it can be countered and contradicted by the action of other national governments. International "agreements" cannot help, because, as we have seen, their observance cannot be ensured, and they can be enforced, if at all, only by resorting to war. Moreover, the expedients, for the most part, go counter to the several national interests of the parties, which are therefore seldom, if ever, willing to agree to adequate remedies. Among independent sovereign states neither security nor the rule of law can be maintained, nor can action to remedy the destruction of the environment be accomplished.

Since national sovereign governments can no longer serve to achieve the common good of their peoples (which requires the solution of global problems), the justification for their sovereign power has been removed and they have in fact become obsolete. What is now essential is the establishment of a global authority (such as the Commission deprecates), empowered to enact and enforce World Law.

For these reasons, the recommendations of the Commission are (as I will shortly demonstrate) largely impracticable, ineffective, and simply the products of wishful thinking unrealizable under the present conditions of recognized sovereign independence of states. Because the Charter of the United Nations declares that the Organization is based on the principle of sovereign equality of its members, no reformation of that Organization or amendment of its Charter can establish global governance, unless that principle is abandoned and a new Constitution for genuine world government is set up, globally accepted, and ratified. The Commission's recommendations fall far short of this requirement.

When they speak of "the global neighborhood" (although much that they say is appealing), what the Commissioners have failed to appreciate is that there is actually no such thing today as an international "community"—rather only an association of sovereign states. A "community" is a society in which common interests are given precedence over individual and special interests. But sovereign governments necessarily give primacy to national interests before all others, and give little or no consideration to the global interests of mankind. Therefore, the hopes and recommendations of the Commission are no more than pious aspirations which do not effectively address and respond to the practical requirements of the present global situation.

Let us now consider the Report in more detail.

GENERAL ASSESSMENT OF THE REPORT

In their favor, it can be said of the Commissioners that they frequently state problems facing the international community with perspicacity, and recognize what would be the more desirable state of affairs. For instance, they rightly assess the growth of the menace from nuclear weapons and the danger of nuclear proliferation; they deplore the evils of the arms trade; they see the problems arising from economic inequality among the nations; and they are clearly aware of the dangers of population growth and ecological degradation resulting from population pressure. They wisely observe that today security is not limited to defense but includes conservation of the environment, and they also recognize the extent to which the world has become unified by technical advances. The desirability of maintaining the rule of law worldwide is emphasized, as well as the significant development of a global civil society. At the same time, the Commissioners admit the existence of deepening disquiet over the activities and deficiencies of the United Nations. The aims of world government are clearly perceived: sustainable development, the promotion of democracy, equity and human rights; and humanitarian action. The Report sets out what its authors call a global civic ethics which is sound and admirable, and asserts that "good governance requires good government." But it understands this to mean government by nation-states, which cannot, if only because it is not global and has no jurisdiction beyond national boundaries, achieve the aims set out, for they are global in scope and cannot be secured for any one nation to the exclusion of the rest. Nor will national governments act for the welfare of humankind as a whole, but only and always in what they perceive as their own national interests.

As a consequence, the Commissioners invariably fail to carry through the plain logic of their own analyses, and they fight shy of recommending the only effective remedy to current global ills to which their own assessment points. For instance, on page 9, it is admitted that "the perceived need for co-operation between developing states... had to contend with the strong nationalism and regard for sovereignty..." The obvious remedy would be to do away with these obstacles by combining the developing nations into a federal union. This course, however, is eschewed by the Commission.

Security

What the Report says in its opening paragraphs on the changed nature of security may be quoted with unqualified approval:

Rivalry has always been inherent among sovereign states. In the past, states' efforts to increase their own security by expanding their military capabilities and forming alliances with other military powers inevitably threatened the security of other states... To continue in this path is to court disaster... Efforts by the great powers to preserve their military dominance will certainly stimulate emerging powers to acquire more military strength.

At the same time, the emerging powers' attempts to redress the military imbalance can only prompt the traditional powers to reinforce their capabilities. The results of such a vicious circle will be rising political tensions, wasted resources, or worse—war through accident or inadvertence. (p.78)

But no credible remedy is offered to counteract this insufferable state of affairs.

The Commission sets out six norms to be embedded in international agreements, but it gives no indication of how sovereign states are to be induced to conform to them. It simply resorts to the United Nations and its humanitarian agencies, ignoring the extent and repeated examples of frustration of the activities of these agencies by the steady insistence on sovereign claims by national governments, for example, Serbia, Croatia, Zaire, Somalia, Burma, and others. It also appeals to the Charter and possible action under Chapter VII. It endorses the use of sanctions, while admitting their limitations ("The political leaders or groups whom sanctions seek to influence are very often immune from their effects," p. 107). And it condones the use of force (even recommending the formation of an International Volunteer Force) ignoring the fact that waging war is the opposite of maintaining peace.

When it comes to dealing with the nuclear threat, it can do no better than *hope* that the nuclear test ban will be concluded and observed, though mere hope can ensure neither. It *hopes*, similarly, for treaties defining nuclear-free zones, and *calls on* all nations to sign the non-proliferation treaty, as also it calls on the international community to redouble efforts to pursue demilitarization. One is naturally put in mind of the exchange between Glendower and Hotspur in Shakespeare's *Henry IV, Part I*:

> *Glendower*: I can call spirits from the vasty deep.
> *Hotspur*: Why, so can I, or so can any man;
> But will they come when you do call for them?

All this ignores the facts that (1) there is no way of persuading sovereign states to sign treaties that they do not consider to be in their national interests, (2) that paramount among these are security and the assumed need to maintain their military capabilities, and (3) that the only way to ensure the observance of such treaties is to apply sanctions, either economic and military, which defeat the objects of demilitarization and pacification.

A Global Civil Society

The organizations mainly concerned with the common interests of humanity are nongovernmental. The Commissioners realize and approve of the growth in number and influence of NGOs, and see them as constituting a developing global civil society. So far they are right, but they do not draw the appropriate conclusion.

Every community can be viewed in two ways, as a civil society and as an organized political state. On the national level, the boundaries of these two aspects of community roughly coincide: for the most part the same people belong to both; and the important characteristic of the relation between them is that the activities and the civil rights of voluntary associations are (or should be) protected by the law enacted and enforced by the political government. Without this provision, nongovernmental associations cannot confidently achieve their aims. In the modern international scheme, NGOs that pursue the common interests of humankind, bodies like Amnesty International, Greenpeace, Oxfam, Friends of the Earth, the World Wildlife Federation, Save the Children, and hundreds of others, have no legal backing from the international organization, that is, the United Nations. For the most part, they are advocating action which national governments see as in conflict with their national interests (e.g., as Spain and Norway perceive their national interests, protecting the whale or fish populations of the world's oceans is not among them). Accordingly, NGOs are perpetually frustrated in the achievement of their objectives. For example, Amnesty International does invaluable work in monitoring and reporting violations of human rights, but the national governments which perpetrate them remain unrepentant, accusing Amnesty of bias, denying their reports, alleging that they are based on insufficient evidence, on special cases, or the like. As the United Nations simply represents the national governments, those who are not accused do little or nothing to bring the culprits to book, because it is not in their national interest to do so, and in any case they could do nothing other than apply sanctions, either economic or military (the former, to be effective, usually involving the latter), which are unlikely means of remedying the situation. Consequently, the emerging global civil society remains ineffective until it can be given proper legal backing by effective and genuine World Law—a support which International Law does not provide because it cannot be enforced on national sovereign states. Genuine, federal and democratic World Government would provide such legal backing to a global civil society; yet the Commission explicitly repudiates any such idea.

The so-called global governance, to which the NGOs are said so significantly to contribute, is therefore fully illusory. Neither can the NGOs be as usefully effective as they should be, nor does (or can) the United Nations give them the legal status that they require.

Nevertheless, the development of the global civil society is of the utmost importance, for it is factual evidence of the common interests of the peoples of the world in the conservation of global ecology (Greenpeace, Friends of the Earth, et al), in respect for human rights (Amnesty), in combating poverty, famine, and hunger (Oxfam), and in the maintenance of world peace, an interest ostensibly represented by the Stockholm Initiative. Thus, the global civil society represents the crying need for a political organization that will serve these common interests, and give them precedence over parochial concerns, in contrast to the way in which national governments today serve national interests at the expense of the welfare of humanity as a whole. The only such global political organization capable of this role would be federal World Government, and that is the logical conclusion to draw from the evidence submitted by this Report—while it is precisely the one it has not the courage to recommend.

The Report speaks of empowerment of the people (pp. 35-37), but it is extremely vague about its nature and how it is to be brought about, speaking only of education, economic security, women's liberation, improved means of communication, etc., all of which are no doubt important; but the true method of empowering the people is democratic government, and all the Report can offer on this topic is the comment that people are becoming increasingly disenchanted with the political process. To combat such disenchantment, it recommends decentralization within societies. This may, indeed, be salutary, but it will have no effect on world "governance" as long as that is left to an association of sovereign states. Sovereignty in each nation is exercised only by the central government, all that is represented in the councils of the United Nations, where its effect is to nullify efforts to attain the international objectives set out by the Charter. The true principle relevant here is that of federalism, which assigns to the central government matters of common concern, and to local governing institutions those of local interest. This is the proper meaning of "subsidiarity" (which the Commission recommends). Decentralization in world government, therefore, consists in the establishment of a Federal Constitution for the world as a whole, which would distinguish these two classes of interest, and set up democratically based institutions that can serve both of them with proper legal security.

Greater participation of the people in both local and central government is obviously desirable, but it will not be brought about if people disenchanted with politicians refrain from voting, for it is only by voting that their democratic participation is ensured. Direct democracy is possible only in small communities. Where populations are large, representative institutions are the only feasible instruments for popular participation. If government sincerely devotes itself to the common interests of the people, they will not become disenchanted with it; and, whatever may be the case at the national level, there can be little doubt that at the international level, the interests of humankind are far from being addressed under the existing regime, because the United Nations cannot keep the peace, nor can it, nor can NGOs without legal backing, do anything adequate to conserve the environment, so long as sovereign, independent governments give precedence to their own national interests.

Sovereignty and Global Values

The "neighborhood values" set out by the Commission are excellent and sound, but how their observance is to be assured does not appear. Sovereignty is accepted as the cornerstone of the modern interstate system, and tolerated rather than condemned. The norms of sovereignty are enumerated and admitted, and the Commissioners ask that they be respected: namely, equal rights for all sovereign states, territorial integrity and political independence, and the prohibition of intervention in domestic affairs. The stark fact that sovereign states frequently disregard these "norms" is overlooked, and we are not told how they can be enforced (as the Commission recommends) without resorting to armed conflict. Moreover, these so-called norms are precisely the cause of all the troubles in international affairs. The interest in preserving territorial integrity is what impels states to maintain their military capabilities, and to menace their neighbors when they do likewise. The inability of the United Nations to intervene in domestic affairs renders it powerless to deal with civil conflicts, genocidal atrocities, violations of human rights, and environmental destruction.

How can sovereign nation-states be compelled to recognize and discharge their responsibilities? How is corruption to be combated within their borders without intervention in their domestic affairs? How is racism to be outlawed through international action? And most important of all and farthest-reaching, how is the rule of law to be ensured within national borders and internationally among sovereign nations? The Report does not tell us any of this; although it admits that old notions of territorial independence and nonintervention are losing their meaning in an increasingly interdependent world. But it does not reach the obvious conclusion that this transition demands a new form of world organization that establishes this interdependence legally and constitutionally.

The Rule of Law

Throughout the Report, the importance and necessity of maintaining the rule of law are repeatedly asserted. The rule of law is the conduct of government without arbitrary decree or usurpation of power unauthorized by statutory and customary law. It also prescribes the maintenance of peace and order, through law enforcement by police and the courts, without excessive violence; and the prohibition and prevention of the use of unauthorized force. But there can be no rule of law where no effective law exists. In the international sphere, we have argued, there is no effective law, because effective law must be capable of enforcement. International law is not enforceable without resort to war, which is itself a breach of the rule of law.

The Commissioners say that the arguments, which were once advanced by scholars, are less often heard today: that international law is not law in the true sense because there is no police force to enforce it, no sanctions if it were disobeyed, and no international legislature (p. 304). Perhaps such arguments are less often *heard*, but they have certainly been asserted, and are undoubtedly still valid and sound. It is claimed in the Report that the standing of international law is now unquestioned and that although states are sovereign, they are not free to do whatever they want. We are not told by whom the status of international law is unquestioned, or given examples of cases in which states have refrained from breaches of the law when their perception of their own interests has dictated violation. In fact, sovereignty means no less than the freedom to do whatever the sovereign government decides, and if any state does decide to respect the terms of international law, it is only when and because they are embodied in its own sovereign legislation. Otherwise, they are at liberty to interpret the law as suits their own interest, to disregard it, or to violate it at will, until restrained by military force.

History has shown that whenever the "vital interests" of a nation are at stake, international law is ignored by its government. Germany paid no respect to it either before or during the Great War and the Second World War, nor did Japan when it invaded Manchuria and bombed Pearl Harbor. Britain disregarded it when Argentina occupied the Malvinas—using the excuse of self-defense (common in all such cases) without any effort to submit the claim of suzerainty to the World Court. The United States invaded Granada in breach of international law without any such excuse, and Iraq, Israel, and South Africa have all, from time to time, treated its terms with disdain.

"In an ideal world," the Report alleges, "acceptance of the compulsory jurisdiction of the World Court would be a prerequisite for UN membership." This, by its own admission, is pure idealism, but even more than that, it is self-contradictory, because membership of the UN assures a state sovereign independence, while acceptance of compulsory jurisdiction of the World Court would be an abrogation of sovereignty. The Report contends that in the absence of the Court, "self-serving interpretations of international law can be asserted unilaterally in the Security Council and elsewhere." But in the presence of the Court, this already regularly happens. The Report admits that "[t]he Court has jurisdiction only where states that are parties to a dispute have agreed to abide by its decision." Were the rule of law to prevail, no such freedom to abide or not to abide by a court's decision would be vouchsafed. No citizen of any state is at liberty to refuse the jurisdiction or to reject the decision of a court of law, and any who attempt to do either can be compelled to obey without resort to military armament. Sovereign states cannot be so constrained and habitually flout the jurisdiction and the decision of the World Court. The Report itself records how the United States contested the right of the Court to hear the Nicaragua case and refused to participate when the Court ruled in favor of its own competence; and likewise how France refused to appear before the Court or to accept its decision concerning nuclear tests and fallout on Australia and New Zealand. Moreover, even when a state does agree to submit its case to the World Court, if the decision goes against it, it is liable to reject and disregard it. Where the putative subjects of law can thus choose to respect or to flout the jurisdiction and decision of a court, the rule of law cannot be maintained.

The Commissioners suggest steps by which compulsory jurisdiction might be approached, but they all depend on the willingness of states to adopt them, and it is clear that none will do so, nor (without sacrificing sovereign independence) could any, except where it regarded compliance to be in its national interest. The Report further outlines the contradictions and confusions involved in suggestions that the Security Council submit its decisions to review by the Court, giving the example of the demand on Libya to extradite suspects of the bombing of Pan Am flight 103. Quite apart from conflicts in the law, nothing can force Libya, as a sovereign state, to hand over its citizens for trial by a foreign or a reputed international court, save sanctions ultimately involving military threat, which violates the rule of law. So much for the prospects of an international criminal court to try alleged war criminals and the perpetrators of genocide and ethnic cleansing. How could the states of which the accused were citizens be forced to hand them over for trial?

While nations remain sovereign, no rule of law can be imposed on them; and as international law lays down that its only subjects are sovereign states, they will be immune from compulsion. The United Nations, for the same reason, is powerless to maintain the rule of law. International law rests on treaties, called lawmaking treaties, of which the Charter of the United Nations is one; but, we have seen, there is no way, except by military force, to compel sovereign states to abide by agreements to which they have subscribed; that is, there is no means of maintaining the rule of law among sovereign governments without actually violating it.

There is one way, and only one, to ensure the maintenance of the rule of law among the nations, and that is to establish a legislature to enact law, an executive to administer it, a judiciary to interpret it, and police to enforce it. That could occur only by means of the universal ratification of a Constitution for the Federation of the Earth which would abrogate national sovereignty, while it guaranteed the autonomy of all nations with respect to purely local matters (states' rights); which would constitute a democratically elected legislature to enact World Law, a responsible executive, an independent judiciary, a law enforcement agency, and an ombudsmus to protect individuals and associations from injustices and inequities and to guard against corruption.

Economic Interdependence

Chapter 4 of the Report is the longest, and perhaps the most tedious. It gives a lengthy account of existing international institutions and practices designed to facilitate world trade and financial transactions. Suggestions for improvement upon these arrangements are mostly vague and impractical: with little exception, the Commission seems to favor the status quo, merely exhorting governments to behave fairly and to observe standards previously agreed or recommended for the future. Where this has not already occurred, no method of bringing it about is proposed or contemplated. All of the recommendations offered in this area depend on agreement between states, the observance of which, even if it can be reached, is always uncertain and can never be ensured.

The main innovation proposed by the Commissioners is the creation of an Economic Security Council (ESC) as a new adjunct to the United Nations. This group is to consist of representatives of sovereign governments, some 23 in all, for the Commissioners maintain that the Council must be small in order to be efficient. The major economies, they say, would be represented as of right, and membership by other nations would rotate. The ESC is to promote consensus on international economic issues, such as shared ecological crises, economic instability, rising unemployment, and mass poverty, and would be concerned with the promotion of sustainable development. These are all, of course, serious problems, but how the Council is to promote consensus is highly questionable. The Commission asserts that it should not have authority to make legally binding decisions, but would gain influence by competence and relevance. It would have deliberative, rather than executive, functions. In short, it would be powerless.

No indication is given how the Council could persuade governments to do anything other than what their national interests dictate. The Report says it could give signals that could guide the global community. What is to induce any sovereign state to heed such signals does not appear. All this is obviously mere impractical, wishful thinking. How can "competence and relevance" influence the actions of sovereign governments? How could a deliberative body without executive functions do anything to regulate the activities of transnational corporations, or coordinate the policies of national states?

The Report repeatedly deplores the existence of inequality and imbalance between the major economic powers and the developing countries and urges ways of counteracting it, yet the representation of the world's largest economies on the ESC as of right can only enhance such inequality; it would entrench the "hegemonic ambitions" of the most prosperous nations—what the Co-Chairmen so strongly deprecate in their dismissal of the world government.

The Council, we are told, would work closely with the Bretton Woods institutions, but it would not replace them. It would break down institutional isolation, and rationalize and focus the economic activities of the UN. So it would apparently have a centralizing effect. Yet we are also told that "the international community is best served by a plurality of institutions with a diversity of approaches and functions rather than by attempts to create a monopoly of wisdom" (p. 161). Such thinking hardly seems consistent. The Report vacillates between abolishing existing economic institutions in favor of the ESC, and retaining them, lest the present system be upset. In any case, that an Economic Security Council such as is proposed would make little difference to present methods or arrangements is pretty clear, and its potential contribution to "global governance" would be highly dubious. As the Report itself says: "In the absence of a representative high-level body developing an international consensus on critical economic issues, the global neighbourhood could become a battleground of contending economic forces" (p. 162).

Yet again, the insights of the Commissioners point in the right direction, but they do not lead them to advance the right expedient. No new and largely ineffectual organ of the United Nations will do; a more logical solution of the perceived economic problem is a federal world legislature—which, so far from recommending, the Commissioners reject. It is not simply that the global neighborhood could become a battleground, but that without a world legislature the requisite measures cannot be implemented. For example, the Commission recommends that "[an] international tax on foreign currency transactions should be explored as one of a series of options that also includes creating an international corporate tax base for multinational companies." Who is to impose such taxation? Who is to write the legislation which exacts it? Who will collect it and enforce it? The proposed Economic Security Council could do none of these things, and no national government could legislate for more than its own subjects, nor could any such government be compelled to do even that without invoking the whole dubious, unreliable, and globally damaging machinery of economic and military sanctions.

Other economic recommendations are weak or impracticable or both. Against mass poverty, the best the Commission can offer is to urge governments to redouble their efforts to meet the longstanding target of 0.70 percent of GDP for official development assistance, although they admit that the actual contribution has now fallen to 0.29 percent. What will persuade governments to redouble their efforts the Report does not tell us. The World Bank, it says, should be equipped to play a greater role in developing financing, and a strategy should be adopted to mobilize aid flows and to demonstrate value for money. What this strategy should be is not detailed, though in the past the World Bank and the IMF, to ensure "value for money," have imposed restrictive conditions on the economic practices of developing countries that have been to the detriment of the supposed beneficiaries and have imposed greater hardships on their people, while they favored the economies of the wealthier nations. We are not told how such policies are to be reformed or their effects remedied.

Constantly and properly the Report insists on the need for sustainable development; but it does not explain what this means, or what it would involve. The phrase "renewable energy" never appears, and, while it is admitted that energy efficiency is imperative for developing countries, no indication is given of how those countries can become more efficient in the use of energy. The significant estimate of the Electric Power Research Institute in the United States is quoted that all that country's energy needs could be met with a 55 percent reduction of current levels of fossil fuel usage, but no methods are suggested for converting to the use of other sources than fossil fuels, easily available though these other sources are.

To protect and preserve the environment, the Commissioners recommend that strong international support should be mobilized for Agenda 21, but they do not tell us how to accomplish this. They also recommend the use of market instruments, including environmental taxes and tradable permits, urging governments to commit themselves to the "polluter pays principle." But they do not say how governments that find these policies adverse to their national economic interests are to be converted to them. Nor do they explain or suggest how economic rearrangements can be made which demonstrate that environmental conservation is actually in the interests of the people concerned.

To list all the recommendations of the Commission Report and to detail their obvious weaknesses would be unbearably tedious and time-consuming. Suffice it to say that the previous examples are typical. Although the Commissioners recognize the growing economic interdependence of nations and the need for coordination of economic policies, their somewhat halfhearted endorsement of most of the present international economic institutions and methods only goes to support the prevailing anarchy, the consequences of which their description of current conditions illustrates very clearly. As all the recommendations made presuppose the present assemblage of national sovereign and independent states, even so far as they are desirable, they could at best be realized through international agreement, against which the pursuit of national interests would militate, and even if reached could result only in treaties, the observance of which could not be enforced by pacific means.

Reforming the United Nations

The Report declares that global governance involves a variety of people and organizations, but that "a vital and central role in global governance falls to people coming together in the United Nations, aspiring to fulfill some of their highest goals through its potential for common action." Up to the present this potential has not proved to be very strong, especially in the matter of the war in the former Yugoslavia. Moreover, aspirations may be very commendable, but their fulfillment in practice is a very different matter. The aspirations of the original founders of the UN were world peace and prosperity, to which, today, we must add the conservation of the global ecology. But there is little sign of fulfillment of any of these goals by United Nations action or that of any other body.

The causes of this failure are admitted by the Commissioners: the Charter proclaims the Organization to be the creation of "We, the peoples," but it has always been the domain of governments, not peoples. "The United Nations was there to be used," says the Report, "and not infrequently abused; to be an instrument of national interest where it could be; and to be bypassed where it could not be made to serve that interest" (p. 226). Such perspicacity on the part of the Commissioners would be admirable if only they had allowed it to lead them to its logical consequence, that the UN Charter must be replaced by a constitution for a federation of all nations. But this they are far from conceding. They wish to preserve the structures of the UN, proposing some reforms, which we shall presently assess, and asserting that its failings have not been structural, but "have been the collective failings of the member states." How true! What they deplore "is not the failure of some monolithic supranational entity... but the lapses of the members of the United Nations" (p. 228). What they fail to understand is that these lapses are no more than the inevitable pursuit by sovereign governments of the national interests of the states over which they preside. The Charter of the UN requiring, as it does, the preservation of their sovereign independence, ensures that they will use its procedures (or abuse them, if that term be more apt), as an instrument of national interests. Yet the Commission is of opinion that this dispensation was quite right, and that the powers of the UN should remain with its member nation-states, and that "we, the peoples" must act through our national governments. This is the root fault of the whole Report and the main flaw in all its recommendations.

The Commissioners contend that the United Nations was hobbled from the outset by the nuclear arms race and the Cold War, due largely to the Soviet Union's blocking of the Baruch Plan to bring all nuclear activity under international control. What they fail to see is that this phase of the Organization's history was dictated by the national interests of the sovereign members: that of the United States in keeping nuclear activities under the control of a body in which it held a dominant position, and that of the Soviet Union in preventing this advantage to its rival and in its own development of a nuclear capability. As long as its members are sovereign states, the Organization will continue to be hobbled in the same way by their continued pursuit of their national interests, especially by the permanent members of the Security Council, who can veto any measure that does not serve those interests.

On the other hand, we may concede immediately that the subsidiary agencies of the UN are served by competent and devoted officials and that, against odds and despite severe handicaps, they do and have done admirable work in many fields. They are not to be blamed and are not responsible for the reluctance of governments to give them proper financial and other much needed support whenever national concerns are threatened by doing so. We may agree with the tributes paid to these agencies by the Commissioners. Failures are attributed to lack of political will on the part of UN members, and, true as this may be, the reason for the lack of will is not investigated. It is virtually always the priority given to national interests over the needs of the "global neighborhood." The welfare of distant and foreign peoples is treated as, at best, secondary. This cannot be remedied by tinkering with the United Nations Charter; contrary to the view of the Commissioners, the basic fault with the Organization is one of principle, and that is what the Report fails to address.

Because the Charter was drafted fifty years ago, when the international scene was very different from the present, the Commission considers that the time is ripe for reform. In some ways, indeed, the international situation has changed significantly, but in one respect it remains the same. It is still an assemblage of sovereign states, mutually recognized as such, and negotiating in terms of a treaty (the Charter of the United Nation). This, for reasons we have set out, renders that body incapable of settling disputes peaceably whenever the vital interests of the disputants seem to them irreconcilable. Disputes cannot be settled by litigation, because, in such circumstances, the rule of law does not prevail. On page 237, the Report records the fact that the Security Council has authorized the use of military force seven times, yet it deems it prudent to assume that "in the years ahead the UN should continue to be able to play a major role in maintaining peace and security around the world." In what sense, one must wonder, is the authorization of war a means of maintaining peace?

Agreement on measures to conserve the environment suffer likewise, because the precedence given by states to their national interests obstructs agreement, and such consensus as can be reached is inadequate to the needs of the situation, and is fragile, because the terms of any treaty contracted cannot be enforced. In these circumstances, reform of the UN Charter, less drastic than transforming it into a federal constitution, will be of no avail.

The Commission deems the Security Council to be the first organ requiring change. The veto permitted to its permanent members was, it wisely observes, "virtually a contradiction of the other terms of the Charter" (p. 235). But in 1945, it explains, "the realities of power were such that unless other countries accepted the permanent membership of the five, with their right of veto, there would have been no Charter." In short, in the power structure prevailing, the Charter was only acceptable if self-contradictory. What greater condemnation of the Organization could one conceive? To increase the number of permanent members, while retaining the veto, would only make matters worse; so that is ruled out.

Even so, the Commissioners realize that the position of the five permanent members is, for the present, virtually unassailable, because "the world can move towards reform of the Security Council only with their consent"—and so the category of permanent members with a veto will have to remain "for the time being." This basic disadvantage they propose to mitigate by introducing a new category of "standing" members, two from the industrial countries (one from Europe and one from Asia) and three from the larger developing countries (one each from Asia, Africa, and Latin America). These new standing members are not to exercise a veto. What possible difference they would make to the func- tioning of the Security Council it is rather difficult to see, since they could not counteract the veto right of the permanent members. It is also difficult to understand how matters will be ameliorated by the further recommendation that the number of rotating members be increased from ten to thirteen (clearly, the Commissioners are not superstitious).

Meanwhile, the veto is to be phased out. A concordat is proposed between the five permanent members agreeing that they will forgo the use of the veto except in circumstances "they consider... overriding in the context of their national security." To this we might well expect them to agree, for is it not precisely the present position? The use of the veto has always and invariably been justified by the member exercising it on grounds of overriding considerations of security. The veto, says the Report, would then be available only in extreme cases; but what sort of case is to be deemed "extreme," and by whom, is not explained. If a permanent member considers a case to be extreme as a threat to its security, but other members disagree, would the concordat require the veto to be forgone? And if that were the view of the majority of the Council, would the permanent member concerned then refrain from using it? To quote George Bernard Shaw's Eliza Dolittle: "Not bloody likely." So none of these proposed reforms would do anything to improve the functioning of the Council, or contribute in any way to the solution of world problems.

Next, the Commissioners turn their attention to the General Assembly. They confess that it was never intended to be more than a deliberative forum, without real authority, and with capability only to discuss and recommend, to debate and pass nonbinding resolutions. But the Commission has nothing substantial to offer here by way of improvement. It simply appeals for the recognition of the Assembly as a "principal organ," and says that it should be more vigorous and effective, but does not explain how this is to be accomplished. It hopes that it will "play a vital legitimating role"—but what this means and how the hope is to be fulfilled remains obscure.

The widely canvassed suggestions that an assembly directly elected by the people be added to the General Assembly, or one of parliamentarians elected by national legislatures, are rejected as premature. In fact, premature or not, neither would be very helpful, for they would have no legislative powers and, at best, could only perform an advisory function to what is itself no more than an advisory body.

More to the point is the Commission's desire to give more representation to the global civil society by instituting a Forum of accredited nongovernmental organizations and the like. But how this would function is left vague: it would be a matter for the General Assembly to decide. It is suggested that this forum meet in the Plenary Hall of the General Assembly in the run-up to the annual meeting of that body; but what it should do, or how it would influence the decisions of the Assembly or any other organ of the UN, is left unexplained. Clearly, it could do very little and would have very slight, if any, influence; for, at most, it could offer advice and suggestions, which may well be ignored by an Assembly itself without legislative power. At worst, the Forum would merely confuse and complicate the proceedings of the Assembly.

Another proposal is to give the civil society a Right of Petition for action to redress wrongs that could endanger a people's security. The petitions would, apparently, be presented to a Council for Petitions to be set up, consisting of five to seven persons appointed by the Secretary-General and independent of governments. It would, however, be (the Report states) a Council without power of enforcement, and it would simply make recommendations to the Secretary-General, the Security Council, and the General Assembly. Thus the prospect of its having any positive effect would be minimal. The eminence of its members, it is presumed, would give it moral authority; but in the arena of power politics in which international relations are conducted, moral authority carries negligible weight, and this proposal is but another example of the impractical, cloud-cuckoo thinking typical of much of this Report. The proposed Right of Petition is, in fact, a useless sham. To whom would it be open? From whom would petitions originate? How would they be collected or voiced? Through what channels would they be brought to the Council? Who would be competent to respond to, or act upon, them, and how? None of these questions seem to have been considered. But in any case, even if all such questions could be answered satisfactorily, no mere presentation of petitions would alter the limitations under which the UN already labors, or improve the enforcement methods open to the Security Council.

In short, the democracy that the Commission so much wants to foster is far from being promoted or assisted by the proposed reforms of the United Nations, which, as we showed earlier, is not a democratic organization, but simply an association of government representatives. By no means are all the governments they represent democratic. UN officials are not elected by popular vote, nor are any of its assemblies or councils, nor would be any of the new bodies proposed by the Commission. Even for the right of petitioning no democratic procedure is prescribed. The addition to the General Assembly of subsidiary bodies like a Forum of Civil Society, which the Commission advocates, or even a Peoples' Assembly, or an assembly of parliamentarians, which the Commission does not favor, would all be ineffectual unless they could be given proper legislative powers, and that is impossible as long as the member states remain sovereign.

Insofar as the economic and social agencies of the UN are concerned, the Commission seeks, by and large, to do away with all of them and substitute an Economic Security Council, the futility of which we have already demonstrated. ECOSOC (Economic and Social Council) is to be wound up, and UNCTAD (UN Conference on Trade and Development) and UNIDO (UN Industrial Development Organization) are also to be closed down. The reason given is: "As governments set out the policies of the various agencies through their separate governing bodies, it is governments that are best placed to secure coordination" (p. 268). How totally false and misguided! In fact, governments constantly fail to secure coordination, because they are wholly preoccupied with their own national interests; witness the difficulty experienced in obtaining agreement on GATT and the Uruguay Round.

Indeed, the agencies that the Commission seeks to abolish would not be sorely missed if a proper legislature were to be established that could deal effectively with the economic, ecological, and social problems they were designed to tackle, along with many others that they are powerless to resolve. But the Economic Security Council proposed by the Commission could do no better, if as well, and offers no improvement.

The development of regionalism in many areas of the world is welcomed by the Commission, and the tendency, it feels, should be strengthened. It contends that the UN must prepare itself for a time when regionalism becomes ascendant worldwide, and it commends the UN regional commissions. Nevertheless, it entertains some misgivings that, as they grow stronger, regional organizations could turn into conflicting blocs. Here the Commisioners show glimmerings of insight. Regional organizations may well become stepping-stones to world federation, if they at first encourage unification within the regions, and later encourage the idea of still wider federation. But as yet they are certainly a long way from this development. The European Union, the most advanced to date, is still battling against the resistance of Britain to any thought of federalism, as well as the continued reluctance of other members (notably Denmark), while other embryo regional organizations are still very loosely associated. Moreover, even if regional federations were formed, as long as they remained sovereign and independent, whatever modifications were made to the United Nations to accommodate them, the general world situation would not be changed in substance, and problems of conflict resolution and of ecological conservation would remain as recalcitrant as ever.

Beyond amendment of the Charter of the United Nations, the Commission addresses itself to the appointment of the UN Secretary-General, which, it complains, is at present hampered and inhibited by the veto power of the permanent members of the Security Council, preventing the best candidates from being identified or the most competent person from being appointed. Any change in the procedure is bound likewise to be obstructed by the use of the veto, so the recommendation of the Commission that it should not apply in this matter is not likely to be heeded. Reference to the proposed Constitution for the Federation of Earth could have given the Commissioners better guidance. This document provides for a tricameral legislature, one house of which, the House of Counselors, would consist of well-qualified experts elected by professional associations and academic institutions, which among its other functions, would nominate high officials for election by the other two houses.

Finally, the Commissioners lament the fact that the income of the United Nations is insufficient to cover its costs, and that many of the member states do not pay what is expected of them. They deprecate the fact that withholding contributions has become a destructive way of exercising influence. They suggest that this practice be penalized by depriving the culprit of the right to vote in the General Assembly. Of course, it is clear that none of the permanent members could be deprived of their right to vote in the Security Council, because they would veto any motion to that effect. The influence of the General Assembly, however, and of the nonpermanent members of the Security Council, is so weak that the penalty is unlikely to deter many; nor would it make any significant difference to the general conduct of international affairs as it actually proceeds, for the most part irrespective of the United Nations, by negotiation or confrontation between independent states.

THE SANDS OF TIME

Some may wish to argue that, despite their shortcomings, the recommendations of the Commission ought to be heeded and implemented as a stepping-stone to closer integration, forming another stage in what must inevitably be a long process of development. But no such argument can be accepted; first, because these recommendations would not produce any significant advance toward federal unification and would alter the present methods of conducting international affairs hardly at all. Next, it is even more important to remember that humankind today is beset by the most urgent and ominous problems, threatening the very existence of life on Earth. Scientists have more than once warned us that unless the present rate of environmental disruption is promptly countered, it could well run out of control beyond redemption, and that we may already have passed the point of no return. We cannot, therefore, afford to wait for any long, leisurely process of development to improve our methods of "global governance"—a phrase that simply disguises the prevalent power politics that pervades international relations.

As long as states remain sovereign and independent and give precedence in consequence to their national interests over those of the global community, there will be no hope of solving world problems; and the one and only remedy is the establishment of a world government under a democratic federal constitution. Delay may well be fatal, nor is it necessary, because we already have in our hands an excellent and viable Constitution for the Federation of Earth needing only ratification. As this Constitution provides for its own amendment, as deemed necessary by the democratically elected legislature, immediately on ratification and at regular intervals thereafter, no persons or organizations need have any misgivings and can ratify it without qualm.

A CALL TO ACTION

The final chapter of the Report is headed "A Call to Action." It does little more than summarize what has been said and recommended in earlier chapters. However, the Commissioners fear that if reform is left to normal processes, only piecemeal and inadequate action will result. What they themselves have advocated, however, may well be described in just those terms. Further, they urge the General Assembly of the UN to schedule a World Conference on Governance in 1998 (a year which has already been committed to history), its decisions to be ratified and put into effect by 2000. It should now be apparent that any such conference, whenever and wherever it might be held, would be wasting its time. "Governance" as defined in the Report, as is now clear, is no more than a somewhat modified version of what already exists—and what already exists is in fact no governance at all, for sovereign states are by definition subject to no higher authority than themselves, and they neither will nor can (without forfeiting their sovereignty) submit to any form of legitimate governance. The proposed world conference, therefore, would serve no useful purpose.

Time is running out for humanity, and we cannot safely wait until some specified future year before beginning to take action. By that time, it may well be too late to reverse the environmental degradation that threatens the destruction of the rain forests, the ozone layer, and the food chain, as well as global warming causing disastrous climate change that together could spell annihilation for the human race, quite apart from the continuing threat of nuclear war, which has not been ended despite the passing of the Cold War, and against which no assured means of prevention has been found.

We must take action now. We need not wait, as many well-intentioned federalists demand, for some belatedly convened Assembly of World Citizens to draft a Constitution for World Federation, because this has already been done. The complaint that no elected convention drafted the Constitution for the Federation of Earth is neither valid nor relevant. The only important question is whether the Constitution is a good one and can be made to work. Its democratic acceptance and ratification by a significant proportion of the population of the Earth is all that is needed to legitimize it. So if any World Conference is to be called, it should be *now*; and its purpose should be to ratify the Constitution for the Federation of Earth right away, with the possibility of amendment if and as a sufficient majority of representatives think necessary. This is the one remaining hope for the solution of current world problems, which are utterly beyond the competence of either national sovereign states or a United Nations composed of sovereign, independent members.

The call to action that is appropriate and urgent is for the immediate establishment of a genuine World Government, one that can enact genuine World Law enforceable, not on sovereign states, for that is impossible without warfare, but upon individuals, which is possible without resort to weapons of mass destruction. Only thus can the worldwide rule of law be maintained, world peace be assured, and some real hope of reversing ecological destruction be entertained. If this call to action is not heeded, then the prospect for humanity is very dark indeed.

Chapter 7

A Critique of "Our Global Neighborhood"

Philip Isely

In the Co-Chairmen's Foreword, the authors state: "The strongest message we can convey is that humanity can agree on a better way to manage its affairs and give hope to present and future generations."

But the Report of the Commission on Global Governance is extremely lacking in clear definitions of specific proposals to accomplish "a better way." Almost all its proposals are formulated in a very nebulous way. Those given specific titles usually lack clear descriptions of what is proposed, clear structural concepts, specific means to put them into effect, a precise description of their authority, and what is to be accomplished by the proposal.

Concerning the basic concept of "global governance," which is a phrase repeated several hundred times in the text of the Report, the authors state at the outset (p. xvi) and repeat later (e.g., pp. 4, 336) that they do not mean global government or world federalism. They say: "We are not proposing movement toward world government, for were we to travel in that direction we could find ourselves in an even less democratic world than we have—one more accommodating to power, more hospitable to hegemonic ambition, and more reinforcing of the roles of states and governments rather than the rights of people."

By this innuendo, world government is equated to undemocratic procedure and tyranny or dictatorship or autocracy, although in the spirit of obscurantism these specific words are not used. However, nowhere in the Report is there any substantiation or further reasoning given for rejecting world government and world federation.

From the statement in the Foreword, authorized by Co-Chairmen Shridath Ramphal and Ingvar Carlsson (which is presented as the viewpoint of the entire Commission), it may be supposed that if world government leads to less democracy and to imposition by powerseeking agents, then all national governments must have demonstrated the equation of government to less democracy and more tyranny, and, of course, this must be true of state governments and local governments, for is there any intrinsic difference between government at local, state, national, and world levels?

In Chapter 1, the Commission purports to formulate the concept of global governance, as compared with government. The concepts in this chapter, which form the basis for using the term "global governance" throughout the Report, are extremely imprecise and nebulous. The need for a constitution to define the process of governance is ignored or thought to be irrelevant. The process by which world laws may be proposed and decided is not defined. The way in which people should be represented in a legislature is ignored. The responsibility for executive and administrative departments to carry out legislation decided by elected representatives is ignored. The need for a world court system to be responsible under constitutional law and legislative law is ignored. The entire Report gives evidence of lack of understanding by the Commission members of responsible, effective procedures for democratic government under constitutional provisions and safeguards.

It may be noted, as an aside, that those persons who in both public and private speaking and writing have been using interchangeably the terms "world governance" and "world government" must be more careful of their language. If what is truly meant is "world government," then the term "world governance" should be avoided, since the Commission on Global Governance has now expressly captured the use of the term "global governance" as definitely not to mean world government or world federalism.

Much is written in the Report about the "empowerment of people"—of the need for people to have the right and opportunities for greater participation in deciding on the management of public affairs. The recommendations of the Report, however, do not include giving people the right or opportunity to actually vote for any delegate to a representative world legislature or world parliament, nor to cast a deciding vote on anything.

The best that the Report comes up with is to institutionalize the "Right of Petition," and a vague proposal for a global "Forum of Civil Society." Several pages are devoted to description of each of these concepts, but even after very close reading of these pages, many questions remain about what, if anything, of substance has actually been proposed.

The Right of Petition, which the Commission concedes may require amendment of the UN Charter, sounds good at first blush. But exactly to whom will "the people" have the right to submit their petitions? Of course, to the higher authorities: that is, to the UN Security Council, or the General Assembly, or the Secretary-General. People are definitely NOT to have the right to vote for their representatives to world parliament, or to vote in a deciding way upon anything. Instead, they will have bestowed upon them the formal right to petition.

Roll the years of history back to before the Magna Carta of the year 1215!

Instead of being subjected to the imposition of constitutional and elected democratic world government, the people are to be given the right to petition— to petition the king! However, it is even more of a farce: the king in this case, as represented by the General Assembly of the UN, the Secretary-General, and the Security Council, has no real governing authority.

But that is not the full story of this vaunted Right to Petition by which the people are to be empowered. On page 261 of the Report, we read that this Right is to be "strictly circumscribed." First, the Right to Petition may only "deal with complaints about threats to the security of people." Second, petitions must go through a "screening process." For screening, the petitions are to be addressed to a "Council for Petitions" composed of "a high-level panel of five to seven persons... appointed by the Secretary-General and the General Assembly." Nothing is actually said about who may actually formulate a petition, or by what procedure a petition may be submitted to the Council for Petitions, but it would appear to be by a much less direct process than that enjoyed by the serfs and lords of ancient days.

In a more foggy way, and without Charter amendment, the Commission proposes a "Forum of Civil Society." This Forum, without any voting or legislative rights in the UN process, is to be composed in some undefined way by representation of "300 to 600 organs of Global Civil Society"—more commonly referred to as nongovernmental organizations (NGOs). To begin the Forum of Civil Society, the commission proposes (p. 259) that the President of the UN General Assembly shall convene a "working group of organizations of international civil society and members of the UN Assembly to develop the proposal" without Charter amendment.

After getting organized, the Forum of Civil Society is to meet each year prior to the session of the General Assembly, and may then submit its "considered views" to the General Assembly. By reading scattered sections of the Report on pages 258, 259, and 345, the information is gleaned that this Forum will be composed of representatives of organizations which are accredited in an undefined way to the General Assembly, of course without vote. This Forum is offered as a substitute for the long-proposed Citizens Assembly and the more recently proposed Parliamentary Assembly, to be attached to the UN General Assembly, under the provision of Article 22 of the UN Charter. The main difference is that the Forum of Civil Society is NOT to be composed by elections, neither by the people nor by world citizens nor by members of national parliaments. God forbid any process of directly elected representation. People are simply not to be trusted with any plan for direct election and voting.

Thus, the Forum of Civil Society, which in any case will not be fairly representative of the tens of thousands of nongovernmental organizations in all of the countries of the world, not to mention the people, will at very best have only a voice for submitting resolutions to the General Assembly, which may be disregarded. In turn, the Commission does not propose giving the General Assembly any more world legislative authority than it now has, which is zero.

This, then, is the double sop thrown to the people of the world by the Commission on Global Governance, this is the "empowerment of the people": a strictly circumscribed "right to petition," limited to "security" issues, even less than commoners and lords had prior to 1215, and a manipulated discussion forum without legal standing, both entirely powerless. This mind-befuddling sop is substituted by the Commission for a clear way for the people to elect delegates on a fairly and universally defined basis to a legislative world parliament with constitutional authority to solve global problems. This foggy and innocuous way for the people to have a "voice" in world affairs is proposed by the Commission as a "major step forward" (p. 260), and as preferable to constitutional, representative, and responsible world government.

Although denying people the right to elected representation in a world legislature, or to vote in any other aspect of world government or world governance, the Commission in many passages of the Report repeatedly urges and emphasizes the necessity to comply with world law, and the necessity to enforce world law or international law. Moreover, the Commission's definition of world law is extremely fuzzy and hard to pin down. Since the Report rejects at the outset any concept of world government, it certainly does not include an elected and representative world legislature or parliament to debate and adopt world laws.

We are left to conjecture that what is meant by "the rule of law worldwide" (see the kindergarten-level discussion of international law beginning on page 304) is, in reality, when it comes down to tangible specifics, the so-called law defined by treaties and other less binding agreements among sovereign states. The UN, of course, is not empowered to adopt world laws, because only national governments can agree on treaties, which history records they can also break whenever convenient. This is the ancient, obsolete and spurious system of "let's pretend" law which international diplomacy hides behind, but which the Commission now says should be better respected and obeyed.

Treaty law, which has been proven impractical and disastrous as a method for the management of world affairs during more than 300 years of wars and mismanagement of human affairs on Earth, is then to continue as the bulwark for world law that the Commission recommends. The several major defects of treaty law are well known. First, it is not decided by a legislature to which the people elect their representatives, so it cannot be called a democratic process. Second, treaty law is not universally and equally applicable, but applies only to those nations which ratify the particular treaty, however few or many, and varies in application from one treaty to the next. Third, treaty law among nations applies only to international affairs or the conduct of affairs between or among nations, and is not applicable to individual citizens directly. Fourth, since most of the problems of global human society cannot be defined in terms simply of relations among sovereign nations, it is impossible for treaty law to solve most of the global or supranational problems of people living on Earth. Fifth, any nation may withdraw unilaterally from a treaty.

Although the Report places great importance and emphasis on "strengthening the Rule of Law worldwide," none of the defects of treaty law just mentioned are recognized by the Commission. Despite this crucial oversight (or deliberate neglect), a headline of the Report (p. 325) reads: "The very essence of global governance is the capacity of the international community to ensure compliance with the rules of society."

To try to understand a bit better what the Commission means by the "rules of society" and "international law" we may go back to page 306, where the Report quotes Article 38 (1) of the Statute of the "World Court," which lists several sources for "international law," which are mostly of a general nature, including: "international conventions... international custom... general principles of law recognized by civilized nations... judicial decisions of equity... etc."

The Report eventually concedes (p. 311): "Treaties are the principal source of jurisdiction in contentious cases before the World Court." Treaties are formal and ratified agreements between and among sovereign nations, and are not the ordinary laws or rules of civil society applicable to individual citizens. Who rightly, and with respect for justice, should be compelled to comply with laws which are neither decided by, nor subject to the decisions of, a legislative body elected by those subject to the laws?

After all the many pages and passages and pious admonitions in the Report about the enforcement and compliance with the rule of law, i.e., the rule of so-called "international law" (the enforcement of treaties among sovereign nations), the Report finally comes down to one short specific paragraph about enforcement on page 438: "We do not emphasize formal enforcement measures, but failing voluntary compliance, Security Council enforcement of World Court decisions and other international legal obligations should be pursued under Article 94 of the (UN) Charter." At this point, it is necessary to refer to the UN Charter, to quote Article 94: "If any party (i.e., nation) fails to perform the obligations incumbent upon it under a judgment rendered by the Court, the other party may have recourse to the Security Council, which may, if it deems necessary, make recommendations or decide upon measures to be taken to give effect to the judgment." So, specifically, what does this mean? For an answer, we must go back to Chapter 7, Articles 39 to 47 of the UN Charter, which the Report fails to mention, but which are implied if any enforcement action is to be taken.

To summarize, Articles 39 to 47 define how the UN is to enforce decisions of the Security Council, including decisions "to give effect to the judgment" of the World Court. Articles 39 to 47 define how the Security Council is to *engage in war* to enforce its decisions. Of course, such blunt language is not used, but it is war nevertheless. War is the act of exercising force against entire populations to obtain compliance or the submission of national governments. In times past, war was fought primarily by contending armies and other military forces, to prove that might makes right. But war today has different forms. The UN Charter defines the actions of war to be taken by the Security Council in several stages.

First is a pre-fighting stage of requesting or demanding compliance. Next is the stage of economic boycott and sanctions, severance of economic relations, and strangulation of the civilian population. That is war. Next is blockade of commerce and travel and communications, which is enforced by military strength or threats to use such force, which means tighter strangulation of civilian populations. If this does not obtain compliance, then the next series of steps defined by Articles 43 to 47 comprise the use of military force "by air, sea or land forces" in whatever way the Security Council may decide, and by requiring member nations of the UN to provide the needed military contingents.

Use of the term "peace forces," in this Report and elsewhere, is strictly a misleading euphemism. Any organized "forces" which are equipped with guns, bombs, tanks, military aircraft, warships, troop carriers, etc., are military forces which engage in war.

The basic nature of these several stages of warfare is that force, beginning with economic sanctions and proceeding to armed military action, is taken against entire populations of innocent children, women, and men, with no means of identification, arrest, and prosecution of the specific individuals who may be responsible for noncompliance with "international law" or Court decisions. This procedure of war is what the Commission on Global Governance actually relies upon for law enforcement, instead of the procedures of civil society for civilian police to identify, arrest and prosecute those individuals who may be responsible for violations.

To be entirely clear on this critical issue, the procedures for obtaining compliance with "international law," on which the Commission depends, may be summarized as follows:

1. The people and nations of the world are exhorted to comply with world or international laws, for which the people are denied representation by an elected legislature to make the laws: i.e., if not government without representation, then governance without representation.

2. Decisions to obtain compliance are to be made by a court system which is entirely divorced from any functioning of a world legislature, which is divorced from any comprehensive world constitution, and which is therefore essentially operating in a legal void.

3. Finally, to obtain compliance and enforcement, the Commission resorts to the time-dishonored practices of war against entire populations.

4. The various decisions of the Security Council to carry out the several stages of enforcement by war are made, in the last analysis, by the five permanent members of the Security Council.

5. In practice, this means enforcement of world law against weaker nations, for, obviously, no decision of the Security Council could be taken to enforce any international law against any member of the Security Council having the power of veto. Thus, enforcement may be taken only against weaker nations as decided by those who have the veto power.

This is the system which the Commission upholds to enforce respect for law and compliance with the rule of law. This system of world tyranny and war enforced by the Security Council is what the Commission prefers to a constitutional federal world government, under which the people are guaranteed the right to elect their representatives to a world parliament, which then adopts world laws by consent of the governed, with enforcement by civilian police action when necessary to apprehend individual law-breakers rather than make war against entire populations.

The Commission also recommends an "International Criminal Court," to be set up immediately and separately from the International Court of Justice—the so-called World Court. The International Criminal Court, like the main World Court, is to function without an elected world parliament to define and adopt world laws of any kind, and is to function outside of any comprehensive world constitution, thus putting it in an irresponsible and capricious legal void. No means of enforcement of decisions of such a world criminal court are defined, other than those already described for the World Court. Thus, we would have another instrument for the rule of world governance without representation for those to be governed.

Another area of concern given much attention by the Commission in its Report is the problem of widespread poverty in the world, together with related social conditions—a problem which has been getting steadily worse during the past 30 years or longer. Numerous pages of the Report are devoted to detailed descriptions of this situation. But for remedies, the Report is full of nice-sounding admonitions and vague generalities, but nothing that touches on basic solutions or corrections.

The Report accepts the major existing world economic and financial institutions, including GATT (the General Agreement on Tariffs and Trade), the new World Trade Organization, the International Monetary Fund, and the so-called World Bank, without proposing any basic changes that would turn these institutions into effective instruments for eliminating world poverty. The Report accepts the present trend, in fact, the extreme pressures for privatization and structural readjustments in the capitalist system mold, albeit with some pious admonitions to treat poverty-stricken people and countries in a more gentle and helpful way. Otherwise, forced "structural adjustments" as prerequisites to obtain recycling of loans, and the current "extensive movement in favor of market driven approaches since the end of the 1970s" (p. 26), are not seriously questioned.

As for GATT, which is now to be recast as the World Trade Organization, the Commission recommends (p. 222): "All governments should quickly enact legislation to implement the Uruguay Round agreement of the General Agreement on Tariffs and Trade and to set up the World Trade Organization." This recommendation is made despite the very strenuous criticisms and opposition to GATT and the emerging World Trade Organization by numerous environmental and labor organizations, on the grounds that the GATT treaty works to undermine all kinds of hard-won laws and regulations to protect the environment in many ways, and that the enforcement of the GATT treaty will force wages down in the "more developed" countries, and will also keep wages down in the poverty-stricken "developing" countries. This recommendation for immediate ratification and implementation of the GATT treaty is also made despite the Commission's own acknowledgment (p. 166) that "many developing countries have felt marginalized from the (GATT) process, which is still monopolized by the United States, the European Union, and Japan."

In fact, despite pious sentiment about ending poverty, nowhere in the Report is there any serious and substantial analysis and criticism of GATT and the emerging WTO—which is defined as a treaty of some 22,000 pages—for flagrant failure to protect environmental standards, and for subjecting wage standards and other social security standards to downgrading pressures of profit-seeking "market forces." All is to be the proper arena for "free" trade among approximately 37,000 transnational corporations which dominate international trade and investments today.

In the context of GATT, the Commission does make one recommendation, and that is to set up a Global Competition Office. As phrased on page 222, "The WTO should establish new rules to strengthen global competition and a Global Competition Office should be set up to provide oversight." Nothing is said here about the environment or wage and social security standards. This "competition" office is apparently simply to ensure fair competition among all of the profit-seeking 37,000 (and growing) transnational corporations. It may be noted that these corporations dominating world trade are mostly headquartered in the strongest countries economically, that is, the US, Japan, the UK, Germany, France, and so on. The purpose of "competition" is obviously not to facilitate and enable developing countries to employ their citizens in producing to supply the needs of people in the developing countries, nor to lift themselves out of poverty; it is rather to serve those who are already dominant.

As an aside, it may be noted that the 22,000 pages of the GATT treaty, which is to serve as the legal guidelines for the emerging World Trade Organization, would comprise about 44 printed books of 500 pages each. We suppose that the Commission members are all quite familiar with this equivalent of 44 500-page books, and that, no doubt before recommending immediate ratification, they had carefully read the entire work—which will give lifetime employment to tens of thousands of lawyers for decades in arguing about the detailed application of the stipulations and exceptions in each of the 22,000 pages.

Still in the area of economics, one of the few innovative proposals of the Commission is for a new Economic Security Council (pp. 153-160, 263-269, 342). The new ESC is not to be given any actual power to make legally binding decisions (p. 155), but will function by making studies and recommendations.

A striking feature of this proposal is that the new Economic Security Council is to replace the present Economic and Social Council of the United Nations, which will require an amendment to the UN Charter. The present Economic and Social Council, having broader functions than only economic (see Articles 61 to

72 of the UN Charter), is comprised of 54 members elected by the General Assembly of the UN and is thus reasonably representative of UN membership; in particular, it is well representative of the "developing" countries, and the major powers do not have a controlling vote. In contrast, the new Economic Security Council proposed by the Commission is to have a small and limited membership "able to capture the priority attention of key economic ministers in major countries" (p. 158). More precisely, for membership and control of the new Economic Security Council, which is to have no more than 23 members, the Commission (p. 159) proposes: "First, the world's largest economies would be represented, as of right... Second, there would also have to be balanced representation between regions."

It can easily be seen that in place of the present, rather broadly representative Economic and Social Council, where the "developing" countries have the most votes, the new ESC will give control "as of right" to the major powers now dominating the world economy, and with social concerns left out. So much for pious sentiments about the plight of the poverty-stricken majority of the Earth in the less advanced countries.

The present nearly 1000 nongovernmental organizations, accredited with observer status to the UN Economic and Social Council, are to be transferred by "an improved process for continuing review and accreditation" (p. 278) to the General Assembly. In fact, it is these accredited observer NGOs which are to comprise, in new clothes, the proposed Forum of Civil Society. We may assume that the "improved process for continuing review and accreditation" will make sure that no organization with serious criticisms of the UN system, or favorable to its replacement by constitutional democratic world government, will be able to sneak in.

As part of the process of setting up the new ESC and WTO, the longstanding UNCTAD (United Nations Conference on Trade and Development), which has always tended to represent the interests of the less developed countries, will also be scrapped, according to the Commission's recommendation.

Concerning one of the major stumbling blocks in the functioning of the UN, which has perverted service to humanity from the outset, that is, the controlling votes in the Security Council by the five permanent members, the Commission strongly condemns the veto power held by the United States, Russia, United Kingdom, France, and China, who were given this key power as the victors in World War II. The Commission says this must be changed, but without clearly facing up to the fact that any change in this system for control would require the agreement of each of the five nations now holding veto power.

Instead, the Commission tiptoes around this dominating situation by means of proposing a two-stage process for "phasing out" the veto power (pp. 233 -241, 344-345). The first proposed stage is for the General Assembly to elect a "new class of five standing members" to the Security Council, which is to be enlarged from the present ten nonpermanent members to thirteen. It is not clear what is to be the real value of having this new class of five standing members, since they will not have any more voting power than the rest of the rotating members. As for the veto, in this first stage, the Commission asks the five permanent members having the veto to please and kindly "enter into a concordat agreeing to forgo its use save in circumstances they consider to be of an exceptional and overriding nature." So what else is new?

For the second stage, the Commission wistfully suggests that there "should be a full review of the membership of the Council... around 2005 [i.e., ten years from the time of writing] when the veto can be phased out." Surely all of the five permanent members, who have insisted on their veto rights for the past 50 years, without budging an inch, will see the sweet reason of this suggestion.

The Commission also, incidentally, proposes that the Security Council when enlarged to a total membership of 18, shall require a vote of 14 to make any decision (p. 345), including by necessity the unanimous vote of the 5 permanent members. This will increase the number of votes from the present 9 out of a total of 15 members, to the new requirement of 14 concurring votes. In practice, this will make it more difficult for any decision to be reached, and, in particular, make it more difficult for the permanent members to control even the current behind-the-scenes financial arm-twisting by the most powerful. It seems highly unlikely that those now in control will vote for a UN amendment to weaken their power by this proposal.

For purposes of financing global activities under "global governance," the Commission does not examine or propose any specific budget, and does not estimate what might be required to solve global problems as compared with military expenditures. Apart from dues to be paid by member nations, with no means to enforce payment or collection, the Report mentions a few sources for global revenue (p. 220) like charges on airline tickets, ocean maritime transport, and "user fees" for "some common global resources." The Commission fails to examine the multitrillion-dollar costs for salvaging and maintaining the global environment and the costs for dismantling nuclear weapons, and disposing of accumulated radioactive poisons, or the actual financial requirements for coping with any other global problem, including how to truly end world poverty. The Commission is very definite, however, that "we specifically do *not* [emphasis added] propose a taxing power located anywhere in the UN system... global revenue receiving arrangements of whatever kind have to be agreed globally and implemented by a treaty or convention" (p. 218). This, we remember, is the time-honored and time-proven method for the successful (?) financing of all governments and governances.

Concerning the problems of nuclear weapons, chemical-biological weapons, and other weapons of mass destruction, as well as other military expenditures, including the spread of smaller arms and bombs everywhere, together with the persistent problem of disarmament, the Commission, while bemoaning the horrors of the situation, can offer nothing better than continued negotiations among sovereign nations—negotiations which have been fully unsuccessful in reducing military arms since the end of World War II.

To reinforce disarmament sentiment, the Commission stoutly recommends (pp. 340-341) that "the international community should reaffirm its commitment to eliminate nuclear and other weapons of mass destruction progressively from all nations, and should initiate a ten-to-fifteen-year programme to achieve this goal, to include extension of the Non-Proliferation Treaty, and a treaty to end all nuclear testing." No questions are asked about why sovereign nations did not disarm after the Hague Peace Conferences of the 1880s, the end of World War I, the Kellogg-Briand peace pact of 1928, the end of World War II, and during the years of continuous disarmament conferences (accompanied by continuous increases and the spread of armaments worldwide) since 1946. The central issue (obstacle) of continuation of the system of national sovereignty is ignored.

While seriously underestimating total world arms expenditures at only $815 billion dollars in 1992, the Report projects a goal of reducing world military expenditures to the modest total of only $500 billion (pp. 125, 341) by the year 2000. That, of course, would be better than nothing, but practically speaking, who is really being defended by the continued expenditure of that much?

To help achieve this somewhat modest goal, the Commission recommends a Demilitarization Fund "to provide positive incentives for reductions in military spending (p. 126) by the developing countries... to focus on support of defense conversion activities." In a Global Military Expenditures table on page 124, the Report shows that in 1992 the "developing" countries spent $125 billion, while the "industrial" countries spent $690 billion. We suppose that this conclusively demonstrates that the developing countries pose the biggest threat, and thus will need the most help from the Demilitarization Fund.

The Commission also recommends a "mandatory Arms Register, and prohibition of the financing or subsidy of arms exports by governments," but seems to forget that under its nebulous proposal for "global governance," there is no way to make anything mandatory—short of war.

We cannot help but observe that having rejected, as "leading to less democracy," any proposal for World Government (such as the Constitution for the Federation of Earth, which would require total disarmament to proceed upon ratification), the Commission prefers the obviously more democratic procedure of wasting $500 billion or more per year on the entrenched benefits of the autocratic military-industrial system under national sovereignty.

The Report of the Commission on Global Governance is replete throughout with a great many high-sounding and enticing admonitions and generalities for improvements and doing things better, while leaving all the basic operating structures of the United Nations essentially unchanged. In this critique, I have not mentioned many of the admonitions scattered along the way, principally because no specific ways are defined to accomplish most of the suggestions.

In trying to understand the incomplete and vaguely formulated proposals of the Commission, it is also necessary to continually turn pages back and forth to understand what is actually not really well defined. It is something like trying to pick up a form modeled in wet sand, which crumbles in your hands, and you are left not knowing what it really is that you do not have. Specifics and definite structures and procedures are what the Commission evidently abhors, and this lack helps make its Report sound good—although upon closer examination the document is revealed to be contradictory, befuddling, and misleading.

As a final proposal (p. 351) and consolation prize to all those who may have been looking hopefully and eagerly for something good and useful to come out of the Commission on Global Governance, the Commission recommends "that the (UN) General Assembly should agree to hold a World Conference on Governance in 1998, with its decisions to be ratified and put into effect by (the year) 2000."

The Report expresses (p. 350) "fear that if reform is left to normal processes, only piecemeal and inadequate action will result." But the Commission, in its final recommendation, can only foresee another five years, if not more, of stumbling around in a netherworld (or never-never world) of irresponsible and undefinable terms of "world governance." Although each Commission member was provided with a copy of the Constitution for the Federation of Earth, and with "A Bill of Particulars: Why the UN Must Be Replaced" (a publication of the World Constitution and Parliament Association, included as an appendix to this chapter), the Commission was unwilling or unable to come to grips with any clear concept for responsible federal world government to replace the proven obsolete and unworkable UN system. Instead, the Report relies on the universally discredited system of solving problems and managing world affairs by treaties—a system (or non-system) which has been obsolete for more than 200 years, and which has been proven unworkable and disastrous by two major world wars, scores of other wars, a multitrillion-dollar nuclear arms race whose toxic byproducts have poisoned Earth for tens of thousands of years into the future, and a steadily advancing climate-change crisis of staggering proportions (which was recognized by leading scientists more than 20 years ago), not to mention scores of other enormous and accumulating unsolved world problems.

Near the beginning of the Report and also at its end, the Commission on Global Governance emphasizes the need for "enlightened leadership." On page 353, the Commission stresses, "The world needs leaders made strong by vision, sustained by ethics, and revealed by political courage that looks beyond the next election." Unhappily, this reviewer must conclude that the Commission and its members have demonstrated in this Report none of those laudable qualities.

If this Report, *Our Global Neighborhood*, were just another book among many, offered for thoughtful discussion about world problems, perhaps not so much fuss need be made about its dire shortcomings. However, the aim of the Commission, as summarized on page 377, is a sustained campaign to promote the recommendations of the Report: "The Commission decided at an early stage that it would engage in active efforts to disseminate the Report, and promote its ideas and recommendations. This will be done mainly through speaking engagements, working with governments, international organizations, NGOs and other civil society organizations, and the media; organizing workshops and discussions; and distributing material."

To the extent that the Commission succeeds in its avowed campaign, which is enhanced by the VIP nature of the Commission members, the result will be to obscure and confuse what truly needs to be done: that is, to replace the UN immediately with a constitutional federal world government, which is already generations overdue. The effect of the Report, if taken seriously and without understanding what it fails to propose, will be to help mislead both the people and the governments of the world into more years of aimless wanderings in a foggy and extremely hazardous wilderness of avoiding the required practical measures to cope genuinely with world problems.

APPENDIX TO CHAPTER 7

A BILL OF PARTICULARS
Why the United Nations Must Be Replaced

PART I

Failures of the United Nations Organization to Serve Human Needs during the past five decades and some of the proliferating global problems which the UN is not solving.

1. *War*

Although the United Nations Organization was created in 1945, as stated in the preamble, "to save succeeding generations from the scourge of war," war preparations and wars have continued as a major priority and activity of almost all member nations of the UN

Since 1945, hundreds of millions of people have been murdered or maimed in wars or had their homes and communities destroyed by wars. Mostly civilians. Since 1945, more than 100 nations, including two-thirds of the present Members of the United Nations, have been involved in several thousand wars, and probably fifty or more wars are now going on including insurrections.

Since 1945, the people of Earth have been robbed of many trillions of dollars squandered on the nuclear arms race, resulting in increasing global insecurity, with more than 50,000 nuclear bombs aimed and ready to fire, whereas the explosion of less than 100 is sufficient to wipe out human civilization on Earth by causing the onset of nuclear winter as well as by outright destruction and long-lingering radioactive poisoning of the environment.

Since 1945, more scientific and engineering talent of the world has been engaged in the design and production of weapons of war than in any other activity.

Since 1945, apart from nuclear weapons, other weapons of mass destruction and deadly capabilities have been vastly expanded in quantities, in technological varieties, and in destructive power, all contributing to total global insecurity.

Since 1945, most member nations of the UN, both small and large, poor and rich, have given top priority to equipping themselves with modern weapons of war, regardless of needs for housing, nutrition, education, utilities, and other basic needs and services for their citizens.

Since 1945, trade in armaments and weapons of war has zoomed to ever larger proportions, so that guns with magnifying killing and destructive capacities are everywhere, and wars among nations and ethnic nationalities erupt everywhere.

Since 1945, all of the disarmament conventions, commissions, studies and resolutions of the UN have failed to stop the increase and spread of military arms for war, have failed to stop the introduction of new technologies for more destructive weapons, have failed to stop more nations from acquiring nuclear weapons, have failed to achieve disarmament.

Since 1945, the building of vast factories to produce weapons of war presents another complex, expensive, and socially explosive problem of conversion to production for peaceful human needs, so that the production and sale of unneeded weapons continues with no global agency able to facilitate and supervise the needed conversion to serve peaceful needs.

Since 1945, the ensuing arms race and military programs of the member nations of the UN (euphemistically called national military defense, but in actuality war programs) have caused almost all national economies to become war economies, tied to the priorities given to war preparations.

Since 1945, all production of nuclear weapons and weapons of mass destruction should properly be defined as war crimes, committed by most member nations of the UN, and in largest measure by the five permanent member nations of the Security Council, but the UN is silent on this.

2. Environmental Destruction

Despite much attention given to global environmental deterioration by the UN General Assembly, by the United Nations Environment Program, and by UN sponsored conferences, the UN has been unable to implement actions necessary to reverse major environmental damages and to sustain a good livable environment on Earth.

Although it has been known for many years that the rain forests of Earth are needed to recycle 50% or more of Earth's oxygen supply, and to store excess carbon dioxide, the UN has been unable to stop continued destruction of the rain forests at very rapid rates, and at current rates most of the rain forests will be gone within two generations.

Already delayed action to save the rain forests gravely endangers all of humanity by resulting atmospheric imbalances, while reforestation of rain forests is extremely difficult because of bad soil and water conditions after rain forests are removed.

Although it has been known for many years that the burning of fossil fuels is raising the carbon dioxide level in the atmosphere so that the resultant heat trapping will cause disastrous climatic changes, nothing has been done by the UN to stop oil and coal production and burning for fuel.

Although the technical feasibility for safe, sustainable and plentiful energy supplies from solar and hydrogen sources has been known for many years, no intensive global "crash" program has been launched to develop such sources rapidly to replace oil and coal.

Although the reduction of carbon dioxide emissions by 20% has been encouraged at various conventions, this will not stop the other 80% from continuing to cause a rise in CO_2 levels in the atmosphere, and the UN has no way to achieve even the 20% reduction.

An international treaty, non-enforceable, is being promoted by the UN to limit ozone depleting chlorofluorocarbons to 1990 levels, but at 1990 levels, atmospheric ozone will continue to be destroyed, and there is no way to enforce a reduction to 1990 levels, thus promising increased dangers.

Besides chlorofluorocarbons, there are many other gases and sources of gases which deplete the ozone, which rise in the atmosphere over a period of years, and for which there are no regulations, thus assuring continued dangerous ozone depletion for the foreseeable future.

Although it has been known for many years that the phytoplankton in the oceans are needed to recycle 50% or more of the Earth's oxygen supply, as well as store excess carbon dioxide and begin the food chain for fish and sea life, and that ozone depletion will result in destruction of the phytoplankton by ultra-violet rays, this problem has not even been taken up at the UN.

To reverse the catastrophic climate changes which are sometimes recognized as probably already underway, requires a very massive and globally coordinated program of many inter-related parts, which will cost many hundreds of billions of dollars per year for many years if human civilization on Earth is to be saved, but the UN is totally unprepared and unable to launch or administer such a program.

The most drastic result of climate changes, following upon imbalances of carbon dioxide in the atmosphere and heat trapping, will be agricultural failures worldwide and consequent global starvation of a magnitude reaching into the billions of people, but this problem is not even mentioned seriously at UN conferences or in the UN General Assembly or Security Council.

The end of the current inter-glacial period which has already run its historic course of 11,000 years, and the onset of another "ice age," which is the greatest emergency confronting human civilization, is never mentioned seriously by any UN Agency or at any UN Conference.

When taking up the issue of ownership and development of the oceans and seabeds as the common heritage of humanity, the decision taken at the UN sponsored "Law Of The Seas" conferences was to give 200 miles offshore to each nation with a seacoast, which is 200 miles containing the most accessible resources of the common heritage of humanity, and also the areas needing the most protection by global intervention from pollution.

Although radioactive wastes and residues from the production of nuclear power have been accumulating since nuclear power production started 41 years ago, and it is known that these radioactive wastes and poisons are a deadly threat to human life for thousands and tens of thousands of years, the UN has done nothing to stop the production of nuclear power with the resulting accumulation of radioactive poisons, despite the additional fact that there are no safe disposal procedures known for the accumulating life-threatening nuclear wastes.

Now that the threats to human life on Planet Earth from the enormous oversupplies of nuclear weapons are being recognized (when even one nuclear bomb is an over-supply), and now that the objective of dismantling some nuclear weapons has become a diplomatic negotiating point, there is no compelling and safe procedure ready for the extremely complicated and enormously expensive and dangerous work of dismantling these weapons. Meanwhile, the nuclear bombs which proliferated during all the years of UN surveillance become older and more unsafe each year.

Currently dismantling procedures include storage of nuclear explosive components, available for re-assembly into bombs and subject to dispersal to other countries; and the use of nuclear material from bombs in nuclear power plants which poison the environment for thousands of years.

Since 1945, enormous quantities of other toxic wastes have been accumulating from a great many industrial processes, which are dumped in the oceans or shipped from the "advanced" industrial nations to "less advanced" countries, and the UN has no program for safe disposal or control over this global problem.

Dozens of other urgent and extreme environmental problems continue to proliferate and become worse, such as soil erosion and deterioration of agricultural lands globally, depletion and pollution of fresh water supplies globally, depletion of ocean fisheries globally, oil spills and discharges everywhere, multiple atmospheric pollutions globally, and the UN is unable to do anything except make studies, collect documentation, establish commissions to study the problems, and hold conferences which cannot make any binding decisions to solve the problems.

The people of Earth are living under an increasing poisonous and ugly global haze, which spreads everywhere, and even if mentioned at UN meetings the UN is unable to eliminate the sources which cause this haze, even if it constitutes a threat and burden to life everywhere.

For a full bill of particulars in this area, an intolerably lengthy document would be required. The foregoing constitutes only a partial listing of the global environmental problems with which the UN has been unable to cope.

3. *Economic and Social Conditions*

Although the Economic and Social Council of the United Nations was entrusted with wide areas of concern "with respect to international economic, social, cultural, educational, health and related matters," in all of these areas conditions have deteriorated for most of the people and countries of Earth since 1945, while a minority have prospered.

Pleas which were brought before the UN by nations of the "non-aligned movement" for "a new international economic order," to improve conditions in and achieve greater equity for the developing countries, were never acted upon, and have since been ignored.

Instead, developing countries were loaded with short term loans both for development purposes and for armaments, at unsustainable rates for repayment.

To resolve these problems, the International Monetary Fund (IMF) and the International Bank for Reconstruction and Development (IBRD) (both listed as UN Specialized Agencies), together with consortiums of private banks, kindly consented to recycle the debts by combining both overdue and principal interest into new principal amounts, thus re-financing the debts again and again on short terms which could not be repaid.

Since many of the developing countries had initiated various social welfare programs and public enterprises to serve the needs of their people, the debts were recycled only on stringent conditions of curtailment or elimination of social programs, liquidation of public enterprises, devaluations of currencies, privatization, and further austerity measures.

By insisting on treating each country separately, the UN affiliated IMF and IBRD, and the helpful consortiums of big banks, proceeded on a divide-and-conquer basis to bring most developing countries over the years into economic subjugation, without the possibilities for development to serve the needs of their people with equity.

Technology transfers so that developing countries could develop modern production of all kinds of both capital and consumer goods have been consistently avoided or done only partly in the context of operations of multinational corporations. Developing countries for the most part are treated as sources for raw materials and resources to be used by the "advanced" countries for their own industrial and commercial purposes.

Production by modern technological innovations in the advanced countries has rapidly expanded, to the point where there are almost no markets in international trade for goods which might be produced in developing countries by indigenous industries.

The major exceptions to the lack of markets for goods produced in less developed countries are the enterprises of multinational corporations which establish factories in less developed countries to employ labor at very low wages to produce goods for sale in the markets of the richer countries. But only a few of the less developed countries have been chosen for serving the needs of the rich in this way. The rest are not needed.

All the while, since 1945, the gap in incomes for most of the peoples of the less developed countries, in comparison with incomes for peoples in the more developed countries, has been constantly growing larger.

At the same time, by the system of loans and repayment schedules extended to the less developed countries, as supervised by the UN and by specialized agencies of the IMF and the IBRD, the net transfer of capital, by reason of debt and interest payments, has consistently been from the less developed and poorer countries to the already rich.

Unemployment in the "less developed" countries commonly ranges from 15% to 40% or 50%, while unemployment at 8% to 10% in more developed countries is considered unfortunate but acceptable. The problem is much greater when account is taken of marginal and partial employment, and employment at struggling subsistence levels.

Since 1945, the UN has taken no steps towards the introduction of a single global currency, which could eliminate the manipulations and devaluations of variable currencies always to the detriment of most people.

Since 1945, no system of global finance and credit has ever been devised for the primary purpose of serving the human needs of people everywhere, on a basis of equity for all.

Two resource exploitations encouraged in many developing countries have been (a) lumbering for export of raw logs and (b) cutting down of rain forests to provide land (but only with short-term fertility) for growing cattle for meat exports. Both provide cash required to repay loans and thus have the approval of the UN agencies IMF and IBRD, while making lumbering and cattle entrepreneurs rich.

But both extensive lumbering and the cattle industry result in destroying the rain forests which are the lungs of the world to recycle oxygen and carbon dioxide. The result is gross environmental destruction in many ways, as well as resultant migrations of displaced persons to the overcrowded cities.

The cities of almost all developing countries become ever larger and sprawling aggregates of poverty, pollution, inhuman living conditions, and expanding crime, while major cities of many "developed" countries are not too far behind in all of these problems.

Meanwhile, under the watchful eyes of the UN and its affiliated financial agencies, a brisk commerce in armaments and military supplies burgeons in almost all developed countries, with spill-over of high powered guns to all kinds of poverty stricken civilians, insurgent groups and criminals.

Meanwhile, the General Agreement on Trade and Tariffs (GATT), also a UN affiliated project, is being developed behind closed doors and with no representation for interests of "the people" (labor, small farmers, environment, social welfare) to be enforced arbitrarily according to rules to make the world safe for profit-seeking transnational or multinational corporations and their collaborators. The objective is to guarantee and maximize profits for exploitive private enterprise by, among other things, the elimination of such "unfair" trade practices as protection for wage and labor standards, costly environmental protection, subsidies to protect local agriculture and agricultural communities, and the costs of social welfare in general. (Note: There is nothing intrinsically wrong with "multinational" corporations, but only in whose interests they are owned and managed.)

However, a new threat has emerged during the past decade: AIDS. Emerging and growing most rapidly in poverty stricken African countries, this threat is growing worldwide, in both "developing" and "developed" countries, with no end and no solution in sight. In some "developing" countries, as much as 20% of the population is reported HIV positive. To the uncontrolled and spreading epidemic of AIDS is now added the resurgence of tuberculosis, particularly in expanding poverty stricken areas.

Prior to AIDS, the sale of drugs manufactured from "third world" agricultural sources has been one horrible answer to securing limited incomes for some poor farmers while drug privateers get rich. Now the spread of AIDS goes along with the previous commerce in drugs to make socially impossible situations in both rich and poor countries.

Since the end of the "cold war," the UN with its associated IMF and IBRD has willingly cooperated in the universal application of programs for "privatization" and "free market" profiteering, which has resulted in enormous difficulties for most of the people both in the countries of the former USSR and of Eastern Europe, and also throughout the world of "developing" countries—all under the assumption that "privatization" and "free market reforms" are proven to be the best form of economic organization.

All of the problems mentioned above are resulting in an enormously growing problem of refugees: people seeking to flee to safe places; environmental refugees from ecologically devastated places, and soon because of climatic changes; refugees from ethnic, tribal, and religious wars; refugees from horrible slums, oppressions, and lack of economic opportunity.

Many other deficiencies in performance and failures to cope with global problems remain to be listed in such areas as Protection of Human Rights, World Food Supplies, World Energy Supplies, and others.

PART II
Defects in Organization

Considering the seemingly good purposes defined in the UN Charter, why has the United Nations failed to solve global problems?

It is not because the Ambassadors to the UN from the various countries are incompetent or stupid. They are among the best informed persons in the world. Nor is it because the UN staff is incompetent, nor because of misuse of funds. A change in personnel would make no difference.

The main reason is because the UN is simply not organized to solve global or supra-national problems. Major defects are described below:

The first principle of the United Nations as stated in Article 2 is: "The Organization is based on the principle of the sovereign equality of all its members." The Members are the nations of the world, as represented by their national governments. Throughout Article 1 and Article 2, the frame of reference repeated many times is: "relations among nations," "international disputes," "international peace and security," "international law." The words "world," "global," "supra-national," and "Earth" do not appear in the Charter except in three references to the Second World War and use of the word "world" incidentally once in Article 74 and once in Article 76. The entire Charter is drawn exclusively in terms of relations among Member states or nations. The continuance of national sovereignty is accepted without question.

Actually, most problems of living together on Planet Earth, including most of the problems listed in Part I of this Bill of Particulars, cannot be defined or resolved in terms of relations between or among sovereign nations.

The General Assembly of the UN has no authority to adopt world legislation binding on the nations or people of the world. By Articles 10 to 17 on Functions and Powers, the General Assembly is limited to the following actions: "may discuss," "may initiate studies," "may make recommendations," "may consider." However, it "shall" receive reports and approve the budget of the UN; and is given some responsibilities concerning Trust Territories. Thus, the General Assembly essentially may only make or authorize studies and make recommendations, usually in the form of resolutions, which may be implemented only insofar as agreed to in treaties or conventions ratified by the members' sovereign national governments or parliaments. World problems cannot be solved in this manner.

The General Assembly is composed of delegates appointed by national governments on the basis of one vote for each national delegation, regardless of the populations of the countries represented. The General Assembly is obviously not a fairly representative body for either the people or the nations of the world, and because of this basic defect should not be given legislative authority.

The Security Council as defined by Articles 23 to 51, is given "primary responsibility for the maintenance of international peace and security," particularly concerning conflicts or potential conflicts among nations. But the Security Council, like the General Assembly, also has no authority to adopt binding world legislation to solve any global problem, although it may make recommendations and it may decide on various war-making actions supposedly to maintain peace and security.

The Security Council, moreover, is composed of delegates from only 15 Member nations, appointed by the national governments. Any decision requires a unanimous vote by all of the five permanent Members of the Security Council, which are defined as China, France, the USSR (now replaced by Russia), the United Kingdom, and the USA. This means that any decision can be blocked by any one of the five. If the Security Council were given legislative authority, this would mean rule of the world by the five permanent Members, which would be world oligarchic dictatorship and therefore intolerable. The addition of more members to the Security Council would not change this, since the Five will not agree to relinquish their veto power.

Those articles of the Charter which give the most definite authority to the Security Council to take action are Articles 33 to 49, of Section VI on Pacific Settlement of Disputes and Section VII on Action With Respect To Threats To The Peace, Breaches Of The Peace, and Acts Of Aggression. Detailed procedures are given which specify that the Security Council "may investigate any dispute" and "may recommend appropriate procedures or methods of adjustment."

If the dispute continues or is determined to be a "threat to the peace," the Security Council may decide on further measures "not involving the use of armed force" and "may call upon the Members of the UN to apply such measures (which) may include complete or partial interruption of economic relations...and means of communication." If this is inadequate, the Security Council then "may take such action by air, sea or land forces as may be necessary (which) may include...blockade and other operations by air, sea or land forces of Members of the United Nations." This is, of course, the conduct of war against *entire populations* of countries, including "the interruption of economic relations."

Nowhere in the Charter is the disarmament of nations required, in fact, the opposite. Article 43 specifies that "All Members of the United Nations, in order to contribute to the maintenance of international peace and security, undertake to make available to the Security Council, on its call...armed forces..." And Article 45 specifies that "In order to enable the United Nations to take urgent military measures, Members shall hold immediately available national airforce contingents for combined international enforcement action..." This means that the UN Charter specifically requires the continuation of national military forces, rather than disarmament.

The United Nations does not have a true Executive Branch with Ministries which could be given responsibilities for implementing legislative decisions of a World Parliament. Most of the executive decisions and actions are taken by the Security Council. Towards the end of the Charter, Articles 97 to 101 specify a "Secretariat (which) shall comprise a Secretary-General and such staff as the Organization may require. The Secretary-General shall be the chief administrative officer of the Organization." Further composition of the Secretariat and staff are not defined. This is entirely inadequate for the implementation of solutions to the manifold global and supra-national problems of Earth, which in fact the UN is not designed to accomplish.

The Secretary-General is "appointed by the General Assembly upon the recommendation of the Security Council." This is a slightly concealed way of saying that the Secretary-General shall be the chief administrative officer for the five permanent Members of the Security Council, who in fact control all important operations and decisions of the UN.

Since the decisions of the Security Council require the unanimous vote of the five permanent members, no decision or action can ever be taken which is adverse to one of the permanent members—that is, no action can ever be taken which is adverse to the USA, Russia, the UK, France, or China. Thus, decisions and actions can only be taken adverse to nations which are weaker or in a weaker position. The Security Council is thus organized for the strongest nations to rule the weaker nations, and is an agency for maintaining the status quo rather than to find solutions to problems for the common and equitable benefit of humanity. The Security Council, at the bottom line, is organized essentially to carry out the ancient "bully principle" in international affairs.

An International Court of Justice is specified under Part XIV, Articles 92 to 96, of the Charter—not a "World" Court—which functions in accordance with an annexed statute. The jurisdiction of the Court is limited to "international disputes," but the Court is not given mandatory jurisdiction. The Court has no power to require international disputes to be submitted to it for judgment, but depends on the voluntary agreement of those nations involved. Any nation can decline to be a party to a case brought before the Court, and therefore excuse itself from complying with decisions of the Court.

Actually, the so-called "international law" which comprises the legal framework within which the Court functions and makes decisions, is the result only of treaties and agreements among sovereign nations, and does not represent legislation adopted by a democratically elected World Parliament. Thus, it would be undesirable to give the International Court of Justice mandatory and enforceable jurisdiction until World Law is determined by a democratically composed and fairly representative World Parliament.

The Economic and Social Council of the UN seems to be based on good intentions, yet lacks power to do more than make studies and recommendations, as given permission in Articles 62 to 66 of the Charter.

While originally composed of representatives from 18 Member nations, the number was increased in 1973 to 54 nations. This is still less than one-third of the UN Members, and includes no voting representatives from people. This body would need to be more representative in order to cope with the many world problems with which it should be concerned, although the Charter refers only to "international" economic, social, cultural, educational, health, and related matters.

The much lauded Charter of Human Rights, adopted by the General Assembly and ratified by most Member nations, includes a large number of very well expressed statements to define human rights. However, the UN lacks any means for implementing and enforcing the defined "rights." Further, there are lumped together rights which under any circumstances would take many years or several decades to fully accomplish, and rights which presumably should be immediately enforceable. The Charter, however, makes no such distinction and ratification means little more than lip service. Rights which would take longer to accomplish should be under a separate heading of "directional principles," but with requirements for fulfillment.

Another gross defect in the UN system is the means for controlling international finance, loans, and credits. This is managed by the International Monetary Fund and the International Bank for Reconstruction and Development—commonly called the "World Bank." Both are listed as "specialized agencies" within the UN system, but both are separately organized and not controlled by the United Nations. Yet both are agencies by which decisions of the Security Council are implemented.

Organizationally, both the IMF and the IBRD are headquartered in the USA, along with the UN. However, each is managed by a separate Board of Directors of 24 members each. Voting power in each Board is given to Directors in proportion to the financial power and shares of stock held by each member nation. Thus, between 38% and 39% of the votes for each Board are held by the five nations of USA, UK, Germany, France, and Japan, of which the USA has 17% of the votes. All of the African countries together have less than 10%. All of the countries of Eastern Europe and of the former USSR, except Russia, are represented by Directors from Western Europe. All of the Caribbean countries are represented by a Director from Canada. Most of the Pacific area countries are represented by a Director from Australia.

These two international financial agencies together control the extension of financial credit and loans, the denial and cancellation or suspension of credit and loans, the specific terms for loans and credit (such as various "austerity" measures, economic reconstruction within a country, cancellation of social programs, and privatization), and determine which currencies are recognized as "hard" currencies for international commerce.

By various adroit, sophisticated, informal, hidden and manipulative ways, as well as by voting, these two international financial agencies are used to control the world for the primary interests of the most powerful nations, and to manipulate and implement decisions of the Security Council for the same devious purposes, in particular to implement the basic "bully principle" of the Security Council.

Finally, the budget of the United Nations proper is less than $5 billion per year, which is less than 2% of the USA military/defense budget. How many other Member nations of the UN also have military/defense budgets exceeding the total UN budget? To be practical, a budget of at least a trillion dollars a year is required to cope with critical global and supra-national problems demanding immediate and emergency attention, and continuing into the 21st. century, including numerous environmental crises, reversing climate changes, the dismantling of all nuclear weapons, global conversion to benign energy sources and uses, agricultural and ocean life sustainability, facilitation of economic development to serve human needs equitably, and to cope with all of the problems listed in Part I of this Bill of Particulars. A trillion dollars a year is what the Member nations are together spending on war and military costs, so that a trillion dollars a year to solve global problems is quite reasonable. Unhappily, the design of the UN is completely unsuited to the use of such funds for the proper solution of global problems.

The United Nations Specialized Agencies

In relation to this description of UN defects, something should be said about the good works of many of the "specialized agencies" of the United Nations. Altogether a few more than 40 agencies are associated with the United Nations in various ways, as institutes, programs, commissions, continuing conferences, funds, councils, and specially defined organizations, of which 15 are specifically listed as UN "Specialized Agencies."

Most of the 40-plus agencies are limited to functions of study, research, reports and recommendations. A few are operating agencies, such as the Trustee Council, the Universal Postal Union, the Telecommunications Union, the Civil Aviation Organization, the World Health Organization, the IMF, the IBRD, the growing GATT, and the emerging Seabed Authority.

Most of these agencies are organized under separate "Agreements" among sovereign nations, many originating from studies and recommendations of the General Assembly. However, there is no comprehensive and continuing coordination.

Most of the agencies depend for their funding upon voluntary pledges made by sovereign nations which join together in the separate Agreements or Charters concerning the organization and operation of each agency. The UN has no power, itself, to raise money by any compulsory means for any activity of any UN agency. The total of the budgets for all of the specialized agencies together is not readily available, but probably may add up to the several billion dollar cost of a small fleet of high-powered military aircraft.

Despite the many very good and valuable studies and reports and recommendations of the UN specialized agencies, all of them together have barely made a small dent towards solving the proliferating global problems which are listed in this Bill of Particulars, to which many other unsolved problems remain to be added.

For example, how much progress has the UN Environment Program, started 25 years ago in 1972, made in curtailing destruction of the rain forests? Or switching from production and use of oil for energy to solar energy? How much progress has the UN Development Program, started 31 years ago in 1966, made in facilitating adequate development programs in any country so as to bring unemployment down below 10%, while at the same time assuring fair wages? This does not mean that the agencies are badly managed. It is simply evidence of the impossible constraints under which they try to function.

The best that can be said about the UN Specialized Agencies is that when a constitutional federal World Government with an adequate and mandatory budget of the necessary trillion dollars a year is established, then all viable agencies of the UN can be incorporated within the World Government with adequate funding for effective operations.

Conclusion

In summary, the United Nations is totally unfit to function as a world organization to solve global and supra-national problems, and administer world affairs for the common good of humanity. When analyzed clearly it is obvious that the UN was never designed for such good purposes. It should be equally obvious that the UN Charter should be totally replaced with a well designed Constitution for Federal World Government which defines the necessary structure, functions and powers required to solve global problems and serve the common needs of all inhabitants of Planet Earth.

Yet, at this time in human history, after 50 years of demonstrated failure, of gross defects in every paragraph of the UN Charter, and the manifest impossibility for the UN to solve global problems and serve the peaceful needs of all citizens of Earth, there are many leaders and many organizations proposing to achieve improvements by amending the UN Charter, or by adding ancillary bodies to the General Assembly, or by otherwise "strengthening" the United nations. As long-suffering humanity celebrates the 50th anniversary of UN failure, much attention is being given to such proposals, which diverts the very serious attention which should be given to replacement of the UN, rather than reform. These proposals need answering.

PART III
The Delusion of Amending the United Nations Charter

The procedure for amending the UN Charter is defined in Articles 108 and 109. These Articles both require that any alteration of the Charter must be ratified by each of the permanent Members of the Security Council, as well as by two-thirds of all UN Members—which now total more than 180 nations. Of prime importance is that each Member of the Security Council can veto any amendment, including amendment of the veto power.

The first step towards amendment is "a General Conference of the Members of the United Nations for the purpose of reviewing the present Charter." Such a conference could be convened by a decision of a two-thirds vote of the total membership, inclusive of nine members of the Security Council. However, in view of the opposition of the five permanent Members to amendments, particularly the substantial kind of amendments needed, no review conference has ever been called.

Even if the five permanent Members of the Security Council were agreeable to consider fundamental changes (beginning with elimination of the "veto" power) the entire structure of the UN under its Charter is simply unsuited for changing by amendments into anything resembling a democratic World Organization capable of solving global problems for the equitable benefit of all people and countries of Earth. It is not a matter of changing a word or sentence or paragraph here and there. Hundreds of amendments would be required throughout the Charter. Is that a realistic or practical approach?

What is truly needed is nothing less than an entirely different and new Constitution for Federal World Government. This was fully recognized as early as 1946. The truth of the necessity for World Government has since been covered up and treated as unrealistic, but still remains the basic practical requirement for a peaceful world society able to solve global problems and serve human needs.

To transform the Charter into a workable Constitution for Federal World Government would require changing every section, every article, almost every sentence, as well as thousands of words, each change subject to veto. It should be quite clear that transformation of the UN by amendments into a Federal World Government is entirely impractical and impossible.

In addition, and most importantly, one major area of international control which can never be changed by amendments to the UN Charter, is the area of financial control by the International Monetary Fund and the International Bank for Reconstruction and Development (the so-called "World Bank"). Since these financial agencies are governed by organizational "Agreements" and Boards of Directors which are entirely separate from the UN Charter, even though called UN "specialized agencies," they cannot be touched by amendments to the UN Charter.

Some people and organizations currently try to avoid the issue of amendments by proposing instead "restructuring" or "comprehensive restructuring." This is merely a cute ploy on words, and helps only to confuse people and obstruct clear thinking. Restructuring requires amendments to the Charter. Comprehensive restructuring requires comprehensive amendments to the Charter, as specified in Articles 108 and 109, which is neither realistic nor practical nor possible.

For an analogy, a horse and buggy cannot be transformed into a modern automobile by changing parts. And there is no good fairy to wave a magic wand. The only rational and practical solution is to replace the Charter of the UN completely with a well designed Constitution for Democratic Federal World Government.

PART IV
Proposed Improvements Without Amendments Are Delusions

A. *Add A People's Assembly*

After futilely proposing UN reform by amendments since 1946, some people during the past decade have discovered that Article 22 of the Charter states: "The General Assembly may establish such subsidiary organs as it deems necessary for the performance of its functions."

These people have therefore proposed that without the necessity for amendments, the General Assembly could create an additional People's Assembly or People's Chamber of delegates elected by the people of the world. So they have organized a movement in support of that objective, which has been endorsed and taken up by many organizations. To attempt to achieve changes in the functioning of the UN by this method is worse than useless.

First, the General Assembly is unable to function as a world legislative body to solve global problems or serve global human needs effectively. This is not because of the incompetence or ignorance of the delegates, but because of the way the UN is designed, as documented above.

As previously analyzed, Articles 10 through 17 describe the functions of the General Assembly, referred to in Article 22. Briefly summarized, the functions are: "may discuss"; "may recommend" or "may make recommendations to the Members (i.e., to the National Governments) of the United Nations"; and "shall initiate studies and make recommendations for the purpose of promoting international cooperation." All is to be done in the context of the guaranteed continuance of national sovereignty.

Suppose that after many years the General Assembly is persuaded to add a People's Assembly or People's Chamber to help the General Assembly "perform its functions," and that the people of the world, after further years of organizing, are finally able to elect their delegates to this People's Assembly. What is accomplished?

- Such a People's Assembly will not change the decision-making powers or processes of the General Assembly;
- The added People's Assembly could not enact world legislation nor assist the General Assembly or the Security Council to enact enforceable world legislation on any issue whatsoever;
- The People's Assembly cannot assist the General Assembly to implement non-existent world legislation, which the UN has no authority to implement in any case;
- The People's Assembly will not change the voting procedure in the General Assembly, which will remain at one vote per member nation, as directed by National Governments;
- The People's Assembly will not alter the "veto" power of each permanent Member of the Security Council, which will continue as the deciding power in the UN.

In short, the People's Assembly, if finally accomplished, would only be able to make studies, pass resolutions, and make recommendations to the General Assembly, to assist the General Assembly in the "performance of its functions." That is to say, the People's Assembly could only help the General Assembly do nothing for the practical solution of world problems.

The reason that an organized attempt to get a People's Assembly added to the General Assembly under Article 22 is worse than useless, is that such an attempt diverts the attention and energies and money of well-intentioned people away from what truly needs to be accomplished, which is the replacement of the UN entirely by a well designed constitution for Federal World Government. During the process of trying to achieve a People's Assembly, good people are deluded into thinking they are accomplishing something of value and use in solving world problems, when they are at best accomplishing nothing of legislative or governing substance.

B. *Add A Parliamentary Assembly*

During the last few years, a further proposal has gained popularity, which is to add a "Parliamentary Assembly" to the General Assembly of the UN, also under the permissive paragraph of Article 22 of the Charter. The proposal is for the National Parliaments of the Member nations to choose and send delegates to the Parliamentary Assembly added to help the General Assembly "perform its functions."

The same criticisms made concerning the proposal for adding a People's Assembly apply equally to the proposal for adding a Parliamentary Assembly.

Delegates to a Parliamentary Assembly, if the General Assembly can be persuaded to add such an Assembly under Article 22, would likewise have no legislative powers. The Parliamentary Assembly, despite all the fanfare, could only make studies and pass resolutions to give advice or recommendations to the General Assembly, could only help the General Assembly to do nothing effective to solve world problems.

Worse yet, a campaign to add a Parliamentary Assembly only deludes and misleads good people, including members of national parliaments, into thinking that they are accomplishing something of value to solve world problems, when they are in practical reality accomplishing nothing.

Not even a Chamber of Angels appointed by God or the Gods, under the benign provision of Article 22, could help the General Assembly solve global problems or make the UN Charter "work."

C. *World Governance Without Charter Amendments*

Other proposals have been made to "strengthen" the United nations without amending the Charter. The most precise proposals for "strengthening" without charter amendment have recently been given the descriptive title of "World Gover*nance*." (Not World Gover*nment*.)

"World Governance" is a very nebulous and foggy term which contributes only to confused thinking. World Governance is a term which is used by people who either reject the concept of genuine World Government, or who deliberately want to be vague in order to be accepted, or who may think the UN can be made to "work" without amendments.

In any event, people who like to use the term "World Governance" generally do not propose a World Parliament elected by and responsible to world citizens, do not propose a World Administration given executive authority and responsible to an elected World Parliament, do not propose a World Court system which functions in the context of world laws adopted by a responsible World Legislature, and who obscure clear thinking on all specifics of a constitution for Federal World Government.

If World Governance has any specific meaning it may be as described in a study by the World Watch Institute in 1992 prior to the major world environmental convention in Rio de Janeiro. Strengthening of the UN is generally imagined along the same lines.

By this concept, World Governance starts with treaties or conventions or agreements negotiated among sovereign nations, perhaps initiated by resolutions of the General Assembly. For better enforcement of such treaties or agreements, the following procedures are to be "strengthened" which are already defined for the Security Council by Articles 33 to 49.

a) More stringent procedures for monitoring of compliance with treaties or agreements, or of directives adopted by the Security Council;

b) In case of violations or non-compliance, then strict enforcement first by such non-military means as trade sanctions and embargoes, and denial of financial credits, as well as impounding of financial resources which may be outside of the particular country;

c) If non-compliance or violations continue, then enforcement by military blockade;

d) Perhaps, along the way, obtain the ruling of an "international Court" to justify treaty enforcement by these methods;

e) As a final resort, enforcement is to be firmly carried out by a variety of military measures, which are already defined and approved by the UN Charter, and which of course, mean war no matter how many times the term "peace keeping" is invoked.

The difficulties or folly of "World Governance" and "strengthening" of the UN by such procedures is, first, that most of the problems of the world are not defined simply in terms of relations or disputes or treaties or agreements between or among sovereign nations, and cannot be solved by trying to enforce treaties or agreements among sovereign nations.

Second, the enforcement procedures under this concept of World Governance are carried out against *entire populations*, and punish mostly innocent children, women and law-abiding citizens. This is so with trade sanctions and denial of financial credits, by which today hundreds of thousands and in fact tens of millions of innocent people are suffering great hardship.

By the procedures of military embargoes, and then by overt military force, this system of "strengthening" the enforcement capacity of the UN, or of World Governance, war against entire populations may be carried out all in the name of "peace keeping."

Moreover, World Governance by this concept can only be carried out by the strong against the weak—by decision, of course, of the five permanent Members of the Security Council. World Governance and strengthening the UN by this concept and procedure is simply an obscurantist way of empowering the ancient "bully principle" in international affairs.

In every respect, this is not the rule of law in world and human affairs, democratically agreed with justice for all: World Gover*nance* by this procedure is the opposite of the way for civilized society to proceed.

PART V
The Practical and Immediate Alternative: Replace the United Nations Charter with the Constitution for the Federation of Earth

At this moment in history, early 1997, the fiftieth anniversary of the United Nations has been celebrated, as if the record of years since 1945 shows great accomplishments for the good of humanity. Some people and organizations also proposed to use the 50th anniversary celebration as an occasion to propose amendments to the UN Charter, or to propose other ways to reconstructure or strengthen the United Nations, so that the UN can supposedly better carry out peace keeping, environmental protection and other good purposes.

But both the celebration and the proposals to strengthen and transform the UN are entirely and dangerously misleading.

First, the United Nations during the past 50 years has failed utterly to eliminate "the scourge of war," which was proclaimed as the primary purpose of the UN. Yet in 1995, we were asked to celebrate five decades of the UN, during which many trillions of dollars were squandered on a stupendous nuclear arms race, resulting in conditions of total insecurity for everyone on Earth, and the poisoning of the Earth for thousands of years into the future.

We were asked to celebrate the military arming of more than 180 nations, whose first priority of national sovereignty as guaranteed by the United Nations is military armaments. We were asked to celebrate the failure of the United Nations to solve hundreds of other global and supra-national problems, some of which are detailed in this Bill of Particulars.

Second, the reason that the proposals for amending or strengthening or reconstructuring the UN are *dangerously* misleading, is that too many good people are deceived or seduced or hypnotized or fooled or otherwise misled into endorsing or supporting such futile or militarily enforced proposals, so that they give their energies, money and powers of persuasion to help promote such misleading schemes—instead of helping to replace the UN with a true World Federation under a well designed Constitution for Federal World Government.

Such strong criticism would not be warranted if it were a matter of comparing benign alternative routes to a good world order. That, unhappily, is not the choice, as is so well documented by the history of the 52 years since the UN was imposed by the victors in 1945.

In the first few years following 1945, the well-intentioned world government movement quickly became, for the most part, wedded to the proposition of working through and amending the UN. Most of the thousands of peace organizations during the past 50 years have blindly accepted the UN as the best hope for humanity, followed now by the environmental organizations. Five decades have been lost since 1945 by pursuing the cause of world peace and solutions to world problems within the limitations of the UN, which could never become an agency to solve world problems. The insistence on trying to reach good ends by working through the UN or by trying to amend or improve the UN, has been a very large contributing factor, because of resulting delays, in the stupendous accumulation of all the unsolved and life-threatening global problems detailed in this Bill of Particulars.

It is doubtful that human civilization on Planet Earth can survive another ten years, or even five years, of such misdirection over world affairs; or another ten or five years of blindly pretending that the UN can be transformed or strengthened or restructured to do what only a properly designed and constitutionally authorized federal World Government could possibly do.

The practical replacement of the UN Charter with a constitution for federal World Government could be relatively simple. The reason is that a very adequate Constitution for the Federation of Earth is ready for immediate ratification and implementation. This Constitution for World Government was prepared over a period of years, including four sessions of a World Constituent Assembly held in 1968, 1977, 1980 and 1991, with delegates from all continents.

During the past five years, a Global Ratification and Elections Network has been organized to carry out the ratification campaign in all parts of the Earth, to be followed by the election of delegates to the World Parliament convened under a ratified World Constitution. This global network, called GREN, already includes more than 2000 non-governmental organizations of all kinds, in more than 150 countries, and inclusive of more than 40 million individual members. The campaign is twofold: to get National Governments and Parliaments to ratify, and to get the people of the various countries to ratify for the final authorization of a World Government to serve their needs.

Chapter 8

Reactions of an Ordinary World Citizen to "Our Global Neighborhood"

Jean-Marie Breton

Most registered World Citizens, i.e., those who have received a World Citizen card from the International Registry of World Citizens, are nonviolent pacifist democrats. I can only suppose that few registered World Citizens could read such a book as *Our Global Neighborhood* without experiencing a reaction of great disappointment; but, in fact, I can merely give here my reactions over my own name, and cannot speak in the name of others or of all World Citizens, because every registered World Citizen is free to have his or her own opinions. Nobody (not even the International Registry or any national Center) can speak in the name of all World Citizens. I cannot even speak here in the name of the small group of World Citizens (the "4M") who decided to work with me on a project for the promotion of World Citizenship, because each member of the 4M, too, is free to have his or her own opinions.

But I can give my own reactions as an *ordinary* registered World Citizen: although I approve of most criticisms of the present system in *Our Global Neighborhood*, I do not agree at all with most of its proposals, because they are based on the present State system, on the dogma of absolute State sovereignty; and this dogma is exactly what most World Citizens have been denouncing for 50 years, since we want to establish democratic world institutions, so as to manage and solve world problems at the world level. For the sake of simplicity, I shall follow the order of the Report's chapters.

IN THE FOREWORD

I approve 100 percent of the first six lines of that paragraph which begins in the middle of page xvi, in which both authors recognize that "our work is no more than a transit stop on that journey [to the development of global governance]," but also that "we are in a time that demands *freshness and innovation* in global governance" (my italics). Unfortunately, they (in my opinion) do not go far in this direction!

One page further on I accept also the statement: "This is a time for the international community to be bold, to explore new ideas, to develop new visions, and to demonstrate commitment to values in devising new governance arrangements." But again I deplore the fact that the Report of the Commission on Global Governance is not bold at all, and, although "committed to values," does not develop any new visions at all!

In one respect it may be excused: the only new vision possible for humankind developed since 1948 has been world democracy, which has been implemented as a prototype in the "People's Congress" since 1969. This is a body elected, two delegates at a time, by every new group of 10,000 newly registered World Citizens all over the world, which has happened approximately every second year since 1969. All that the Commission had to do was to accept (or modify) this idea and to propose to extend the prototype to the world as a whole.

Also, on page xix, I do accept the sentence: "Time is not on the side of indecision. Important choices must be made *now*, because we are at *the threshold of a new era*. That newness is self-evident; people everywhere know it, as do governments, though not all admit it." [Italics added.] So why have the authors not drawn the obvious conclusions?

But, on the contrary, I do not accept at all the choice (or the dilemma) which the authors offer to us immediately afterwards: either "security" or "going backwards to... the sheriff's posse dressed up to masquerade as global action"! What security? Against what risk? Martians? Or the madness of one or several heads of States, or terrorists? Whichever of all these may happen, to avoid it, my preference goes to law and collective responsibility, by placing *fraternity and solidarity* at the center. From madness we could easily be protected—why fear it? Is it not just a pretext to keep up stockpiles of arms and ammunition? If there were no more arms, how could we fear any madman who would be unarmed, and so could not wound or kill anybody?

CHAPTER 1: A NEW WORLD

I do not agree with the key sentence in the first half of page 4: "Yet States and governments remain primary public institutions for constructive responses to issues affecting peoples and the global community as a whole." These responses can be given, I firmly believe, only by *citizens* and Peoples. But I do completely agree, as a scientist, with the second half of page 4, where it is said: "There is no single model or form of global government, nor is there a single structure or set of structures. It is a broad, dynamic, complex process of inter-active decision-making that is constantly evolving and responding to changing circumstances. Although bound to respond to the specific requirements of different issue areas, governance must take an integrated approach to questions of human survival and prosperity... Recognizing the systemic nature of these issues, it must promote systemic approaches in dealing with them."

And on page 5 of the Report, while I agree (1) that "the governance mechan-isms must be more inclusive and participatory—that is, more democratic" and (2) that "a multifaceted strategy for global governance is required," I do *not* accept as sufficient the mere "reforming and strengthening of the existing system of intergovernmental institutions." However, I agree that the new world institutions "will require the articulation of a collaborative ethos based on the principles of consultation, transparency and accountability. It will foster global citizenship and work to include poorer, marginalized and alienated segments of... society. It will seek peace and progress for all people, working to anticipate conflicts and improve the capacity for peaceful resolution of disputes. Finally, it will strive to subject the rule of arbitrary power—economic, political or military—to the rule of law within global society." But unfortunately, the subject of this long passage is not the same for me as their "it," which refers to inter-State cooperation, while I have written above: *"new world institutions."* In my view, these are to be decided by citizens and Peoples.

Page 6 (after a first paragraph to which I subscribe entirely) contains an apo-logy for the UNO, which is but a forum of 185 envoys of national States, i.e. representatives of the 185 sovereign bodies which oppress the world's peoples. The UNO is exactly the contrary of a democratic world organization. Of course most of its international organizations may be retained, but with *very deep transformations* from the top (which ought to consist exclusively of world civil servants) to the bottom; the world executive function should no longer work for States, but as a tool in the hands of the World Parliament and of a world judiciary power (such as I have described in my book, *l'Emergence du Droit Mondial* (Paris: Club Humaniste, 1993). But the detailed definition of the world executive function must be left to the future World Constituent Assembly.

I shall not elaborate on the evidence of such statements as those appearing on pages 7 and 9 of the Report concerning the rapidity of change. Freedom for the rich to engage in financial speculation has worse and worse consequences: the poor people become always poorer, and the rich people become always richer, which makes the world less and less human. We live in a world which is very, very hard indeed (not to say unlivable, hence the increase in suicides) for the poor and the weak.

How can one believe that "the North-South dichotomy is becoming less sharp" (p. 10), if it is true that "disparities within nations and regions" are increasing at the same time? All the differences become sharper and sharper, while the mass media make them more unbearable for the disadvantaged. The North-South dichotomy is becoming *worse and worse*, as it has always been since the beginnings of colonization— hence the (supremely evident) "need for vision" (p. 12): a vision that this Report does not have in the least; while the World Citizens have always had it. Why did the authors not ask the World Citizens what that vision should be?

I do not underestimate the pedagogic value of the second half of this chapter, which contains good statistics and a scientific description of the economic, social and environmental changes since 1960. But these all lead to the same conclusions: that the excessive power of those who have money makes a very inhuman world, and that this has to be remedied very urgently.

If the two pages on the "empowerment of people" (pp. 35-37) seem quite adequate, and certainly move in the right direction, again, they do not go far enough when they conclude ingenuously that "the widening signs of alienation from the political process call for... new forms of participation and for wider *involvement of people* than traditional democratic systems have allowed." [Italics added.] The question is, What forms?—and already for 50 years the World Citizens have been refining their answers.

CHAPTER 2: VALUES FOR THE GLOBAL NEIGHBORHOOD

I agree (who would not?) with most "neighborhood realities" which are presented on pages 41-43, because they reveal some of the most acute problems of interdependence which have resulted from technical progress in the last half century. The authors even use the terms "*transnational* movements" and "common humanity" in the second paragraph of page 43. The third paragraph even admits that "millions are so deprived... [and] it does pose a challenge to its governance to reduce alienation among neighbors." But, again in the last paragraph, it is regrettable that the States, the worst robbers and exploiters, are called upon for help!

Of course, I also do agree (who would not?) with the "neighborhood values" presented between pages 43 and 54: they are so universal! But I do not find in this book any remedies against the most harmful illness affecting mankind today: *the crisis of consciousness and conscience*. As Sri Aurobindo in 1919 (and many other philosophers) put it, the crisis of conscience is the only crisis; all other present world crises (economic, social, of education, of faith, etc.) proceed from this fundamental one. If the human being loses his conscience, he loses everything, because conscience is his link with Nature (which is a living being) and with the Cosmos (which is no less a living being).[1] Nowadays, most ecologists (and, among them, some "green" politicians and activists) are trying to give back to the majority of citizens this sense of responsibility, which is an important part of *conscience*. But this effort is still too limited—although it is a good beginning and an encouraging sign for optimists that humankind is not altogether lost!

I am asking for remedies; they consist, of course, in world enlightenment, the *upgrading of the level of consciousness* through education, and in informing all citizens in the world of what is hidden from them by state government propaganda, by corruption, the military-industrial complex, the arms and drug trades and many other such clandestine influences. The Report speaks of *global civil ethics* (p. 55) and I have proposed, in my book on the emerging World Law, a Charter of Mankind (cf. Chapter 8). This latter would naturally include a "global civil ethics."

Most World Citizens, no more than myself, do not have fixed, unchangeable ideas about what should be included in the details of future world institutions. We simply agree, at least most of us do, on the idea that these institutions should be *democratic* and designed by global, transnationally and democratically elected world constituents. But what is world democracy? I shall recall some further principles when I comment on Chapter 7.

I agree, of course, with most "values for the global neighborhood" (pages 43-68). About the "democratic tide" (pp. 57, 63), World Citizens will be delighted to read (p. 62) that *"Democracy... is a global entitlement, a right that should be available and protected for all."* [My italics.] And I do agree, too, with the framed note at the bottom of page 58: "Democracy, Peace and Development" (a citation from Boutros Boutros-Ghali), and with most of page 61. Combating corruption and adapting old norms are evident necessities (page 67, the second paragraph is good on democracy). As for sovereignty, World Citizens certainly accept that "sovereignty ultimately derives from the people," and most of that paragraph in the middle of page 69; but *not* the following statement: "existing norms regarding sovereign equality, territorial independence and non-intervention need to be strengthened in two ways." No! No! No! They should not be strengthened in any way at all, but rather eliminated altogether.

I prefer what I read on page 70: "The exercise of sovereign power must be linked to the will of the people. Unless the abuse of sovereignty is stopped, it will be impossible to increase respect for the norms that flow from it... In an increasingly interdependent world, old notions of territoriality, independence and non-intervention lose some of their meaning. National boundaries are increasingly permeable—and... less relevant. A global flood of money, threats, images and ideas has overflowed the old system of... dikes that preserved state autonomy and control... It is now more difficult to separate actions that solely affect a nation's internal affairs from those that have an impact on the internal affairs of other states, and hence to define the legitimate boundaries of sovereign authority." Nevertheless, with questionable consistency, the Commission concludes on page 71 that "the principle of sovereignty and the norms that derive from it must be further adapted to recognize changing realities." This is, by far, too feeble. Most States have abused their powers, the authors admit, but they do not infer the consequence: that the States, being the worst robbers, bandits, and even murderers in the world, should give back to its rightful claimants the sovereignty which they have usurped from its natural owners, the citizens.

The states (in fact, their predecessors, Kings and Emperors, centuries ago) have arrogated to themselves the sovereignty of the citizens, for very well-known historical reasons. But now the citizens have come of age; they are capable of managing their own affairs themselves. We are able to manage the world ourselves, with justice and equity, as has never been done before. We no longer need any despot, autocrat or tyrant. Every People is able to make its own decisions for itself where its management is concerned. Every People can elect its Members of Parliament on its own, at its own level, and accept an elected President if it decides that is still necessary (but has no need of a tyrannical State ruling over several Peoples or subdivisions of dismembered Peoples). The world must be managed by citizens and Peoples, in harmony, for their happiness, not by inhuman "nation-states" (a hypocritical name for independent sovereignties) which make, sell, buy, and use, arms, to augment their own power, instead of acting only for the welfare of their citizens.

The kind of world democracy which is needed and wanted by everybody (except the few people who profit from the States' governments and the excesses of the abusively free capitalistic system) relies on principles of which I have given a few examples in the fourth chapter of my book: it all starts from the spirit of *world fraternity, solidarity and civism*; a moral conception: no political democracy without economic democracy; liberty of sharing, based on three political principles:

1st Principle: World sovereignty belongs to every citizen; it is inalienable, imprescriptible, and incident with duties.

2nd Principle: Every People ought to do its best for the happiness of all its members: every citizen may therefore apply at any time to join a People. The latter has the right to refuse.

3rd Principle: Every People has an inalienable and imprescriptible right to existence, respect for its identity and autonomy. To each of these rights corresponds a duty, the first of which is respect for Human Rights.

Next come the necessary conditions for a world democracy (I summarize here what I have developed more fully elsewhere): equality before the Law, freedom of opinion and expression for every citizen and People, duties of participation and cooperation, and universal suffrage with protection of minorities. The world's democratization is a process that is only beginning. The "Declaration of the Thirteen World Citizens of World-Wide Reputation" (1966) and the world Declaration no. 10 issued by the "Peoples' Congress" clearly both demand WORLD NON-VIOLENT DEMOCRATIC PERMANENT REVOLUTION, which is the only way to make it possible to set up and develop the world institutions which are indispensable for humankind.

Again, there is a beautiful paragraph on page 74 of the Report: "It is time to begin to think about self-determination in a new context... rather than the traditional context of a world of separate states... Self-determination is a right of all nations and peoples, as long as it is consistent with respect for other nations and peoples." And I should add here "citizens," while the Commissioners think of them only one page further on: "Concern for the interests of all citizens, of whatever racial, tribal, religious or other affiliation, must be high among the values informing the conduct of people in the world that has now become a neighborhood. There must be respect for their rights, in particular for their right to lead lives in dignity, to preserve their culture, to share equitably the fruits of national growth, and to play their part in the governance of the country." I would say, in short: all Human Rights which are listed in the Universal Declaration of 1948. As for the Peoples, I am astounded that such an honorable Commission did not even mention the Universal Declaration of the Rights of Peoples (Algiers, July 4th, 1976). This excellent text should be improved (especially in its preamble!), and then taught in all schools throughout the world, together with the Universal Declaration of Human Rights.

Moreover, among many Peoples, there are minorities: the UN adopted in 1992 Resolution no. 1992/16 of the Human Rights Committee, which tells all authorities of this world (at present mainly States) everything that they must do to protect the rights of ethnic, religious or linguistic minorities. Unfortunately, these rights are not effectively protected. The situation of minorities, without exaggeration, is worse than ever. This proves, again, that you can count on few States to observe the resolutions of the United Nations, or to deal fairly with their Peoples, especially with their minorities. Whatever they are, groups of families, or sections of Peoples, Peoples or groups of Peoples, minorities should be respected, protected and integrated into Peoples and groups of Peoples, exactly like all other persons in the world. And this should be written into a Charter for Humankind to be drafted as soon as possible by elected representatives of all citizens of the world (see my book, Chapter 8).

CHAPTER 3: PROMOTING SECURITY

In my opinion, this is certainly the worst chapter in the Report, because it does not penetrate to the causes of conflict. There are excellent Institutes of Studies concerning conflicts in many places throughout the world, like the University of Uppsala in Sweden, to whose work reference could have been made. Why are there conflicts? Why do they occur? Because of divergences of interests, certainly; but also because arms vendors tariff in arms to governments, Peoples and private militias. But besides the conflicts (which can always be settled by negotiation or arbitration) and the use of force, there is a third factor: it is what professors of political science call "the aggressiveness of man." Man is said to be an aggressive creature, and nothing can be done about it! I suggest that the human being can be taught to use violence only in case of an actual immediate danger to his or her life or physical integrity. In other cases violence should always be outlawed. We may define analogous rules for moral violence, which is another plague of modern societies.

In all cases, divergences of interests should be solved by legal process and the proper organization of the economy (see Chapter 4). And the production and sale of arms should be forbidden all over the globe, with very heavy sanctions against guilty people.

Reasonably, the authors of the Report plead for the prevention of crises, and on page 93 they declare: "The international community [this is subtly misleading because it is a name for an entity which is not yet represented at all] should improve its capacity to identify, anticipate and resolve conflicts before they become armed confrontations." Have you ever met "the international community" in the street? Is it anywhere represented by elected deputies or whatever? No! But it should be, and it would have been long since, did the States not retain the powers which they usurped from the citizens centuries ago. For the time being the proposal above remains a pious wish.

The authors of *Our Global Neighborhood* are perfectly right to declare on page 94 that "One fundamental reason for the failure of the world community to prevent war is the unwillingness and inability of governments to respond to every crisis or threat of a crisis." But their proposals are linked with the UN, which is still a league of nonunited States and a forum for their delegations.

"Ending the Threat of Mass Destruction," "Eliminating Nuclear Weapons"— these titles on pages 114 and 115 sound very good, as well as "Demilitarizing International Society" on page 122; but unfortunately the Commissioners do not tell us at all how to reach these excellent and urgent goals! The description of overarmament, from pages 123 to 130, is correct and should give cause for thought to all heads of States, all parliaments and all conscious decision-makers all over the world. To "inculcate a culture of non-violence" (page 131) is evidently one of the most urgent measures to be taken at all levels and in all branches of education. But only a World Peace Education Council (composed exclusively of world civil servants and Education Ministers of Peoples) can implement this demand—although, in fact, among ordinary persons, "average citizens" like ourselves, nobody wants war.

Hence I can assure the reader, true peace and disarmament will come only from the non-violent peace activists, laymen and other world citizens, and their representatives in a world legislature which can maintain the rule of law worldwide; and this may come sooner than many people think. Governing officers, ministers and executives, and some "politologists" may tell you that the governments have lost most of their powers, but those powers remain in the hands of military-industrial complexes; and it is this real power, with the abuse of money (see my Chapter 4), which has to be urgently eradicated. These are the two main evils of modern times.

CHAPTER 4: MANAGING ECONOMIC INTERDEPENDENCE

An ordinary world citizen, like me, falls in with what the Commissioners call (on page 147) "the democratic ideal of universal participation," but certainly not as being in opposition to "speedy, efficient decision-making"! The authors here do fall into some confusion between (long-term) efficient decision-making and the (short-term despotic) concentration of power in the G7 and WTO (former GATT). The only good long-term objective is to give *dignity and happiness* to the maximum number of people in the world; and that is not at all the objective of these dominant groups, who think only of the maximum financial profit for their States and their multinational firms.

In order to manage economic interdependence, any reasonable world citizen will agree to create "a global forum that will provide leadership in economic, social and environmental fields" (p. 149). The advantages of global economic governance, as listed on page 150, give rise to no misgivings. The only question is: How? The idea of an Economic Security Council (pp. 155-162) with the four aims listed on page 156, and made to address world problems "for which there is no clear institutional mandate or several overlapping ones" is ingenious but still remains within the State system: It is what we call in French "un cautère sur une jambe de bois" (a poultice on a wooden leg).

The remedies proposed on page 202 are not too bad for the immediate future, but they remain also within the framework of the existing economic and financial world situation, dominated by the "free" (i.e., savage, wild, and anarchic) capitalistic system: that is, the law of the jungle. How could a pure, sincere, humane citizen of the world think for one second of remaining forever in a financial jungle where thirty times more money is circulating for speculation than is used for actual exchange of goods and services? Money should not be available for hoarding or speculation.

As for the environment (p. 208: "Protecting the Environment"), the World Citizens created in 1992 the CILAME (Comité International de Liaison pour une Autorité Mondiale de l'Environnement—International Liaison Committee for a World Environment Authority), whose aim, a very clear one, goes far beyond all the explanations in pages 208 to 216, as far as they are based on the continuation of the action of the States, who do whatever they want—or rather what their military-industrial complexes want! None of the technical proposals on pages 210-217 can be studied at the world level, except by a world authority on the environment, independent of all States (which neither UNEP nor GEF is).

CHAPTER 5: REFORMING THE (SO-CALLED) UNITED NATIONS

This is an excellent chapter, especially the proposal for a Forum of Civil Society (pp. 258-260) and I hope, as most World Citizens certainly do, that it will soon be created. But all other proposals stay within the very bad, very unfair, present UN organization, which favors States instead of Peoples. In place of that so-called United Nations Organization, which is a non-democratic anarchy, I, like most World Citizens I have met, especially in the "4M," advocate the creation of a world government by a World Constituent Assembly, which should be elected by all the citizens of the world (we could say: elected by the democratically elected representatives of all Peoples, if all Peoples had democratically elected representatives—which is not yet the case—far from it!).

Contrary to what the authors contend on pp. 227-232, the UN is not "us" at all. Its civil servants have indeed developed a high spirit of world service for Humankind, but unfortunately they are most frequently frustrated by the States—especially the most powerful ones!—at the moments of decision. Hence most proposals presented in this chapter are short-term medicines and lead to nothing other than the reinforcement of the powers of the States, instead of diminishing them.

If I have said that this chapter is one of the less bad ones in this book, it is because of pages 253 ("Global Civil Society") and 254 ("Non-Governmental Organizations"). But these are merely beautiful titles, and I am sorry to say, nothing follows. With respect to a Peoples' Assembly (p. 257) all the Commissioners can say is, "we encourage further debate about these proposals," whereas the debate has already been going on among World Citizens for years, who have concluded that a Peoples' Assembly can only be the second in the future World Parliament, because the first, for reasons of world democracy, should be the *Citizens* Representative Assembly. And on page 258 we have the star turn: the "Forum of Civil Society." Bravo! On one condition: that the UN first be replaced by the World Parliament, which is bound eventually to come anyway; why not sooner rather than later?

In fact, the authors are better prophets when they write on page 288 that "regionalism" (in their understanding of this word, which I shall discuss further) "has the capacity to contribute to building a *more harmonious and prosperous world.*" [Italics added.] By regionalism they should mean, in fact, continental structures, which ought to be much strengthened to solve and manage the continental problems (e.g., territories, population migrations inside the continent, fair distribution of continental resources, ground transportation, roads and railways, etc.) at the continental level, according to the principles of global federalism; but in a Peoples' system, not in a State system.

We do not mean that everything in the UN should be destroyed; but the main structures, the top structures, should be completely abolished and replaced by a World Parliament. Much of the administrative appararus of the UN may, with modifications, be usefully retained. But the fundamental decision-making structure should certainly be completely changed.

CHAPTER 6: STRENGTHENING THE RULE OF LAW WORLD-WIDE

This is the most timid chapter in this Report: why not speak of developing World Law, as I have done in my book, *The Emerging World Law*? In fact, a good introduction to such a chapter would have been its conclusion, as it appears on page 332. But to ensure a Rule of Law requires that Peoples be the legal and judicial agents, not States—the Peoples; and, obviously, the citizens as well.

Again, as in most other chapters, as long as the Report traces the history (page 303) and shows the drawbacks (pp. 304 to 307) of the existing system, one cannot but agree. However, most regrettably, the "ideal world" described on pages 308 to 311, and on pages 318, 321 and 322, is *not ours*: moreover, it still relies on the *absolute sovereignty of states*, for which, as I have shown in the first two chapters of my book, there is complete lack of judicial, as well as human, foundation. I have also shown how desirable it is to give back the sovereignty to the citizens and the Peoples.

As for a world criminal court, it has been a demand made by World Citizens for decades and a centuries-old demand by humanists. The "ideal" international criminal court described in the second half of page 324 is (again) *not ours*. And it ceases to be "ideal" as soon as it involves the Security Council, such as it is now, and then further, at the end of the same page, the Commission requires that such a court be "established by treaty." States do not want to reduce their sovereignty as has been obvious for centuries; hence only a World Constitution proposed by democratically elected representatives of all the citizens of this planet can include an actual world criminal court, as well as an actual world parliament and world judiciary system.

Nevertheless, I agree with the spirit of pages 330 and 331—but not with the letter, when the authors speak of treaties or States.

CHAPTER 7: A CALL TO ACTION

On page 335, I cannot but approve the idea of "a global civil ethic to guide action." On "governance, change and values," again I approve, except in the second half of page 337, where there is too much timidity with regard to the absolute sovereignty of States (some of whom are the worst robbers and killers), which is the evil of the twentieth century.

"Promoting Security": I agree with the spirit of the proposals presented on pages 338-341, but they are merely a first step—obviously, all states should be completely disarmed.

"Managing Economic Interdependence": To build a global forum, an Economic Security Council: yes, but *not within* the UN system, which is within the States system. That ESC should be elected by the citizens, at least indirectly through elected representatives of consumers, merchants and producers. But I *totally* disagree with the proposal on page 343 to "enhance the role of the IMF," which belongs to the present State system and permits the misuse of money by speculators.

"Reforming the United Nations": The Report declines (on page 344) to dismantle the UN "to make way for a new architecture of global governance," although this is highly necessary in my opinion, since I believe (and have demonstrated in my book) that the State system is perverse and evil and that only the citizens and Peoples may decide what is good for the management of affairs at the world level. The next sentence is symptomatic of the trouble when it says "provided governments are willing," for everybody knows that they will *never be willing*, especially to undertake the reforms of the Charter which the Report proposes next, on pp. 345-347.

"The Next Steps": Pages 348-352 again are much too timid; except for one part of a sentence which I accept as it is (p.350, fourth paragraph): "We need that spirit today, together with a readiness to look *beyond* the United Nations and nation-states..." (my italics). Unfortunately this is the only sentence in the whole book which goes that far.

"The Need for Leadership" (pp. 353-357): I agree again with the spirit of these last pages, and especially of this last sentence (p. 356): "Enlightened leadership calls for a clear vision of solidarity in the true interest of national, rather, world well-being—and for political courage in articulating the way the world has changed and why a new spirit of global neighborhood must replace the old notions of adversarial States in eternal confrontation." Also the last two paragraphs on page 357 are very encouraging: they give a good analysis, but no solution for the "far future."

As a World Citizen, I should say that humankind should start from the ideal world society which it wants and deduce what should be the successive steps by which to reach this ideal. And I suggest that this process, already initiated by World Citizens, be continued by them in cooperation with all interested NGOs and MPs from all countries and continental organizations (the EU, the OUA, the Inter-American Organization, etc.).

I have mentioned above, more than once, the level of competence of the world institutions to be created, their fields of competence have been clearly defined in many mundialist publications like the *Mundialist Summa*, a three volume encyclopedia of mundialist ideas, and *One or Zero* a smaller summary edited by Guy Marchand and published by the Club Humaniste. They include both the world level survival problems (wars, hunger, poverty, rarest resources, damage to the environment, terrorism, etc.) and world-level management problems (everyday protection of human persons and the environment, distribution of rarer resources, control of the economy, demography, disarmament, poverty, violation of human rights, and all social problems, dealt with merely by arbitration between continents, with individual exceptions, in accordance with the six principles of global federalism, and so on). As I have explained in my book, only two powers ought to exist at the world level: legislative and judicial. The executive functions should be fulfilled by Peoples and citizens (see Chapter 12 of *The Emerging World Law*) to execute the decisions of the two legitimate world powers concerned with world-level problems. If on particular matters, those two powers happen to have conflicting opinions, they should first discuss them and try to come to some compromise, and, if they cannot, arbitration institutions should be provided for in a legal text, not in a world constitution (though this document should be very short, only a few pages, as I see it, since all the basic principles could be set out in a Charter of Humankind, as described in Chapter 8 of the above-mentioned work).

A last remark on this seventh and last Chapter of the Report: a real "call to action" is more likely to be issued by a *movement*, like the "4M" (World Movement of Mundialist Activists)!

CONCLUSION

By way of a conclusion I should say that this Report *lacks a soul*. It lacks an ideal, hence it proposes very little change, only short-term and short-sighted change, at that. Any change should come from a long-term ideal view, and then proceed from that to objectives, then to organizational plans, as a good architect begins by asking his customer what kind of life he wants to lead before designing the plans of a house. The ideal I propose is not original: the happiness of all humankind through love, non-violence and World Law.

The word "supranational" occurs only once in the whole Report, while it is the most important concept for describing the level of the necessary continental and world institutions.

Yes, indeed, this Report is hardly "a convincing path towards a better world." Like most World Citizens, I am far more ambitious: we want a much more *democratic* world, with democratic world institutions designed actually to *solve* the world-level problems, with the participation of all citizens (directly through democratically elected representatives). Our new world constitution should be drafted by a World Constituent Assembly, whose members should be elected (directly for most Peoples, and through MPs for those Peoples who would prefer this latter procedure). They should be selected for their high moral probity and their independence from any State or financial interest.

The existing "Peoples' Congress," consisting of 20 Delegates elected transnationally by 100,000 citizens from all over the world, is the preliminary committee which should be given the means to prepare this huge work: the global election of the world Constituent Assembly. I think that a world transnational foundation should be set up for this purpose. Incidentally, the World Citizens have also created the World Community Fund against Hunger, which works in underdeveloped countries. It has also drawn up a World Charter of Solidarity, an important component element for the project of a World Charter of Humankind, which I have already mentioned.

Finally, the basis for any future is humanism, fraternity and solidarity first! As a non-violent pacifist and esperantist World Citizen and a member of the Human Rights League, after reading this Report, I can only say: "World citizenship, global civil ethics and democratically elected world institutions are our last chance!" This is what Lamartine tells us in a more poetic way:

The world, in lighting its way ahead, rises to unity.

NOTE

1. Contemporary physicists have discovered that the physical universe is a single, indivisible, whole; and biologists have found that the entire biosphere is one ecological community. Human practices are today disrupting this system, endangering our own survival as well as that of all other living species, in a way that can only be described as immoral.

Chapter 9

A Pragmatic Route to Genuine Global Governance

James A. Yunker

The recent collapse of the Soviet Union and the concomitant recedence of the Cold War have significantly reduced the probability that the prospects of humanity upon this planet will vanish in a nuclear holocaust sometime within the next 20 to 30 years. This is certainly cause for rejoicing—it is one less thing for the present generation of humanity to worry about. But if we look farther into the future, say 50 or 100 years into the future, it is not so clear that humanity's recent deliverance from the perilous Cold War situation that blighted the second half of the 20th century will result in a significant, long-run reduction of the threat of nuclear disaster.

The polarization of the world community along ideological lines resulted in a considerable amount of stability and cooperation within the competing communist and noncommunist blocs of nations. Allied nations tended to tolerate and cooperate with one another as a means of enhancing their security against the terrible menace presented by the other bloc. Now that this terrible menace has suddenly evaporated, security is no longer such an overriding consideration, and the centrifugal forces will become stronger. The world has already witnessed a remarkable demonstration of the power and persistence of nationalistic separatism in the splintering of the ex-Soviet bloc. Especially unfortunate was the former Yugoslavia, in which the splintering process was accompanied by a great deal of violence and bloodshed. Nor is the West immune from this force. For example, the province of Quebec is hovering on the brink of secession from Canada. A secession of this magnitude could reinvigorate other separatist movements throughout the Western world.

Aside from the prospect that resurgent separatism will generate a substantial number of new sovereign and independent nation-states (which multiplies the opportunities for conflict and warfare between these states), the recedence of the

Cold War is setting the stage for more confrontational and divisive politics within nations. Conditions are becoming far more favorable for the rise of irresponsible, extremist demagogues who will inflame tendencies toward chauvinistic patriotism and xenophobic paranoia in order to gain power. Such an individual was Adolf Hitler. When one considers the personality of Adolf Hitler, is it plausible to suppose that had he come to power at a time when nuclear warheads and ballistic missiles were included in the arsenals of nations, he would have been deterred from his plans for national revenge and expansion? The future may see more Adolf Hitlers—and in the nuclear age, only one such individual could be disastrous.

No person endowed with a modicum of rationality and goodwill wants to see this happen. Almost all of humanity earnestly desires that the probability of this eventuality be reduced to the lowest feasible level. Moreover, the ending of the Cold War would appear to be creating an obvious and dramatic opportunity for progress. The ending of World War I saw the founding of the League of Nations. The ending of World War II saw the founding of the United Nations. Could not the ending of the Cold War result in yet another significant step forward toward imposing the rule of law on the family of nations? It certainly could—but not necessarily. World War I and World War II were "hot" wars in which millions were killed. The deadly peril of relying on the balance of power to maintain peace within a family of fully sovereign and independent nation-states was manifested in an extremely potent manner. World War III, had it occurred, would have killed far more people than both World War I and World War II combined. But it did not occur. The Cold War imposed a great deal of psychological strain and anxiety upon a generation of humanity—but this burden was negligible in comparison to the tangible costs of World Wars I and II. Therefore, the prospects for significant progress at this particular time in history are perhaps not as substantial as they might at first appear.

One indication that this is, in fact, the case is the recently published *Our Global Neighborhood: The Report of the Commission on Global Governance*. This substantial document, the outcome of a collective effort by hundreds of political figures, public servants, and academics from around the world, is filled with lofty sentiments and high-minded generalities with which it would be difficult, if not impossible, to disagree. But, in the judgment of this author, the actual, substantive, tangible proposals put forward in the Report are too unconnected, tentative, incomplete, and impractical to accomplish much of benefit to humanity. My prediction is that the proposals will mostly be ignored, and from those few which are, in fact, implemented, no obvious, demonstrable benefits will be garnered.

The basic problem with the Report is its lack of a large, coherent, integrative vision which might be capable of exciting and inspiring the human imagination. This is a classic problem with any document "written by a committee." In the case of the Report of the Commission on Global Governance, the "committee" was very large indeed. The abundance of individuals who contributed to the

Report, of course, lends it a high degree of legitimacy—but high legitimacy may not be of much help if the substantive content of the document is slight and insubstantial. When as many people as were involved in the production of the Report have to agree on content—and when the subject matter is as controversial as the issue of international cooperation—then it is a good bet that the content will, indeed, be slight and insubstantial.

The following quotation from the Report (p. 336) manifests its central shortcoming:

States remain primary actors but have to work with others. The United Nations must play a vital role, but it cannot do all the work. Global governance does not imply world government or world federalism. Effective global governance calls for a new vision, challenging people as well as governments to realize that there is no alternative to working together to create the kind of world they want for themselves and their children. It requires a strong commitment to democracy grounded in civil society.

This paragraph is dominated by warm, mushy, feel-good sentiments which any individual possessed of a shred of rationality and civilization would be hard-pressed to dispute. The third sentence in the paragraph, unfortunately, effectively renders these sentiments null and void: "Global governance does not imply world government or world federalism." This sentence demonstrates that, despite the reference elsewhere in the paragraph (one of many such references in the Report) to a "new vision," the Report is, in fact, devoid of any such vision. The Report, in fact, accepts and operates within the present reality that the highest level of government authority in the world is that of the nation-state. Nation-states are exhorted in the Report to scale ever greater heights of mutual toleration and cooperation. But no significant institutional means—in the form of a world government or world federation—is proposed by which nation-states would be assisted in scaling these ever greater heights. The Commission's very name is a misnomer: humanity cannot achieve meaningful "global governance" without a global government. Personally, I cannot see how semantic dishonesty can appreciably assist the cause of human civilization in the long run. What the Report actually deals with is "global cooperation," and the appropriate name for the Commission would have been the Commission on Global Cooperation.

It is not that global cooperation is not a good idea and a worthwhile cause. Conceivably, some of the specific proposals in the Report could benefit the cause of global cooperation, even if that cause continues to be pursued within the present institutional framework of fully sovereign nation-states engaging in various alliances (one such alliance being the United Nations). But in the judgment of this author, it will be necessary to establish a *new institutional framework* before the cause of global cooperation will be pursued in a truly effective manner. This new institutional framework would, in fact, involve a supranational federation (i.e., a world government or world state). The tentative name I have suggested for this federation is the "Federal Union of Democratic Nations." Detailed description and evaluation of this proposal are available in my book *World Union on the Horizon: The Case for Supernational Federation* (1993). Readers interested in a full exposition of this approach are referred to that source.[1]

My purpose here will be to compare and contrast the approach taken to global cooperation in my own work, *World Union on the Horizon*, with that taken in the Commission's work, *Our Global Neighborhood*. First, I briefly discuss the envisioned Federal Union of Democratic Nations. Then I evaluate some of the specific proposals in the Commission's Report in light of this alternative approach to global cooperation. The thrust of the argument is that the proposed Federal Union of Democratic Nations would be a more effective instrument toward global cooperation than would be the implementation of the Report's proposals—*and* (a very big "and") that such a Federal Union is indeed a feasible and viable option at the present juncture in human history.

THE FEDERAL UNION OF DEMOCRATIC NATIONS

The Commission's phrase "global neighborhood" is catchy, trendy, and well-intentioned. But it is also shallow and cutesy. It may not have the sweep and dignity necessary to awaken real enthusiasm toward the objective of worldwide peace and progress. The phrase seems largely inspired by the tremendous advances in transportation and communications of the twentieth century. Thus we have such marvels as CNN's live television coverage of the assault on the Russian White House in 1993. But instantaneous communications and rapid transportation are double-edged swords as far as the cause of worldwide peace and progress is concerned. One has to *know* one's fellow man in order to hate and fear him. The journalistic communications media (CNN, etc.) are largely business enterprises, and sensationalism is their watchword. Thus, their primary purpose seems to be to make people all around the world painfully aware of how many bad things are happening everywhere, and how many evil people there are who are contributing to these bad things. This creates a psychological attitude in which the concept of worldwide peace and progress tends to be dismissed as a utopian fantasy. At the same time, the contemporary speed of transportation aggravates apprehensions concerning foreign invasions— as in the paranoid fantasies of militia groups in the United States involving airborne invaders delivered by armadas of black helicopters.

The term "neighborhood" implies a small, peaceful, orderly, and inviting residential area in which people live together in serene and mutually supportive harmony. It may be a clever rhetorical device to try to apply this warm and appealing concept to the entire world. Or, to the contrary, it may be so transparently preposterous and dishonest as to be meaningless and totally ineffective with the vast majority of people for whom the Report's message is intended. When we think about the actual, real-world neighborhoods in which some of us are lucky enough to live, whether they be located in large cities or small towns, an absolutely central and essential element is that police protection exists and is effective. If a crime is committed, the police descend, and the perpetrator is arrested and hauled off to jail. If a riot commences, the police descend in force, and the disturbance is quelled. It is simply a delusion to think that real-world neighborhoods owe their harmonious serenity to nothing more than the civilized goodwill of the residents. The fact of the matter is that the existence and effectiveness of larger civil governments are essential to actual neighborhoods as we know them.

This is not to say that peace, cooperation, and mutual respect within an actual neighborhood must be continuously enforced upon its population by an armed and vigilant police force. To some extent, social values and norms become self-enforcing as the population internalizes these values and norms. According to Freud, the socialized individual suppresses various destructively self-centered impulses of the "id" by means of both an "ego" and a "superego." The ego, established in early childhood through parental and other discipline, suppresses these impulses out of fear of more or less immediate punishment. The superego, established in later childhood by means of positive reinforcement in the form of exhortation, praise, and rewards, suppresses these impulses because they are contrary to the social code. The individual subscribes to and abides by the social code because doing so is ordinarily beneficial to that individual in the long term. A similar progression is probably relevant at the social level. Members of a social group (such as a neighborhood) initially engage in mutual cooperation and support out of fear of the consequences should they take an alternative route. But eventually they engage in these kinds of behavior (to some extent at least) out of an internal conviction that they are the right thing to do.

It is probably unrealistic to expect human individuals to develop effective superegos without first developing effective egos through exposure to some degree of external enforcement (parental and/or civil) of social values and norms. And it is probably equally unrealistic to expect human societies, whether they be local residential neighborhoods or the world society of nation-states, to achieve a strong *internal* motivation toward proper behavior independent of exposure to any appreciable degree of *external* motivation toward proper behavior. Similarly, it is probably unrealistic for the Commission on Global Governance to propose that nation-states behave in the manner in which they *would* behave if they were united in an effective world state—without this effective world state actually existing.

Of course, since we are discussing that which is "unrealistic," it must be conceded that at the present time, an extremely strong consensus exists within the human race that any sort of a meaningful world state would be totally impractical. Either such a state would be so loose and disorganized as to be virtually useless (a replication of the United Nations), or it would have to be so powerful and totalitarian as to have a devastating impact upon personal freedom and human welfare. That is to say, a world state is believed to be totally "unrealistic."

I myself accepted the consensus judgment on this matter until, as an under-graduate student at Fordham University in the early 1960s, I experienced what can only be described as a "vision" of social progress on a global scale. This vision continues to inspire me to this day—albeit I have been made unhappily aware of how extremely difficult it is to communicate this particular vision to others. But despite many disappointments over the years, I continue to harbor the hope that the problem is not so much with the vision itself, as it is with my limited powers of communication, and that eventually, despite my limited powers of communication, the vision will be shared by a significant number of others. The fundamental elements of the original vision of the early 1960s are as follows.

There are three primary obstacles to the formation of a viable and effective world state: (1) a deep-seated ideological conflict between democratic market capitalism and oligarchic planned socialism; (2) the tremendous economic gap between the living standards of the richest and poorest nations of the world; and (3) the tremendous force of nationalism in the modern world. These obstacles are obviously formidable—but they are not unbreachable. There exist plausible, workable means by which all three of these obstacles could be overcome.

As to the ideological gap between the communist and noncommunist worlds, this gap could be bridged by a democratic market socialist system. Such a system would incorporate two basic principles from the noncommunist side: the market system and political democracy. It would also incorporate one basic principle from the communist side: socialism, as defined in terms of public ownership of the preponderance of land and capital. Since its introduction into mainstream economic thinking in the 1930s by Oskar Lange, the market social-ist concept has undergone considerable development. Of the several possible varieties of market socialism, that one which seems to this author the most promising in a practical sense is profit-oriented market socialism. Under this variety, most large-scale business enterprises would be publicly owned, but they would be instructed and motivated to maximize their profits. Thus, the economy would operate almost identically to the market capitalist economic system as it currently operates in the United States, in the nations of Western Europe, and, to an increasing extent, in many other nations of the world. The salient difference would be that the profits of the publicly owned business enterprises, instead of going, as they do under capitalism, mostly to a small minority of wealthy capitalists, would instead be equitably returned to the working population as a social dividend supplement to labor income. My own particular variant of profit-oriented market socialism I have dubbed "pragmatic market socialism." Throughout my career as an academic economist, I have kept up a steady stream of contributions on market socialism in general and pragmatic market socialism in particular, comprising to date three books and approximately 20 articles. For the interested reader, a good entry point into this work is my 1992 book: *Socialism Revised and Modernized: The Case for Pragmatic Market Socialism.*[2]

While the case for pragmatic market socialism is indeed extremely sound just based on the adverse internal characteristics of contemporary Western capitalism (specifically, the extravagantly unequal distribution of capital wealth), the decisive aspect of this case in my own mind has been the external situation, i.e., the international situation. At the time of the original vision in the 1960s, clearly the ideological confrontation between communism and noncommunism was the most immediate and ominous peril to human destiny. This confrontation was fueling a nuclear arms competition which threatened to engulf the world in a devastating nuclear war. In a practical sense, this situation made the "external" case for pragmatic market socialism (its potential role as a bridge over the ideological gap) far more important than the "internal" case (its potential role as an antidote to extravagantly unequal capital wealth distribution). As of the latter 1990s, of course, the external case for pragmatic market socialism has largely disappeared, owing to the collapse of the Soviet Union. The ex-Soviet Union and its erstwhile satellites, are ostensibly making haste to replicate democratic market capitalism, as practiced in the leading Western nations, within their own societies. It seems inevitable that the People's Republic of China and the other remaining communist nations will eventually follow the Soviet example. Therefore, the ideological war between communism and noncommunism is ostensibly in its final stages, and noncommunism has apparently won the war. Although pragmatic market socialism is no longer required as an ideological bridge between East and West, I do not regret the time and energy I have devoted to the development of this concept over the last three decades. Pragmatic market socialism would still be a very desirable reform for the presently capitalistic nations—and it may eventually be recognized as such.

While it may be that the degree of progress in reducing the ideological obstacle to world peace and cooperation has been somewhat exaggerated by many people, it is certainly indisputable that this obstacle has been significantly reduced. Therefore, the impediments to world government have been correspondingly reduced. But even if the ideological obstacle were to be totally removed, that would still leave two very formidable obstacles fully intact: the economic gap and the force of nationalism.

With respect to the economic gap, what is needed to bridge this gap is a global economic development effort, along the lines of the post-World War II Marshall Plan, but on a far larger and more ambitious scale. The effort should have an explicit purpose: a high degree of equalization of living standards across all nations of the world—subject to the constraint that living standards in the richest nations continue to rise at a reasonable rate. The critical question, of course, is whether this objective is feasible: whether it would be possible to achieve a high degree of equalization in living standards across the world, within a reasonable length of time, without incurring either a decline of living standards within the richest nations, or a dramatic reduction in the rate of rise of these living standards.

Using the tools of my profession of economics, I personally have developed some important evidence that the answer to this key question is, indeed, in the affirmative. The first version of this research was published in the *Journal of Developing Areas* in 1976 and a second, refined version in *World Development* in 1988.[3] These articles report on simulation experiments with a computer model of the world economy. Results from these simulations suggest that a very substantial degree of equalization in world living standards might be achieved within a planning period of only 35 years, at a modest cost in terms of a slightly lower rate of rise in the living standards of the richest nations. Specifically, the baseline simulation in the 1988 article (reported also in Table 4.1 in *World Union on the Horizon*) indicates that the gap in per capita consumption between the richest and poorest regions could be reduced from 1,100% to only 12% in 35 years, while implementation of this program would reduce total percentage growth in per capita consumption in the richest region over the 35 years from 87.8% to 71.5%. Thus, the cost of the program to the rich nations would be substantial but not unreasonable. In terms of a percentage of national income, the cost of the program to the United States would be 3.2% in the initial period, rising gradually to 4.4% at the end of the planning period.

The prevailing, consensus attitude of contemporary, mainstream economics concerning the prospects for dramatic economic progress in the poor nations of the world within the foreseeable future must be described as wearily pessimistic. According to this prevailing attitude, the results which I have obtained from these computer simulations are simply "too good to be true." The conventional wisdom maintains that putting major resources into a worldwide economic development program would be tantamount to pouring these resources down a rat hole—they would be swallowed up by corrupt bureaucrats, and little or nothing would be accomplished in terms of raising the living standards of the general population in the poor nations. This widely prevalent viewpoint is, in fact, little more than a superficial rationalization for a policy of shortsighted selfishness. It is both irrational and immoral to dismiss the possibility of a major global economic development effort simply on the *assumption* that such an effort would be futile. The results which I have adduced in this area argue strongly for at least an experimental implementation of such an effort. If the pessimistic attitude just described is in fact borne out, then, indeed, the effort would have to be terminated. But at least the rich nations could then terminate their resource contributions to the worldwide economic development program with a clear conscience—because it would have been empirically demonstrated that the program was not achieving its objectives.

If a substantial amount of economic equalization *cannot* be achieved within a reasonable period of historical time, then the prospects for a viable, permanent and effective world government are indeed very slight. But just as it is irrational and immoral to simply *assume* that a worldwide economic development program would be unsuccessful, so too it is irrational and immoral to simply *assume* that a world government would be unsuccessful. Just as a worldwide economic development program deserves a fair chance to prove itself, so too does a world government. But it cannot be just *any* world government. It is necessary to think very carefully about what is possible and what is not possible at the present juncture in human history. It is necessary to develop a specific proposal for world government which achieves an acceptable balance between the competing objectives of establishing a useful supranational government entity, and, at the same time, protecting the legitimate interests of the existing nation-states. Regrettably, it seems that the majority of proponents of world government in the past have been inadequately concerned with the very serious problems confronting world government, and inadequately assiduous in trying to find specific institutional proposals which respond adequately to these problems. Many of these proponents seem to imagine a government with strong central powers, along the lines of the contemporary United States of America, immediately established, with all the nations of the world, without exception, voluntarily subjecting themselves to this government. In the judgment of this author, there is simply no feasible way of getting from here to there, at least in the absence of some horrific global catastrophe such as a nuclear World War III.

My own effort to find a solution to the ideological obstacle to world government has been the concept of pragmatic market socialism. It appears that this concept is no longer needed for this purpose—and that is all well and good, since the potential contribution of world government to human welfare is far more important than the potential contribution of pragmatic market socialism. Again, my own effort to find a bridge over the economic gap is the worldwide economic development program discussed above. The continuing need for such a program is, to my mind, self-evident. Were such a program implemented, it would, in due course, very likely eliminate the economic obstacle to world government. This would leave the power of nationalism as the third and last major obstacle to world government. I have attempted to cope with this obstacle by means of a carefully considered institutional proposal for world government. Actually, the term which I prefer to "world government" is "supranational federation." The latter term might be deemed a "public relations circumlocution" by some, but I believe that it is merited on grounds that the proposal is indeed significantly different from the standard, conventional notion of a "government" in the popular mind. My proposal for a Federal Union of Democratic Nations is intended to achieve the "acceptable balance" referred to above between the competing objectives of establishing a useful supranational government entity, and, at the same time, protecting the legitimate interests of the existing nation-states. Whether or not the proposal does indeed achieve this objective must be for others to decide. The principal elements of the proposal are as follows.

The Federal Union of Democratic Nations would be a legitimate, full-fledged state entity with the power to promulgate and enforce laws, the power to levy taxes and engage in public works, and the power to raise and maintain military forces. Its leaders would be directly elected by the citizens and its administrative apparatus would be substantial and in continuous operation. It would have a capital city, regional offices, and the standard symbols of state authority: a flag, an anthem, emblems, and so on.

At the same time, there would be numerous restrictions on the power and authority of the supernational federation in order to forestall tendencies toward oppressiveness and totalitarianism. In the first place, as suggested by its name, the Federal Union would be a federal, rather than a unitary, state. That is, it would supplement—not replace—the national states taking membership in it. These member nations and their respective governments would not merely be formal entities within the supernational federation; they would retain substantial degrees of sovereignty, autonomy, and independence. Key restraints on the supernational state would include the following: (1) member nations would retain the right to raise and maintain military forces; (2) member nations would retain the right to withdraw (secede) from the supernational federation at their own unilateral discretion; (3) a dual voting principle would be employed in the legislative assembly; and (4) special budgetary provisions would be enacted to prevent legislative deadlocks from freezing the operations of the federation.

Formally established by a Federal Union Constitution, the Federal Union of Democratic Nations would comprise the standard three branches of government: (1) a legislative arm called the Union Chamber of Representatives; (2) an executive arm guided by a Union Chief Executive; and (3) a judicial arm called the Union High Court. All three would be directly elected by the population: Union Representatives would have terms of five years, the Union Chief Executive a term of ten years, and Union Justices terms of 25 years. Component branches of the executive arm would include the Ministry of the Interior, Ministry of Finance, Ministry of Justice, Ministry of Science, Education, and Culture, Ministry of Planning, Ministry of External Development, Ministry of Security, Ministry of Non-Union Affairs, and World Development Authority.

The specific institutional proposals are developed in light of the various perceived problems and hazards inherent in the concept of a world state. The first and foremost of these is the possibility that a world state would attempt to impose upon member nations uncongenial social systems (e.g., communism—or capitalism). Second to this, but still extremely important, is the possibility that a world state would attempt quick and drastic redistribution of income and wealth from the richer to the poorer member nations. This potential policy is referred to as "Crude Redistribution," and it is sharply contrasted to the preferred policy of "Common Progress" (by which living standards in *all* nations would increase, but the *rate* of increase would be higher in the poorer nations than in the richer nations). The position which I argue is that a supernational federation will only be feasible and viable if the supernational government completely, totally, and unequivocally renounces Crude Redistribution in favor of Common Progress. Many specific proposals are designed to allay fears and apprehensions based on the possibility of misguided social activism and/or Crude Redistribution.

The single most fundamental proposal which would militate against the world state becoming an instrument of oppression is the right of secession. This right would be reinforced by the right of member nations to maintain independent military forces. It is proposed that all military forces of the Union, whether maintained by the member nations or by the Union itself, wear the same uniform, have similar weaponry, and be considered formally as components of the overall Union Security Force. But in the event of fundamental and irreconcilable conflict between the Union and a particular member nation, the nation would have both the formal authority and informal means (i.e., its own military) of resuming its independence from the Union.

Secession would be a drastic step and, if widely prevalent, would threaten the viability and existence of the Federal Union. Certain key proposals are designed to forestall the emergence of such serious conflicts between the Union and its member nations that secession would be contemplated. Among the most important is the dual voting system in the Union Chamber of Representatives. According to this system, any proposed measure would have to be passed by a 60 percent majority on two bases: the population basis and the material basis. In the population vote, a Union Representative's voting weight would be equal to the proportion of the population of the entire Union represented by the population of his or her own Union District. In the material vote, that same Union Representative's voting weight would be equal to the proportion of the overall revenue of the entire Union represented by the revenue raised in that Representative's Union District. Thus, the richer nations, as providers of most of the Union's revenues, would retain more power in the legislature than would be the case if voting weight were based exclusively on population represented.

Although much attention is devoted in *World Union on the Horizon* to the "negative" issue of impeding undesirable policies and activities by the supernational federation, substantial attention is also devoted to the "positive" aspects of supernational federation. For example, concentration of the space exploration effort within a single political entity encompassing a very large proportion of the human population might well lead to a more vigorous and successful effort. This effort would be the sole concern of the Ministry of External Development. The same is true of the Union's pursuance of a World Economic Development Program under the guidance of the World Development Authority—with the understanding that this program would be conducted along the lines of Common Progress and not Crude Redistribution.

The psychological importance of the Union as a symbol of human unity and solidarity cannot be overemphasized, and this importance dictates, among other things, that the capital city of the Federal Union must be a very impressive and attractive location. In addition to the usual imposing public buildings, the capital city should contain numerous superior tourist attractions: museums, theaters, a botanical garden, a zoo, and perhaps a major amusement park along the lines of Disneyworld. In short, the capital city should be made into one of the great tourist meccas of the world.

There are many other important practical issues. For example, with respect to immigration, it is conceded that although free movement of goods and capital within the Union should be pursued from the outset, the elimination of the present national barriers to immigration will have to await the success of the

World Economic Development Program. With respect to a common language, the argument is that there should be only one official language within the Union, and that this language should be English. The hope would be that this would be made acceptable to non-English-speaking nations by the requirement that all schoolchildren in English-speaking nations study some other language to the same extent and intensity that schoolchildren in other nations study English.

There are various other objectives and areas of activity for the supernational federation. For example, certain organizational and regulatory functions pertaining to international transport, commerce and communications, as well as global environmental protection, some of them already well developed at the present time under the auspices of the United Nations or other multinational entities, could be taken over by appropriate ministries of the Federal Union. It should not be excessively difficult to establish a common currency within the Union under the aegis of the Ministry of the Interior. The Ministry of the Interior could also engage in the collection and dissemination of economic and social statistics pertaining to the member nations. Among the projects of the Ministry of Science, Education, and Culture might be the support of a few elite universities, newly founded by the Federal Union at various locations throughout the federation. The Ministry of Planning would have nothing to do with direct economic planning of the sort that was long favored in the Soviet Union and some other communist nations. Rather it would operate as a permanent, large-scale "think tank," which would carefully analyze and evaluate various policy concepts and proposals emanating in embryonic form from legislators and executives in the supernational government. Its reports would then become inputs into practical decisionmaking by these legislators and executives.

If the Federal Union of Democratic Nations develops properly, nonmember nations will experience increasing incentives to join the Union. To begin with, participation in the Federal Union free trade area would represent very tangible economic benefits. Moreover, the poorer member nations would receive preferential treatment in the World Economic Development Program. Member nations of the Union would also enjoy more security against the threat of foreign invasion by nonmember nations. But aside from these practical matters, there would be the extremely important, albeit intangible, psychological element in Union membership. The history of nation-states and nationalism, among other things, demonstrates the attractiveness to individual human beings of being part of large-scale social undertakings. Human beings are social animals, and they derive a high degree of comfort and encouragement from active participation in society. All other things being equal, they prefer being part of larger organized social groups than smaller organized social groups. Perhaps it is a matter of some fundamental, primitive impulse toward risksharing: the larger the group sharing the risk, the less risk to each individual member of the group. Also no doubt there are considerations of power and capability. As a rule, larger organized social groups possess more power and capability than do smaller organized social groups, and to some extent at least, larger group power and capability tend to translate into tangible benefits to the individual members of the group. The expectation of these benefits in the future creates a psychological incentive to participation, even if the current benefits are not in fact particularly obvious or dramatic.

Of course, the incentives of nonmember nations to join the Union will be greater to the extent that the Union's citizenry maintains a relatively high level of unity and harmony. This is not to say that a utopian condition of beatific bliss is either possible or necessarily desirable. It goes without saying that there will inevitably be a great deal of vigorous, even acrimonious, political discussion and controversy within the Federal Union into the foreseeable future. But such discussion and controversy could and should be conducted within a context of deeply shared purpose and mutual respect. Political issues should generally be regarded as temporary problems and difficulties which will eventually be surmounted by the Federal Union—not as permanent liabilities which call into serious question the fundamental value and very existence of the Federal Union. This positive attitude toward political controversy would be facilitated by the development of what might be termed "supernational patriotism."

There is a subtle interplay between "real factors" and "psychological factors." The real factor in this case is the existence of the Federal Union of Democratic Nations, its physical substance in terms of buildings and people, its active participation in the governance of society. The psychological factor is the impact upon human mentality of the Federal Union, of its provision of a higher focus of loyalty and allegiance than the focus presently provided by the national governments. The more successful the Federal Union is in terms of its practical operations, the more rapidly will the psychological attitude of supernational patriotism grow and progress. At the same time, the more developed becomes the spirit of supernational patriotism, the more successful the Federal Union will tend to become in its practical operations and endeavors. The objective is the simultaneous, interactive development of both real and psychological factors in a kind of snowballing process toward a very high level of effectiveness and unity. It cannot be anticipated that progress will be continuous and linear. No doubt there will be setbacks, periods of retrogression and apprehension, disappointments and defeats. But this has, indeed, been the history of humanity throughout all past ages. Despite all the tragic reverses experienced by humanity throughout its long history, the general trend has definitely been onward and upward. Supernational federation offers us a major opportunity to consolidate, continue, and accelerate the onward and upward trend established by human history up to the contemporary age.

CRITIQUE OF THE COMMISSION REPORT

The phrase "Federal Union of Democratic Nations" has a fateful, sonorous ring to it. It is a phrase potentially capable of commanding serious attention and generating real enthusiasm. The phrase "global neighborhood," on the other hand, is trifling and inconsequential. It is reminiscent of the children's television program *Mr. Rogers' Neighborhood*. The phrase sounds as if it were devised by a team of advertising professionals accustomed to writing copy intended to sell blue jeans, soap powder, perfume, or toys. It may be argued, of course, that the world is not ready for a Federal Union of Democratic Nations. This could certainly be true—but if it is, indeed, true, then it is probably also true that the world is equally unready for a global neighborhood along the idealistic lines envisioned by the Commission on Global Governance. The Commission's proposals are clearly on the side of truth, justice, and goodness. But truth, justice, and goodness are far too abstract to provide, in and of themselves, effective motivation to most human beings. Most human beings require a more concrete and tangible focus around which to organize their worthy impulses toward truth, justice, and goodness. No such focus is to be found in the Report of the Commission on Global Governance. In contrast, the proposed Federal Union of Democratic Nations, or some other viable plan of world government, might indeed provide such a focus.

The central problem with the Commission Report is its explicit rejection of the notion of world government. With the calmly complacent dogmatism of a medieval theologian, the Report sets forth the proposition that any movement toward world government at the present time would create "an even less democratic world than we have now—one more accommodating to power, more hospitable to hegemonic ambition, and more reinforcing of the roles of states and governments than the rights of people" (p. xvi). No evidence, analysis, or argument is adduced in support of this proposition. To the authors of the Report, the proposition is apparently considered so pristinely obvious, so indisputably self-evident, and so fundamentally axiomatic, as to render any hint or vestige of justification needless, pointless, and superfluous.

To this author, who has engaged in a great deal of hard thinking about world government over a period of decades, and who has thereupon published a carefully considered, closely reasoned, book-length advocacy of world government, such thoughtless acceptance and recitation of the conventional blind prejudice against world government is highly frustrating, to say the least. There is no evidence in the 400-plus pages of the Commission Report that any sort of careful, critical attention was devoted to any of the numerous plans for world government which have been put forward over the last 50 years since the end of World War II. My own plan is, of course, only one of many. Apparently, the Commission never bothered to consider any of these plans. It would appear that the simple term "world government" was, in and of itself, enough to terminate the normal processes of intellectual inquiry, and to elicit a veritably Pavlovian response of denial and rejection. One can only wonder at the convoluted and distorted perspectives, at the veritably delusional attitudes, responsible for a lengthy and pretentious document on "world governance" which casually but definitively rejects the concept of world government. Why bother?

What, indeed, is the point of the exercise? As it stands, this Report is little more than a wish list of "nice things which we ever-so-civilized members of the Commission would like to see happen." The need for, and usefulness of, such lists are marginal at best. The Commission's wish list is analogous to what a child of an impoverished family might draw up for purposes of mailing to Santa Claus. If such a child lists a pony as a desired Christmas present, the pony is not going to appear on Christmas morning—simply because no Santa Claus exists to bestow such a gift. To my mind, the Commission on Global Governance is, in effect, addressing itself to Santa Claus—a nonexistent entity. It is highly doubtful that its wishes will be granted. The overall effect of the Report is thus fatuous and borderline ludicrous.

For example, any sane and civilized person wishes for nuclear disarmament. On this issue, the Commission Report delivers the following pronouncement (p. 340-341):

Work towards nuclear disarmament should involve action on four fronts:

- the earliest possible ratification and implementation of existing agreements on nuclear and other weapons of mass destruction;
- the indefinite extension of the Non-Proliferation Treaty;
- the conclusion of a treaty to end all nuclear testing; and
- the initiation of talks among all declared nuclear powers to establish a process to reduce and eventually eliminate all nuclear arsenals.

Is it necessary to have hundreds of first-rate intellects from all over the world labor mightily over a period of years to inform us of this? Hardly. Without any indication of how such worthy goals may be facilitated, such a list amounts to nothing more than a series of banal platitudes.

In my own work *World Union on the Horizon*, I do not waste the reader's time with inane lists such as the one above, reproduced from the Commission Report. There is no need to argue that such things are desirable from the point of view of the long-run survival prospects of the human race. Everyone agrees on that. The problem is that such things are regarded by some subgroups within the human population as inconsistent with their short-run survival prospects and/or inconsistent with the preservation of their material welfare. The real task is to get these subgroups to recognize that the retention of their nuclear armories is not only hazardous to the long-run general interest of the entire human race, but also quite hazardous to their own short-run self-interest as well. They would be much more likely to recognize and accept this latter proposition if they were citizens in good standing within a functioning, effective world polity.

Consider Russia, for example. Ten years ago, Russia was insulated from a potentially hostile outside world by several peripheral republics of the Soviet Union, plus a buffer zone of Eastern European satellites. Ten years ago, Russia possessed, in addition to a massive inventory of strategic nuclear weapons, gigantic "conventional" armed forces as well. Now Russia has been stripped of all its peripheral republics and satellite states. Now Russia's military forces, nuclear and conventional, are withered down to a tiny fraction of their former size. Under the circumstances, Russia can hardly be expected to dismantle the remnants of its nuclear armory. What would happen, for instance, if a reunified and resurgent Germany, looking back wistfully at the ambitions of the Third Reich, decided that it could make better use of Russian natural resources than Russia itself? How would Russia protect itself against a potential German invasion? By relying on the United Nations? In 1991, the United Nations proved that it could deal with aggression by a small Middle Eastern nation without nuclear weapons (Iraq). But could it deal with aggression by one of the principal world powers—a world power armed with nuclear missiles? Quite possibly not. Quite possibly it would show itself to be as ineffectual against aggression by a major world power as the League of Nations proved itself to be during the 1930s. On the other hand, a handful of operational nuclear missiles which could be launched at Berlin and other German cities would be a far more reliable deterrent against potential German aggression than the United Nations, "world public opinion," etc. It is to be expected, therefore, that Russia will *not* engage in complete nuclear disarmament, so long as the world system remains basically geared to the present pattern of self-righteously sovereign nation-states bonded together only by paper alliances.

Consider, as a second example, the United States. The United States has a great deal of material prosperity to preserve and protect. That level of material prosperity naturally elicits a substantial amount of envious resentment elsewhere in the world. Without substantial conventional and nuclear arms—especially nuclear arms—the United States would be vulnerable to invasions by the populous poorer nations of the world. Nor are all of these nations at a safe distance. At the moment, Mexico confronts a rich and powerful northern neighbor. Any thoughts that Mexico might entertain about rectifying the terrible human rights violations imposed on Mexican emigrants to the United States, and at the same time recovering the huge territories in the American Southwest which were forcibly taken from Mexico in the Mexican-American War of 1848—such thoughts are suppressed on account of the military power of the United States. But let us imagine that Mexico confronted a rich northern neighbor which maintained skeleton conventional military forces and no nuclear missiles at all. The calculus would be changed—greatly changed. Apprehensions of this sort mean that the United States will dismantle its last nuclear missile only after every other nuclear missile in the world has been dismantled. Practical United States policymakers do not expect to be put into this position within the lifetime of anyone now living. As is the case with Russia, the United States expects to retain at least a "few" (i.e., a few dozen or possibly a few hundred) nuclear missiles into the foreseeable future. It is utopian nonsense to expect Russia or the United States to engage in total nuclear disarmament so long as the present-day nation-state system remains basically intact.

It is not that I expect the establishment of a Federal Union of Democratic Nations, as described and evaluated in *World Union on the Horizon*, to lead instantly to worldwide nuclear disarmament. Now that the nuclear genie is out of the bottle, it will not be an easy matter getting it back into the bottle—world government or no world government. Indeed, the Federal Union proposal which I have set forth envisions the likelihood that a considerable number of member nations will retain military forces—including nuclear weaponry—under their effective national control for a prolonged period following establishment of the Union. Such forces would be *formally* incorporated into the Union Security Force, but in the event of serious conflict between the Union and any particular member nation, that nation could easily establish effective control over the military forces which it maintains within its own borders. Nevertheless, the critical advantage of the existence of a world government in the form of a Federal Union of Democratic Nations is that it would gradually foster both material and psychological conditions under which the perceived need within nations to control nuclear and other weaponry for purposes of national security would gradually wither away.

Hopefully, this perceived need would eventually wither away sufficiently for total nuclear disarmament to occur. But there should be no sense of urgency on this matter. Member nations should not be pushed and prodded to divest themselves of nuclear missiles. The attitude should be: When the time is ripe, this will happen. In *World Union on the Horizon*, I do not waste time dwelling upon the long-run advisability of nuclear disarmament, simply because this advisability is sufficiently obvious to all rational individuals (presumably, only rational individuals will read my book). Nor do I propose that nuclear disarmament be on the continuing agenda of the Federal Union. Let the member nations decide for themselves how much in the way of nuclear and conventional arms they need. If the Union operates as it should operate, the member nations will gradually see for themselves that they need progressively less in the way of all types of armaments, and they will gradually divest themselves of these armaments. Attempting to hasten this process would well be counterproductive and possibly fatal to the cause of world government.

Although the horrific possibility of nuclear war has dominated human thinking ever since the tragedies of Hiroshima and Nagasaki, it is necessary to keep this possibility in proper perspective. Of the hundreds of millions of people killed by human conflicts throughout the twentieth century, the casualties of Hiroshima and Nagasaki constitute only a tiny fraction. Even if complete nuclear disarmament were to be achieved, and all human conflicts in the future conducted solely and entirely with so-called conventional weapons, the death and destruction could still be devastating. In contemplating future conflicts, it is essential that proponents of world government (including myself) remain rational, reasonable, and realistic with respect to the potential effectiveness of world government in limiting such conflicts. It would be foolish to expect the establishment of a world government along the lines of the Federal Union of Democratic Nations, or indeed along any lines whatsoever, to bring human conflict to a complete and instantaneous halt. It seems extremely unlikely that all nations of the world would become charter members of a supernational federation. Those nations maintaining their independence might elect to go to war among themselves, or even to attack member nations.

Civil wars might erupt, both within member nations and within independent nations. It is unrealistic to expect that the existence of a supernational federation will deter all such conflicts. It is also unrealistic to specify that the supernational federation would always and invariably endeavor to quell such conflicts by force of arms. For example, if a civil war were to erupt within a member nation between one faction wishing to remain within the Federal Union and another faction wishing to establish independence, that nation should be suspended from membership pending the outcome of the conflict. Under no circumstances should components of the Union Security Force from outside that nation intervene in the conflict. The matter should be left to the population of that nation, to be settled by peaceful democratic means hopefully, but by force if necessary. A guiding principle must be that external force can never be used either to incorporate new member nations into the Union, or to forestall departing member nations from reestablishing their independence.

No doubt many "traditionalist" proponents of world government will fail to comprehend the necessity for an "open door" policy with respect to the membership of the proposed Federal Union of Democratic Nations. This is understandable. Nations have often employed force to quell independence movements within various regions. In some cases, such conflicts have escalated into all-out civil wars. To the people of the United States, of course, the best-known historical example of this was the American Civil War of 1861-1865. This devastating conflict was fought to prevent the departure of the Southern states from the United States. The conflict was successful in maintaining the territorial integrity of the United States, and it had the additional effect of eliminating the institution of slavery from the North American continent. The overwhelming majority of the American people today believe that the American Civil War was a just war with favorable long-run consequences to the nation. Even within the Southern states, a considerable majority now accepts this proposition. Therefore it is now believed that had the population of the Northern states, under the guidance of the newly elected President Abraham Lincoln, acquiesced peacefully in the departure of the Southern states from the United States, this would have been a terrible mistake with severely adverse effects on the development of Northern and Southern states alike. The belief that the American Civil War was a just and beneficial war easily generalizes into a belief that an essential element of nationhood is unwillingness to countenance the departure of component regions of the nation.

But it is a logical fallacy to conclude, on the basis that the American Civil War was a just and beneficial war, that a supernational state could not be willing to countenance the departure of component nations of the state, and yet retain the essential nature of a state. If in 1861, the United States of America had allowed the peaceful secession of the Southern states, the United States of America would have still been a nation—albeit a less extensive and powerful nation. If Canada were to allow the independence of Quebec, Canada would still be a nation. The dissolution of the Soviet Union does not imply that Russia is no longer a nation. In like fashion, a supranational state would still be a state even if a minority of nation-states were to reassert their independence following a period of membership. It is absolutely essential to be absolutely clear on this point. If the conditions of membership in the supranational federation involve the following proposition: "Once you join, an effort to leave will be met by force," then very few nations will venture to join. On the other hand, if the right of peaceful and unobstructed departure is clearly and explicitly granted, there is a very good likelihood that only a very few member nations will ever elect to exercise this right.

Most of the humanitarian disasters over the last two decades—in Cambodia, Somalia, Rwanda, and Bosnia—have not, in actual fact, involved international aggression. Rather they have proceeded from internal ethnic and ideological conflicts. When these disasters occur, there is normally a hue and cry among compassionate people demanding outside intervention by the UN, the US, NATO, and so on. Unfortunately, compassion and naivety tend to go hand in hand. Normally, these conflicts are so vicious, and the warring parties so self-righteously fanatical in the pursuit of their objectives, that quelling the conflicts would require very heavy losses among the intervening military forces. Thus, it is understandable that less compassionate people—the majority—are unwilling to incur these losses in order to benefit very different people in very remote parts of the world, many of whom in any case do not appreciate the intervention (intervention is appreciated only by the losing side, which is often the minority).

It is the belief of this author, notwithstanding my advocacy of a plan of world government, that these kinds of conflicts should be allowed to burn themselves out without any outside intervention beyond efforts at mediation. Personally, I do not support military interventions by the United Nations in various internal conflicts at the present time, and I also do not propose that the Federal Union of Democratic Nations, should it be established, become involved in such interventions in the future. This should be qualified to apply to the *near* future, by that meaning perhaps 20 to 30 years following the Union's foundation. Within that period of time, the disintegrative forces would be too strong to risk the serious threat to the long-term preservation of the Federal Union represented by large-scale military intervention into localized conflict situations. Conceivably, in due course the unitary spirit within the Union would become strong enough to permit large-scale military interventions into these situations on humanitarian grounds without seriously undermining the stability of the Union. But that day cannot be rushed, and it would be unwise to try to rush it. It is not that these localized conflict situations are not appalling. It is just that the conditions are not yet ripe for the forcible suppression of these situations by outside military intervention. It is *more* likely that conditions *will* become ripe for this within a reasonable period of historical time if humanity does establish a supranational federation than if humanity does not establish such a federation.

The Report of the Commission on Global Governance is, naturally, replete with nobly compassionate references to, and anguished rhetoric about, the plight of human beings victimized by localized conflict situations. The following is a typical passage (p. 16):

A disturbing feature of the contemporary world is the spread of a culture of violence. Civil wars brutalize thousands of young people who are drawn into them. The systematic use of rape as a weapon of war has been an especially pernicious feature of some conflicts... The ascendance of the military in many countries has contributed to an ethos inimical to human rights and democratic values... Conflict and violence also leave deep marks on the lives of children, innocent victims who are rarely able to rid themselves of the legacy of war...

Appalled as it is by all these terrible things, the Commission declines to consider or even contemplate the potential contribution of a world government to the lessening of these conditions. At the outset, world government is excluded from a discussion of "world governance" on grounds that it is self-evident that the establishment of a world government would worsen these problems. While a proponent of world government such as myself is sorely tempted to attribute this viewpoint to stupidity or hypocrisy, in fairness to the Commission it must be more plausibly attributed to judgmental paralysis stemming from deficient vision. This is a problem which has afflicted humanity throughout our history, and which has greatly retarded the rate of progress which might otherwise have been achieved. But the problem has been surmounted in the past, and hopefully it will be again in the future.

Now that the ideological conflict between communism and noncommunism is winding down, the single most important remaining obstacle to effective world government is the economic gap. What is to be done about the economic gap? My own answer, elaborated in Chapter 4 of *World Union on the Horizon*, is a global economic development program on a heroic scale. The Report's timid answer is: Form a deliberative/study group to be known as the Economic Security Council (ESC). We already have a Security Council (SC) as the focus of effective power in the United Nations, whose purpose it is to try to cut down on the amount of death and destruction imposed by armed conflict in the world. Now we shall have an *Economic* Security Council (*E*SC), whose purpose it will be to think very hard about what might possibly be done to assist the billions of impoverished people living in the world. What a daring, bold, ingenious, and forward-looking idea! (Please excuse the sarcasm.)

The level of success achieved by the Security Council of the UN in the 50 years since its establishment has not been overly inspiring. During most of that 50 years, humanity lived in daily dread of nuclear catastrophe. The Cold War has recently receded, but no one believes that the Security Council had anything to do with this deliverance. The "hot" Cold War conflicts in Korea and Vietnam proceeded with supreme indifference to the UN in general and the Security Council in particular. So did several other conflicts such as the Iraq-Iran war.

The expulsion of Iraq from Kuwait could be cited as an achievement of the UN, but in all probability, even if the UN had never been formed, the United States and its European allies would probably have dealt firmly with the Iraqi invasion of Kuwait just to keep the price of oil down. If the beneficial effects of an Economic Security Council, should it be formed, on the world poverty problem are comparable to the beneficial effects of the original Security Council on the world violence problem, then we would be well advised not to get our expectations up too high.

The fact of the matter is that the only feasible means of overcoming the world poverty problem within a reasonable period of historical time lies in a global economic development program on a vast scale. Such a program would involve a massive shift of new capital resources from the rich countries to the poor countries. Whether such a program would be successful cannot be predicted in advance. This is an empirical question which can only be answered by means of undertaking the effort and observing the outcome. If the outcome is disappointing, then the effort should and would be abandoned by the rich nations. In all likelihood, the abandonment of this effort would coincide with the dissolution of the world government. It is almost impossible to imagine that a supernational polity could remain stable in the long term despite such drastic divergences in regional living standards as exist in the world today. But as I stated earlier, it is both irrational and immoral to simply *assume* that a massive global economic development program would be unsuccessful. Rather such a program *should* be undertaken—it *should* be given a fair and reasonable chance to prove itself. I am very dubious that the Economic Security Council proposed by the Commission will, in and of itself, accomplish anything consequential toward the recognition and acceptance of this proposition by the populations of the rich nations.

In the judgment of this author, there is a higher likelihood both that the required economic development program *will* be undertaken, and that it *will* be successful, if there is a world government in operation than if there is not a world government in operation. This is the one area in which the world government should, indeed, push its authority to the limit. It is the one area in which it will have to take legitimate, calculated risks. It is to be expected that the rich nations will manifest a considerable amount of reluctance and resistance to the required contributions. These contributions will constitute the largest single source of disintegrative pressures. The need to maintain these contributions at a high level is the reason why the supernational federation should not squander its resources and "use up its credit," so to speak, in such endeavors as sending elements of the Union Security Force to suppress various localized conflict situations analogous to Somalia, Bosnia, and so on.

In conclusion, I am forced to describe the Report of the Commission on Global Governance, on the whole, as an exercise in futility. It provides a heavy dose of pious hand-wringing about the numerous ominous problems confronting humanity. It also provides a lengthy list of nice things which the human race ought to be doing to surmount these problems. But it refuses to consider the single most plausible institutional innovation which could indeed significantly facilitate these nice things: the establishment of a world government. Imagine a person suffering from a potentially deadly ailment. An operation is indicated. A dangerous operation, to be sure—but the alternative is even more dangerous. Now imagine another person, representing himself as a doctor, saying to the afflicted one: "Well, I think this operation is too dangerous. I think you should instead put your trust in the power of prayer." This metaphor represents the substance of what the Commission on Global Governance is saying to the human race.

NOTES

1. James A. Yunker, *World Union on the Horizon: The Case for Supernational Federation* (Lanham, MD: University Press of America, 1993).

2. James A. Yunker, *Socialism Revised and Modernized: The Case for Pragmatic Market Socialism* (New York: Praeger Publishers, 1992).

3. James A. Yunker, "A World Economic Equalization Program: Results of a Simulation," *Journal of Developing Areas* 10(2): 159-179, January 1976, and "A World Economic Equalization Program: Refinements and Sensitivity Analysis," *World Development* 16(8): 921-933, August 1988.

Chapter 10

Summary and Conclusion
Errol E. Harris

None of the authors of the foregoing essays have anything but admiration and approval for the aims and objectives entertained by the Commission on Global Governance; they all envision a global community in friendship and harmony; they concur with the type of global ethic that the Commissioners commend; they admit the importance of a global civil society and the influence for good of the work of NGOs; they applaud the inclusion of environmental preservation as a factor in the security of peoples; they all believe that government should be responsible to the people and desire that the people should have more power; and they all insist on the necessity for the maintenance of world peace and enforcement of the Rule of Law.

What they deprecate, on the other hand, is the Commission's failure to recognize the obstacles presented to the achievement of these aims by the persistent and inevitable priority given by sovereign states to their own national interests to the detriment of global considerations, and the impossibility of ensuring world peace as long as sovereign states, as they are bound to do, give precedence to defense considerations, build up their military strength in consequence, and generate an arms race in the attempt to maintain a balance of power between opposing blocs. As the Commissioners fail to admit that International Law cannot be enforced on sovereign states without waging war and that the United Nations cannot, therefore, keep the peace as long as it respects Article 2 of its Charter, they fail to see that the desired ends of the Commission can never be achieved within the United Nations structure under the restraints imposed on it by the obligation to respect the sovereign independence of its member nations. The Commission proclaims the need for a drastic change in our thinking about international relations, yet it refrains from any clearcut specification of such change, and it fails to give any evidence of itself having adopted the radically new outlook it espouses.

The philosophical background to modernity that must be taken into consideration in any assessment of the Report is set out in Chapter 1 ("A Planetary Paradigm for Global Government") by Professor Glen Martin. This he contrasts with a planetary approach to moral and political thinking, which, in the present epoch, should be the ground on which any political critique must rest. He complains that, while the Commission rightly recognizes the problems, it fails to penetrate to their causes. He gives us a thorough analysis of the deficiencies of *Our Global Neighborhood*, and stresses the philosophical and practical need to adopt a global (relational) outlook in world affairs.

Professor Martin is substantially right in his analysis of the elements in the modern spirit which give rise to the predicament in which we find ourselves today. He is unerring in his perception that the future demands a paradigm recognizing the crucial interrelation of whole and part, and the need to transcend Newtonian presuppositions of atomism with all their disastrous consequences. The paradigm for the future must derive from a fundamental holism, rooted in Einsteinian (and, we may add, quantum) physics, and ecological biology.

As Martin points out, the Renaissance-era liberation of "reason" from the shackles of medieval dogmatism and authoritarianism was unfortunately contaminated with other ingredients which have led, today, to very destructive tendencies. Reason in the seventeenth and eighteenth centuries was centered on Descartes' *ego cogitans*, and this, while it had enormously liberating effects, also generated an individualism which infected political thinking from John Locke to Herbert Spencer, such as Dr. Martin deplores, and this was undoubtedly associated with the "liberalism" of Adam Smith and John Stuart Mill.

But "reason" has two phases: one as understanding and another as speculative reason. The eighteenth century was in the grip of the former, as we still are, for the most part, today; the latter has yet to prevail, and is what is implicit in Dr. Martin's planetary paradigm. Several of the writers to whom Martin refers have failed to take heed of what Hegel wrote about master and slave in his *Phenomenology of Spirit*, and it may be well to draw attention here to the dialectical development of the consciousness of self that is involved. The urge to dominate is only one (primitive) moment in this process; and the opposition of self to not-self is a necessary phase, indispensable to what Professor Martin calls the relational self. Conflict between self and other is dialectically reconciled in mutual recognition and respect, in which each self finds itself at home in its other. So we are led to a resolution of the modern problem which concurs with what Martin contemplates.

The problem of the sovereign nation-state is a sixteenth-century outgrowth from the conflict, first, between emperors and popes in the Middle Ages, and then from the centralization of power in the hands of monarchs as opposed to their feudal fief-holders. The theory of sovereignty, as it evolved in the works of Hobbes, Spinoza, Rousseau, and Hegel, placed the supreme power in the rulers of the nation, whom the last three of these thinkers identified with the people; but this was in a period when states in international relations were, as Hobbes put it, "in the state of nature," an anarchical situation in which to this day they remain. But now, as Einstein saw, circumstances have radically changed, and warfare ("ultima ratio regis," inscribed on his cannon by Louis XIV) is no longer tolerable with nuclear weapons in the hands of the combatants. This is an additional reason for the desperate need for a new paradigm.

The historical and ideological background of the Report is explored by Professor Falk's paper (Chapter 2: "Liberalism at the Global Level"). He contends that the Report belongs in the "liberal" tradition and shows how it defers to the opinions of the powers that be. Professor Falk tries to set out the advantages of the Report and the ways in which it could be important at the present time; but, on the whole, in large measure, he condemns it with faint praise, concluding that it will ultimately function as a lead balloon. He sets out the presumed theoretical presuppositions of the Commission and estimates its likely impact in the contemporary international milieu. At the same time he describes the psychological atmosphere which surrounds it—postmodern disillusionment with government and discontent with the achievements of the United Nations. The "liberalism" which he says it presupposes is that of Woodrow Wilson, on the one hand, and Kant, on the other. But he does not expatiate on the faults of either of these varieties. The third type of liberalism operative in the background is that of Locke and Adam Smith, involving individualism in the political notion of democracy, and the higgling of the market in economics (the two being intimately connected). Professor Falk maintains that the Commissioners defer overmuch to the prevailing "realist orthodoxy," but he omits to mention that this "orthodoxy" is little more than a disguised idealism putting its faith in failed methods of diplomacy and in the United Nations, despite its evident debility. Falk does not hold with this "orthodoxy" himself, and has a great antipathy to "statism," to which it adheres. He pins his faith in global civil society (though he tends to overlook the part played in this loose array of associations by the world federalist movement). While recognizing the Kantian influence underlying the Commission's Report, Falk has not found it necessary to point out that Kant recommends federalism, although it is a federalism which inconsistently retains national sovereignty for the member states. Possibly Professor Falk expects us to recognize this defect as reflected in the general spirit of the Report which he criticizes, although he does not explicitly draw attention to it. However, as the reader proceeds to other papers, it will become apparent to him or her that the defect of the Report is not confined to its failure to find a receptive audience, as Falk maintains, but is also inherent in its inability to meet the real demands of current world problems.

John Roberts' paper (Chapter 3: "Governance—An Opportunity?") is rather different from the others. Although most of the writers address the question of the meaning of "governance," whether in general or as used by the Commission, Roberts considers rather what it might be made to mean than what etymology requires, or the meaning given to the word by those who currently use it. He suggests that it provides an opportunity to avoid the distaste for government of all kinds, which today is so widespread among those who have become dis-illusioned and who have misgivings about all forms of bureaucracy and power-politicking, as too apt to become corrupt, inefficient and self-seeking. "Gover-nance" may, perhaps, be used as a term indicating the renunciation of all that, and the adoption of a federal democratic system which constitutionally guarantees civil and personal rights, as well as the rights of nationalities and ethnic groups, while satisfactorily administering those matters which are of common concern to all. Roberts' discussion is thoughtful and intriguing, and his argument is elegant; but his suggestion has come too late, for the word has now been hijacked to mean either some vague network of cooperation between civic associations, or else the present disposition of international arrangements, or some variation of them that makes little or no difference, in contrast to world federalism. And among the hijackers are the authors of the Report on Global Governance.

The true meaning of the word "governance" and what it implies and involves are the central questions which this book is meant to address. The dictionary leaves one in no doubt that it means "government"; and Professor Ronald Glossop (Chapter 4: "Global Governance Requires Global Government") is convinced that either is impossible without the other. He quotes the Report as saying that "good governance requires good government," but he complains that they interpret both terms incorrectly. In actual fact, the Commissioners define "governance" very vaguely, as several of our authors observe, so that what it turns out to be, for "the global neighborhood," is nothing very different from the status quo ante. It is with this that Professor Glossop takes issue. He accepts emphatically the Commission's statement that "good governance requires good government," while he rejects, with equal emphasis, what they intend by either term—the first as too woolly, and the second as nothing other than national sovereign domination. Professor Glossop is also concerned about democracy and the failure of the Commission to meet its standards. His main argument is that a new paradigm has to be established in political thinking: a shift from national sovereignty to global authority. He stresses the problem of a common language, which he sees as indispensable, both for the global orientation and for democratic communication. And he tackles in a refreshing manner the issue of international law and the reasons for its shortcomings.

Professor Griffin (Chapter 5: "Global Government: Objections Considered") centers his discussion on the questions of the desirability and the possibility of world government. Both have been seriously questioned. The Report summarily dismisses world government as undesirable, with scant discussion, and the impression left with the reader is that the Commissioners believe it to be com-pletely impracticable. Griffin examines the arguments that could be put forward on either side about both issues, irrespective of the Commission's silence, and he demonstrates convincingly that the objections on both counts are without adequate foundation.

The core critique of the Report is to be found in the next two chapters. In

Chapter 6 ("Global Governance or World Government?"), I have drawn special attention to the problem of national sovereignty, to which the Commissioners seem almost totally oblivious, and how their neglect of it vitiates all their recommendations. In Chapter 7 ("A Critique of 'Our Global Neighborhood'") and its Appendix ("A Bill of Particulars"), Philip Isely is fundamentally concerned with the undemocratic character of the United Nations and with the need for its replacement. He deplores the use by the Report of the term "global governance" as vague and imprecise. He deprecates the acceptance by the Commission of the main institutions of the existing international structure and its ineffectual tinkering with them. He castigates the proposals made in the Report as outdated, undemocratic, conceptually fuzzy, ineffective, and bellicose. What is urgently needed for the maintenance of peace and justice is a clear idea of world government, the rapid ratification of a democratic world constitution, and the effective enforcement of the rule of law. These two chapters together form a sort of center toward which the arguments in the other papers converge.

In Chapter 8 ("Reactions of an Ordinary World Citizen to 'Our Global Neighborhood'"), M. Breton expresses the reaction of a World Citizen of mundialist persuasion to the Commission Report. Despite his disavowals, his opinions are fairly typical of the organization which he leads. He is naturally federalist in his outlook, but he differs from Isely in requiring that any constitution for world government must be produced by an assembly of elected representatives of registered World Citizens. This, Isely considers, is a desire to reinvent the wheel, because a Constitution for the Federation of Earth has already been drafted by a Constituent Assembly of qualified people drawn from countries in all five continents. Moreover, the essential requirement is that whatever constitution is adopted should be adequate and satisfactory, no matter by whom it is drafted, and that it should be approved and ratified by those who are to live under it. Democracy can require no more. M. Breton's zeal for democracy is exemplary, and he is clearly under the strong influence of Jean Rousseau. Accordingly, he is unrelenting in his criticism of the failure of the Commission to recognize the undemocratic nature of the institutions it approves and to acknowledge the undemocratic practices of contemporary nation-states, multinational corporations, and the United Nations.

Professor Yunker's concerns in Chapter 9 ("A Pragmatic Route to Genuine Global Governance") are largely economic. He believes that world union is, as he puts it, "on the horizon," and he has little doubt about its advantages, which he details and discusses. He considers that the Commission has altogether missed the boat, and loses itself mainly in the enunciation of platitudes. The obstacles to world government he sees as primarily economic and he has his own proposals for overcoming them. A system he calls "pragmatic market socialism" (a hybrid procedure by which the main assets would be publicly owned, but the profit motive would be retained and the requirements of the market would be met) would address the ideological opposition between capitalism and socialism. Yunker does recognize, however, that with the recent winding down of the Cold War, the potential significance of pragmatic market socialism as a bridge between competing ideologies has been greatly reduced. The major economic impediment to world government at the present time he perceives as the tremendous gap in living standards between the rich and poor nations. He proposes a global economic development effort, along the lines of the post-World War II Marshall Plan, to overcome this impediment. Yunker's political recommendations for a supernational federal government, and his requirements for democratic and civil safeguards, are actually very similar to those of the World Constitution and Parliament Association, and are embodied in the Constitution for the Federation of Earth. Therefore the "horizon" on which Professor Yunker perceives world union to be looming could be much nearer than even he seems to envisage.

It is to be hoped that perusal of these essays will convince readers that "our global neighborhood," in its present situation, is a rather unruly and disordered township, in which dissension, violence, and conflict are far too prevalent; and that the "improvements" recommended by the Commission are, at best, plasters to be patched over sores, the causes of which they do not remove. To realize a truly neighborly global community, something much more radical is clearly necessary. The reader will be stimulated to consider whether the remedy might not lie in adopting for the international arena the same expedients as are used within our national societies to maintain law and order, namely, constitutionally authorized legislation with criminal and civil law enforcement. The reader should investigate the possibility of extending these measures to the global community, and should consider in what forms that might most expediently be accomplished. Attention may then be drawn to what has already been accomplished by the World Constitution and Parliament Association, and the urgent action for which it is calling at the present time. The Commission has deliberately ignored this approach to world problems, and has, in fact, condemned it without good cause. The time has surely come to rethink the whole situation anew, and to strive to do so more consistently.

Appendix I

A Call to Action: Summary of "Our Global Neighborhood"

EXTRACTS FROM THE CO-CHAIRMEN'S FOREWORD

The Charter of the United Nations was written while the world was still engulfed in war. Face to face with untold sorrow, world leaders were determined never to let it happen again. Affirming their faith in the dignity and worth of the human person, they set their minds on the advancement of all peoples. Their vision produced the world's most important political document.

Half a century has passed since the Charter was signed in San Francisco. There has been no world war in that time, but humanity has seen much violence, suffering and injustice. There remain dangers that could threaten human civilization and, indeed, the future of humankind.

But our dominant feeling is of hope. We believe the most notable feature of the past fifty years has been the emancipation and empowerment of people. People today have more power to shape their future than ever before; and that could make all the difference.

At the same time, nation-states find themselves less able to deal with the array of issues—some old, some new—that face them. States and their people, wishing to control their destinies, find they can do so only by working together with others. They must secure their future through commitment to common responsibility and shared effort.

The need to work together also guided the visionary men and women who drew up the Charter of the United Nations. What is new today is that the interdependence of nations is wider and deeper. What is also new is the role of people and the shift of focus from states to people. An aspect of this change is the growth of international civil society.

These changes call for reforms in the modes of international co-operation—the institutions and processes of global governance.

The international system that the UN Charter put in place needs to be renewed. The flaws and inadequacies of existing institutions have to be overcome. There is a need to weave a tighter fabric of international norms, expanding the rule of law world-wide and enabling citizens to exert their democratic influence on global processes.

We also believe the world's arrangements for the conduct of its affairs must be underpinned by certain common values. Ultimately, no organization will work and no law will be upheld unless they rest on a foundation made strong by shared values. These values must be informed by a sense of common responsibility for both present and future generations.

The members of the Commission, all serving in their personal capacities, come from many backgrounds and orientations. Yet, over the last two years together we have been united by one desire: to develop a common vision of the way forward for the world in making the transition from the cold war and in managing humanity's journey into the twenty-first century. We believe this report offers such a vision.

Each member of the Commission would have chosen different words, if he or she were writing this report alone. Everyone might not have fully embraced each and every proposal; but we all agreed on the overall substance and direction of the report. The strongest message we can convey is that humanity can agree on a better way to manage its affairs and give hope to present and future generations.

The development of global governance is part of the evolution of human efforts to organize life on the planet, and that process will always be going on. Our work is no more than a transit stop on that journey. We do not presume to offer a blueprint for all time. But we are convinced that it is time for the world to move on from the designs evolved over the centuries and given new form in the establishment of the United Nations nearly fifty years ago. We are in a time that demands freshness and innovation in global governance.

Global governance is not global government. No misunderstanding should arise from the similarity of the terms. We are not proposing movement towards world government, for were we to travel in that direction we might find ourselves in an even less democratic world than we have—one more accommodating to power, more hospitable to hegemonic ambition, and more reinforcing of the roles of states and governments rather than of the rights of people.

This is not to say that the goal should be a world without systems or rules. Far from it. A chaotic world would pose equal or even greater dangers. The challenge is to strike the balance in such a way that the management of global affairs is responsive to the interests of all people in a sustainable future, that it is guided by basic human values, and that it makes global organization conform to the reality of global diversity.

Many pressures bear on political leaders, as they seek both to be effective and to retain support at the national level. Notwithstanding the drawbacks of nationalism, however, the history of even this century encourages us to believe that from the very best of national leaders can come the very best of internationalism. Today, a sense of internationalism has become a necessary ingredient of sound national policies. No nation can make progress heedless of insecurity and deprivation elsewhere. We have to share a global neighborhood and strengthen it, so that it may offer the promise of a good life to all our neighbors.

Important choices must be made now, because we are at the threshold of a new era. That newness is self-evident; people everywhere know it, as do governments, though not all admit to it. We can, for example, go forward to a new era of security that responds to law and collective will and common responsibility by placing the security of people and of the planet at the centre. Or we can go backwards to the spirit and methods of what one of our members described as the "sheriff's posse"—dressed up to masquerade as global action.

There should be no question of which way we go. But the right way requires the assertion of the values of internationalism, the primacy of the rule of law world-wide, and institutional reforms that secure and sustain them. This report offers some suggestions for such responses.

Removed from the sway of empires and a world of victors and vanquished, released from the constraints of the cold war that so cramped the potential of an evolving global system throughout the post-war era, seized of the risk of unsustainable human impacts on nature, mindful of the global implications of human deprivation—the world has no real option but to rise to the challenge of change, in an enlightened and constructive fashion. We call on our global neighbors, in all their diversity, to act together to ensure this—and to act now.

Ingvar Carlsson	*Shridath Ramphal*
Stockholm	London

SUMMARY OF PROPOSALS

In setting forth the major proposals made by the Commission, we wish to emphasize that all the proposals form a coherent body—not inseparable, but mutually reinforcing. We encourage their consideration as such.

GOVERNANCE, CHANGE AND VALUES

Global governance, once viewed primarily as concerned with intergovernmental relationships, now involves not only governments and intergovernmental institutions but also non-governmental organizations (NGOs), citizens' movements, transnational corporations, academia, and the mass media. The emergence of a global civil society, with many movements reinforcing a sense of human solidarity, reflects a large increase in the capacity and will of people to take control of their own lives.

States remain primary actors but have to work with others. The United Nations must play a vital role, but it cannot do all the work. Global governance does not imply world government or world federalism. Effective global governance calls for a new vision, challenging people as well as governments to realize that there is no alternative to working together to create the kind of world they want for themselves and their children. It requires a strong commitment to democracy grounded in civil society.

The changes of the last half-century have brought the global neighborhood nearer to reality—a world in which citizens are increasingly dependent on one another and need to co-operate. Matters calling for global neighborhood action keep multiplying. What happens far away matters much more now.

We believe that a global civic ethic to guide action within the global neighborhood and leadership infused with that ethic are vital to the quality of global governance. We call for a common commitment to core values that all humanity could uphold: respect for life, liberty, justice and equity, mutual respect, caring, and integrity. We further believe humanity as a whole will be best served by recognition of a set of common rights and responsibilities.

It should encompass the right of all people to:

- a secure life;
- equitable treatment;
- an opportunity to earn a fair living and provide for their own welfare;
- the definition and preservation of their differences through peaceful means;
- participation in governance at all levels;
- free and fair petition for redress of gross injustices;
- equal access to information; and
- equal access to the global commons.

At the same time, all people share a responsibility to:

- contribute to the common good;
- consider the impact of their actions on the security and welfare of others;
- promote equity, including gender equity;
- protect the interests of future generations by pursuing sustainable development and safeguarding the global commons;
- preserve humanity's cultural and intellectual heritage;
- be active participants in governance; and
- work to eliminate corruption.

Democracy provides the environment within which the fundamental rights of citizens are best safeguarded, and the most favorable foundation for peace and stability. The world needs, however, to ensure the rights of minorities, and to guard against the ascendance of the military, and of corruption. Democracy is more than just the right to vote in regular elections. And as within nations, so globally, the democratic principle must be respected.

Sovereignty has been the cornerstone of the inter-state system. In an increasingly interdependent world, however, the notions of territoriality, independence, and non-intervention have lost some of their meaning. In certain areas, sovereignty must be exercised collectively, particularly in relation to the global commons. Moreover, the most serious threats to national sovereignty and territorial integrity now often have internal roots.

The principles of sovereignty and non-intervention must be adapted in ways that recognize the need to balance the rights of states with the rights of people, and the interests of nations with the interests of the global neighborhood. It is time also to think about self-determination in the context of a global neighborhood rather than a world of separate states.

Against the backdrop of an emerging global neighborhood and the values that should guide its governance, we explored four specific areas: security, economic interdependence, the United Nations, and the rule of law. In each area we have sought to focus on governance aspects, but these are often inseparable from substantive issues.

PROMOTING SECURITY

The concept of global security must be broadened from the traditional focus on the security of states to include the security of people and the security of the planet. The following six principles should be embedded in international agreements and used as norms for security policies in the new era:

- All people, no less than all states, have a right to a secure existence, and all states have an obligation to protect those rights.
- The primary goals of global security policy should be to prevent conflict and war, and maintain the integrity of the environment and life-support systems of the planet, by eliminating the economic, social, environmental, political, and military conditions that generate threats to the security of people and the planet, and by anticipating and managing crises before they escalate into armed conflicts.
- Military force is not a legitimate political instrument, except in self-defense or under UN auspices.
- The development of military capabilities beyond that required for national defense and support of UN action is a potential threat to the security of people.
- Weapons of mass destruction are not legitimate instruments of national defense.
- The production and trade in arms should be controlled by the international community.

Unprecedented increases in human activity and human numbers have reached the point where their impacts impinge on the basic conditions on which life depends. Action should be taken now to control these activities and keep population growth within acceptable limits so that planetary security is not endangered.

The principle of non-intervention in the domestic affairs of states should not be taken lightly. But it is necessary to assert as well the rights and interests of the international community in situations within individual states in which the security of people is extensively endangered. A global consensus exists today for a UN response on humanitarian grounds in such cases. We propose an amendment to the UN Charter to permit such intervention, but restricting it to cases that in the judgment of a reformed Security Council constitute a violation of the security of people so gross and extreme that it requires an international response on humanitarian grounds.

There should be a new "Right of Petition" for non-state actors to bring situations massively endangering the security of people within states to the attention of the Security Council. The Charter amendment establishing the Right of Petition should also authorize the Security Council to call on parties to an intrastate dispute to settle it through the mechanisms listed in the Charter for the pacific settlement of disputes between states. The Council should be authorized to take enforcement action under Chapter VII if such efforts fail, but only if it determines that intervention is justified under the Charter amendment referred to in the previous paragraph on the grounds of a gross violation of the security of people. Even then, the use of force would be the last resort.

We suggest two measures to improve UN peacekeeping. First, the integrity of the UN command should be respected; for each operation a consultative committee should be set up including representatives of the countries contributing troops. Second, although the principle that countries with a special interest in relation to a conflict should not contribute troops should be upheld, the earlier view that the permanent members of the Security Council should not play an active part in peacekeeping should be discarded.

New possibilities arise for the involvement of regional organizations in conjunction with the UN in resolving conflicts. We support the Secretary-General's plea for making more active use of regional organizations under Chapter VIII of the Charter.

The UN needs to be able to deploy credible and effective peace enforcement units at an early stage in a crisis and at short notice. It is high time that a UN Volunteer Force was established. We envisage a force with a maximum of 10,000 personnel. It would not take the place of preventive action, of traditional peacekeeping forces, or of large-scale enforcement action under Chapter VII of the Charter. Rather, it would fill a gap by giving the Security Council the ability to back up preventive diplomacy with a measure of immediate and convincing deployment on the ground. Its very existence would be a deterrent; it would give support for negotiation and peaceful settlement of disputes.

The international community must provide increased funds for peacekeeping, using some of the resources released by reductions of defense expenditures. The cost of peacekeeping should be integrated into a single annual budget and financed by assessments on all UN member countries, and the peacekeeping reserve fund should be increased to facilitate rapid deployment.

The international community should reaffirm its commitment to progressively eliminate nuclear and other weapons of mass destruction from all nations, and should initiate a ten to fifteen year programme to achieve this goal.

Work towards nuclear disarmament should involve action on four fronts:

- the earliest possible ratification and implementation of existing agreements on nuclear and other weapons of mass destruction;
- the indefinite extension of the Non-Proliferation Treaty;
- the conclusion of a treaty to end all nuclear testing; and
- the initiation of talks among all declared nuclear powers to establish a process to reduce and eventually eliminate all nuclear arsenals.

All nations should sign and ratify the conventions on chemical and biological weapons, thus enabling the world to enter the twenty-first century free of these weapons.

For the first time, the dominant military powers have both an interest in reducing world-wide military capabilities and the ability to do so. The international community should make the demilitarization of global politics an overriding priority.

Donor institutions and countries should evaluate a country's military spending when considering assistance to it. A Demilitarization Fund should be set up to help developing countries reduce their military commitments, and global military spending should be reduced to $500 billion by the end of the decade.

States should undertake immediate negotiation of a convention on the curtailment of the arms trade—including provision for a mandatory arms register and the prohibition of state financing or subsidy of arms exports.

MANAGING ECONOMIC INTERDEPENDENCE

Globalization is in danger of widening the gap between rich and poor. A sophisticated, increasingly affluent world currently coexists with a marginalized global underclass.

The pace of globalization of financial and other markets is outstripping the capacity of governments to provide the necessary framework of rules and cooperative arrangements. There are severe limits to national action to check such polarization within a globalized economy, yet the structures of global governance for pursuing international public policy objectives are underdeveloped .

The time is now ripe to build a global forum that can provide leadership in economic, social, and environmental fields. This should be more representative than the Group of Seven or the Bretton Woods institutions, and more effective than the present UN system. We propose the establishment of an Economic Security Council (ESC) that would meet at high political level. It would have deliberative functions only; its influence will derive from the relevance and quality of its work and the significance of its membership.

The ESC's tasks would be to:

- continuously assess the overall state of the world economy and the interaction between major policy areas;
- provide a long-term strategic policy framework in order to promote stable, balanced and sustainable development; and
- secure consistency between the policy goals of the major international organizations, particularly the Bretton Woods bodies and the World Trade Organization (WTO).

The ESC should be established as a distinct body within the UN family, structured like the Security Council, though not with identical membership and independent of it.

With some 37,000 transnational corporations world-wide, foreign investment is growing faster than trade. The challenge is to provide a framework of rules and order for global competition in the widest sense. The WTO should adopt a strong set of competition rules and a Global Competition Office should be set up to oversee national enforcement efforts and resolve inconsistencies between them.

The decision-making structures of the Bretton Woods institutions must be made more reflective of economic reality; gross domestic product figures based on purchasing power parity should be used to establish national voting strength.

The role of the IMF should be enhanced by enabling it to:

- enlarge its capacity to provide balance-of-payments support through low-conditionality compensatory finance;
- have oversight of the international monetary system and a capacity to ensure that domestic economic policies in major countries are not mutually inconsistent or damaging to the rest of the international community;
- release a new issue of Special Drawing Rights; and
- improve its capacity to support nominal exchange rates in the interest of exchange rate stability.

For some countries, aid is likely to be for many years one of the main ways to escape from a low-income, low-savings, low-investment trap. There is no substitute for a politically realistic strategy to mobilize aid flows and to demonstrate value for money, including co-financing between official aid donors, the private sector, and NGOs with a view to widening the support base.

A false sense of complacency has enveloped the developing-country debt problem. Radical debt reduction is needed for heavily indebted, low-income countries, involving at least implementation of full "Trinidad" terms, including the matter of multilateral debt.

In response to environmental concerns, governments should make maximum use of market instruments, including environmental taxes and traded permits, and adopt the "polluter pays principle" of charging. We support the European Union's carbon tax proposal as a first step towards a system that taxes resource use rather than employment and savings, and urge its wide adoption.

It is time for a consensus on global taxation for servicing the needs of the global neighborhood. A start must be made in establishing schemes of global financing of global purposes, including charges on the use of global resources such as flight-lanes, sea lanes, and ocean fishing areas and the collection of revenues agreed globally and implemented by treaty. An international tax on foreign currency transactions should be explored as one option, as should the creation of an international corporate tax base among multinational companies.

REFORMING THE UNITED NATIONS

We do not believe the UN should be dismantled to make way for a new architecture of global governance. Much of the necessary reform of the United Nations system can be effected without amending the Charter, provided governments are willing. But some Charter amendments are necessary for better global governance.

UN reform must reflect the realities of change, including the new capacity of civil society to contribute to global governance.

Reform of the Security Council is central to reforming the UN system. Permanent membership limited to five countries that derive their primacy from events fifty years ago is unacceptable; so is the veto. To add more permanent members and give them the veto would be regressive. We propose a process of reform in two stages.

First, a new class of five "standing" members should be established to serve until the second stage of the reform process. We envisage two from industrial countries and one each from Africa, Asia, and Latin America. The number of non-permanent members should be raised from ten to thirteen, and the votes required for a decision of the Council from nine to fourteen. To facilitate the phasing out of the veto, the permanent members should enter into a concordat agreeing to forgo its use save in exceptional and overriding circumstances.

The second stage should be a full review of the membership of the Council, including these arrangements, around 2005, when the veto can be phased out, the position of the permanent members reviewed, and account taken of new circumstances—including the growing strength of regional bodies.

The Trusteeship Council should be given a new mandate over the global commons in the context of concern for the security of the planet.

The General Assembly should be revitalized as a universal forum. Regular theme sessions, effective exercise of budgetary authority, and the streamlining of its agenda and procedures should be part of the process of revitalization. We also propose an annual Forum of Civil Society consisting of representatives of organizations to be accredited to the General Assembly as "Civil Society Organizations." It should be convened in the General Assembly Hall sometime before the Annual Session of the Assembly. International civil society should itself be involved in determining its character and functions.

The Right of Petition proposed for promoting the security of people requires the formation of a Council of Petitions—a high-level panel of five to seven persons, independent of governments, to entertain petitions. Its recommendations will go as appropriate to the Secretary-General, the Security Council, or the General Assembly, and allow for action under the Charter.

In the light of experience, the proposed Economic Security Council and our other recommendations, we propose that the UN Economic and Social Council (ECOSOC) should be wound up. The UN system must from time to time shut down institutions that can no longer be justified in objective terms. We believe this to be true also of the United Nations Conference on Trade and Development (UNCTAD) and the United Nations Industrial Development Organization (UNIDO), and propose an in-depth review to this end. Our proposals on these UN bodies are part of the integrated set of proposals we make for improving global economic governance including, notably, the setting up of an Economic Security Council. Balanced governance arrangements will not result if policy leadership is preserved in the hands of a small directorate of countries, while such institutions as UNCTAD set up to correct imbalances are dismantled.

To help put women at the centre of global governance, a post of Senior Adviser on Women's Issues should be created in the Office of the UN Secretary-General, and similar positions established in the specialized agencies.

The UN must assist regionalism and gear itself for the time when regionalism is more ascendant world-wide. Regional bodies should be seen as an important part of a balanced system of global governance. However, the continuing utility of the UN Regional Economic Commissions now needs to be closely examined and their future determined in consultation with the respective regions.

The procedure for appointing the UN Secretary-General should be radically improved, and the term of office should be a single one of seven years. The procedure for selecting the heads of UN specialized agencies, funds, and programmes should also be improved.

STRENGTHENING THE RULE OF LAW WORLD-WIDE

The global neighborhood of the future must be characterized by law and the reality that all, including the weakest, are equal under the law and none, including the strongest, is above it. Our recommendations are directed to strengthening international law and the International Court of Justice in particular.

All member-states of the UN that have not already done so should accept the compulsory jurisdiction of the Court. The Court's chamber procedure should be modified to enhance its appeal to states and to avoid damage to the Court's integrity.

Judges should be appointed for one ten-year term only, and a system introduced to screen potential members for jurisprudential skills and objectivity. The UN Secretary-General should have the right to refer legal aspects of international issues to the Court for advice, particularly in the early stages of disputes.

The Security Council should appoint a distinguished lawyer to provide advice at all relevant stages on the international legal aspects of issues before it. It should also make greater use of the World Court as a source of advisory opinions, to avoid being itself the judge of international law in particular cases.

We do not emphasize formal enforcement measures but, failing voluntary compliance, Security Council enforcement of World Court decisions and other international legal obligations should be pursued under Article 94 of the Charter.

An International Criminal Court should be quickly established with independent prosecutors of the highest calibre and experience.

The International Law Commission, or other appropriate body, should be authorized to explore how international law-making can be expedited.

THE NEXT STEPS

We have made many recommendations, some of them far-reaching. We would like to go one step further by suggesting a process for the consideration of these and similar recommendations.

During the time the Commission has been at work, we have witnessed the currencies of Europe held hostage by forces of speculation themselves out of control. Powerful economies confronted each other on the threshold of trade wars, while marginal ones collapsed. There was ethnic cleansing in the Balkans, a "failed state" in Somalia, and genocide in Rwanda. Nuclear weapons lay unsecured in the former Soviet Union, and neofascism surfaced in the West.

The United Nations faces much greater demands. Its existence is a continuing reminder that all nations form part of one world, though evidence is not lacking of the world's many divisions. Today's interdependencies are compelling people to recognize the unity of the world. People are forced not just to be neighbors but to be good neighbors.

Our report is issued in the year the UN marks a jubilee. It is not tied to that one event or to the UN system alone. It speaks to a longer time and a larger stage, but the UN and its future are a central part of our concerns. It is important that the international community should use the UN's anniversary as an occasion for renewing commitment to the spirit of the Charter and to the internationalism it embodied, and establish a process that can take the world to a higher stage of international cooperation. This process must be centered on the UN but not confined to it.

Ours are not the only recommendations that will be considered in the anniversary year. The variety of reports and studies presenting the case for change and proposing the form it should take reflects wide recognition that change is needed. That itself does not guarantee action to bring about change. The will to change does not exist everywhere. It would be easy for all the effort to promote reform to be stalled by a filibuster or simply by inertia. Or, paradoxically, it could be overwhelmed by the onset of the very dangers that some of the changes proposed are meant to guard against.

We are prompted to recall the vision that drove the process of founding the United Nations and the spirit of innovation that ushered in a new era of global governance. We need that spirit again today.

We fear that if reform is left to normal processes, only piecemeal and inadequate action will result. We look, therefore, to a more deliberate process. The Charter has been amended on four occasions. But revision of the Charter is the final stage in a process of reform and is not required for many of the changes we propose.

The ultimate process has to be intergovernmental and at a high level, giving political imprimaturs to a new world order whose contours are shaped to the designs developed for the anniversary year.

For such a process to have the best prospect of securing agreement on a new system of global governance, there will need to be careful preparation. Civil society must be involved in the preparatory process, which should reach out to even wider sections of society than the processes leading up to recent world conferences. Many views must be examined, and many ideas allowed to contend.

Our recommendation is that the General Assembly should agree to hold a World Conference on Governance in 1998, with its decisions to be ratified and put into effect by 2000. That will allow more than two years for the preparatory process.

Action on all recommendations does not have to await the final conference. Many of the changes proposed do not need an amendment of the Charter. Some changes are already under way. We encourage action on reform at all levels—provided, of course, that ad hoc decisions do not become a substitute for systematic reform through a fully representative forum.

A special responsibility devolves on the non-governmental sector. If our recommendations and those from other sources are worthy of support, international civil society must prevail on governments to consider them seriously. By doing so they would ensure that "WE THE PEOPLES" are the instruments of change to a far greater extent than fifty years ago. We call on international civil society, NGOs, the business sector, academia, the professions, and especially young people to join in a drive for change in the international system.

Governments can be made to initiate change if people demand it. That has been the story of major change in our time; the liberation of women and the environmental movement provide examples. If people are to live in a global neighborhood and live by neighborhood values, they have to prepare the ground. We believe that they are ready to do so.

THE NEED FOR LEADERSHIP

Whatever the dimensions of global governance, however renewed and enlarged its machinery, whatever values give it content, the quality of global governance depends ultimately on leadership. Throughout our work, we have been conscious of the degree to which the realization of our proposals depends on leadership of a high order at all levels.

As the world faces the need for enlightened responses to the challenges that arise on the eve of the new century, we are concerned at the lack of leadership over a wide spectrum of human affairs. At national, regional, and international levels, within communities and in international organizations, in governments and in non-governmental bodies, the world needs credible and sustained leadership.

It needs leadership that is proactive, not simply reactive, that is inspired, not simply functional, that looks to the longer term and future generations for whom the present is held in trust. It needs leaders made strong by vision, sustained by ethics, and revealed by political courage that looks beyond the next election.

This cannot be leadership confined within domestic walls. It must reach beyond country, race, religion, culture, language, life-style. It must embrace a wider human constituency, be infused with a sense of caring for others, a sense of responsibility to the global neighborhood.

To a very particular degree today, the need for leadership is widely felt, and the sense of being bereft of it is the cause of uncertainty and instability. It contributes to a sense of drift and powerlessness. It is at the heart of the tendency everywhere to turn inwards. That is why we have attached so much importance to values, to the substance of leadership and the compulsions of an ethical basis for global governance. A neighborhood without leadership is a neighborhood endangered.

When we talk of the need for leadership we do not mean only at the highest national and international levels. We mean enlightenment at every level—in local and national groups, in parliaments and in the professions, among scientists and writers, in small community groups and large national NGOs, in international bodies of every description, in religious communities, in political parties and citizens' movements, in the private sector and among transnational corporations, and particularly in the media.

A great challenge to leadership today is to harmonize domestic demands for national action and the compulsions of international cooperation. It is not a new challenge, but it has a new intensity as globalization diminishes the capacity to deliver at home and enlarges the need to combine efforts abroad. Enlightened leadership calls for a clear vision of solidarity in the true interest of national well-being—and for political courage in articulating the way the world has changed and why a new spirit of global neighborhood must replace old notions of adversarial states in eternal confrontation.

The alternative is too frightening to contemplate. In a final struggle for primacy—in which each sees virtue in advancing its national self-interest, with states and peoples pitted against each other—there can be no winners. Everyone will lose; selfishness will make genius the instrument of human self-destruction. But the leadership to avert this is not sufficiently evident. The hope must be people—people demanding enlightenment of their leaders, refusing to accept the alternative of humanity at war with itself. And that hope is balanced by the promise of the leadership that future generations will bring.

In a real sense the global neighborhood is the home of future generations; global governance is the prospect of making it better than it is today. But that hope would be a pious one were there not signs that future generations come to the task better equipped than their parents. They bring to the next century less of the baggage of old animosities and adversarial systems accumulated in the era of nation-states.

The new generation knows how close they stand to cataclysms unless they respect the limits of the natural order and care for the earth by sustaining its life-giving qualities. They have a deeper sense of solidarity as people of the planet than any generation before them. They are neighbors to a degree no other generation has been.

ON THAT RESTS OUR HOPE FOR
OUR GLOBAL NEIGHBORHOOD.

THE COMMISSION ON GLOBAL GOVERNANCE

The Commission on Global Governance was established in 1992 in the belief that international developments had created favorable circumstances for strengthening global cooperation to create a more peaceful, just and habitable world for all its people.

The first steps leading to its formation were taken by former West German Chancellor Willy Brandt, who a decade earlier had chaired the Independent Commission on International Development Issues. A meeting he convened in January 1990 asked Ingvar Carlsson (Prime Minister of Sweden), Shridath Ramphal (then Commonwealth Secretary-General) and Jan Pronk (Netherlands Minister for Development Cooperation) to prepare a report on the new prospects for world cooperation.

Some three dozen public figures who met in Stockholm in April 1991 to consider this report proposed, in their Stockholm Initiative on Global Security and Governance, that an international commission should recommend ways by which world security and governance could be improved, given the opportunities created by the end of the cold war for enhanced cooperation.

Willy Brandt, after consulting Gro Harlem Brundtland and Julius Nyerere, who had headed two previous commissions, invited Ingvar Carlsson and Shridath Ramphal to chair the new commission. The Commission, with twenty-eight members all serving in their personal capacity, started work in September 1992.

The Commission held eleven meetings, six in Geneva (where its secretariat was established) and the others in New York, Cuernavaca (Mexico), Tokyo, Brussels, and Visby (Sweden). It commissioned a number of papers; it had discussions with several of their authors, a number of persons from public life, and representatives of many civil society organizations. Discussions on key issues on the Commission's agenda were arranged by the Common Security Forum, the Norwegian Ministry for Foreign Affairs and the Centre for the Study of Global Governance at the London School of Economics. The UN University co-hosted a public symposium with the Commission in Tokyo. Regional consultations with experts were arranged, with the collaboration of local organizations, in San Jose (Costa Rica), Cairo and New Delhi.

Support for the Commission's work was provided by the governments of Canada, Denmark, India, Indonesia, Netherlands, Norway, Sweden, and Switzerland, two UN Trust Funds established by Japan, the Canton of Geneva, the government of Mexico City, the European Commission, the Arab Fund for Economic and Social Development (Kuwait), the MacArthur Foundation, the Carnegie Corporation and the Ford Foundation (all of the United States), the World Humanity Action Trust (United Kingdom), and the Friedrich Ebert Stiftung (Germany).

The Commission decided at an early stage to remain active in efforts to disseminate its report, *Our Global Neighborhood*, and to promote its ideas and recommendations. These will be pursued through speaking engagements, seminars and workshops; work with governments, international organizations, NGOs, the media; and the distribution of material.

The Commission's secretariat will continue to function in order to coordinate this work:

The Commission on Global Governance
Case Postale 184
CH-1211 GENEVA 28
Switzerland
Tel: +41 22 798 2713
Fax: +41 22 798 0147

CO-CHAIRMEN

Ingvar Carlsson (Sweden); Shridath Ramphal (Guyana)

MEMBERS

Ali Alatas (Indonesia); Abdlatif Al-Hamad (Kuwait); Oscar Arias (Costa Rica); Anna Balletbo; (Spain); Kurt Biedenkopf (Germany); Allan Boesak (South Africa); Manuel Camacho Solis (Mexico); Bernard Chidzero (Zimbabwe); Barber Conable (United States); Jacques Delors (France); Jiri Dienstbier (Czech Republic); Enrique Iglesias (Uruguay); Frank Judd (United Kingdom); Hongkoo Lee (Republic of Korea); Wangari Maathai (Kenya); Sadako Ogata (Japan); Olara A. Otunnu (Uganda); I.G. Patel (India); Celina do Amaral Peixoto (Brazil); Jan Pronk (The Netherlands); Qian Jiadong (China); Marie-Angelique Savane (Senegal); Adele Simmons (United States); Maurice Strong (Canada); Brian Urquhart (United Kingdom); Yuli Vorontsov (Russia)

Appendix II

Summary Outline History of World Federalism
Errol E. Harris

The history of the World Federalist movement goes back a long way, even before the beginning of World War II, with numerous people involved all over the world. In the space available here it will not be possible to go into all the detailed ramifications of the movement, nor even to mention all the persons who were active in it and to whom credit should be given in a full-scale account of the history. All that will be attempted here is a summary outline, which, it is to be hoped, will not omit anything of special importance. For what follows I am much indebted, and wish to record thanks, to Harold Bidmead for permission to reproduce material from his book *The Parliament of Man*, to Gerry Krause for details contained in his manuscript *A Call for Action*, to Philip Isely, whose comprehensive knowledge of the movement provided a mine of information, and to Jean-Marie Breton for what he has shared with me in correspondence.

Although the history of federalism may be said to begin in the ancient world, I shall not go back as far as the Peloponnesian League and the Holy Roman Empire. These, in any event, were not federations proper, but rather confederations, little better than alliances between independent states, and in the latter case hardly that. True federations are unions between states which pool their sovereignties, and which divide jurisdiction between the federal and the state governments, investing powers in the former to regulate matters of common concern, while devolving powers to deal with matters purely local to the state governments.

A world federation to ensure perpetual peace was first advocated in 1795 by Immanuel Kant; but he confused federalism with confederalism, by insisting that the federated states should each retain its own sovereignty, apparently failing to notice the contradiction involved. For a long time, however, the idea remained purely academic, until the world crisis of 1938, when Adolf Hitler's aggression against the eastern nations of Europe initiated a process which a year later exploded into the Second World War.

In historical fact, examples of federalism have been provided by Switzerland, the United States of America, the Dominions of Canada and of Australia, and the Indian Republic, but world federation in the full sense of the term has been seriously contemplated only during the current century. A practical political movement in favor of world government reached its peak in the 1940s, when it was more or less sabotaged by diversion into a movement for the reform of the United Nations, a digression that has continued to the present day in parallel with the drive for genuine world government, which has branched out according to different notions of how it should be achieved.

Ever since the end of the First World War, people have sought by some kind of international union to prevent the recurrence of major conflicts. The League of Nations, the first attempt, was a spectacular failure, ending with the outbreak of an even more devastating Second World War. Afterwards the United Nations was set up, described as a "League with teeth." But it has been as unsuccessful as the former body in settling disputes. In fact, its Charter prescribes the means and pretexts for waging war, and the Organization has itself been involved in at least three bloody conflicts. Nuclear arsenals have grown despite the awesome threat involved of mass holocaust, and the solution of global problems is more remote today than it has ever been. The League of Nations and the United Nations, however, were not federations, but were more in the nature of confederations, for both have professedly and practically been based on the principle of national sovereignty of the member states, which is an insuperable bar to federalism proper.

Under the dire stress of the Nazi threat, and Hitler's rapid advance on the Continent, Churchill made an offer to the French of political union with Britain. The offer was not accepted, but many statesmen and thinkers realized quite early on that the root cause of war was the sovereign independence of nations, and advocated, both theoretically and practically, the pooling of sovereignty in federal union as the only effective cure for the evil.

Even before all this, in the United States a campaign for world government had been commenced by Lola Maverick Lloyd and Rosika Schwimmer, and in England James Avery Joyce initiated the World Citizens movement, paralleled in the USA at the instigation of M. Thomas Chou. After the war, in Britain and the United States, as well as in several Continental countries, World Federalist movements appeared. In 1947, the World Movement for World Federal Government was formed, which thereupon held its first World Congress in Montreux, Switzerland.

Before the outbreak of the Second World War, just after the crisis days of Munich, Clarence Streit produced *World Government or Anarchy? Our Urgent Need for World Order*, followed later by *Union Now: A Proposal for a Federal Union of the Free*; and W. B. Curry published *The Case for Federal Union*.

There were several other writers proposing similar ideas, in particular, H. N. Brailsford (*The Federal Idea*), Sir William Beveridge (*Peace by Federation?*), and Lord Lothian (*The Ending of Armageddon*). After the war, many more books advocating world federation appeared, and a number of politicians made public statements in favor of progress towards that end. Among them, as recorded by Harold Bidmead, some of the more notable were (besides Lord Lothian and Sir William Beveridge): Sir Archibald Sinclair, Sir Alfred (later Viscount) Duff Cooper, Arthur Greenwood, Herbert Morrison, Harold Nicholson, and Lieut.-Col. Moore Brabazon. A group of British Members of Parliament formed an Association of Parliamentarians for World Federation. At much the same time, a movement was started in Great Britain, which called itself "Federal Union," advocating a democratic federation of free peoples to administer matters of common interest, while leaving to the member governments affairs that were purely national. The intention was that this federation should eventually embrace all the nations of the world. Inspired by Streit's book, a similar organization developed in the United States, which collaborated closely with Federal Union in Britain, and additional branches were formed in many other countries around the world.

Immediately after the war, the federal idea caught on quite readily, and appealed to large numbers of people, both politicians and the general public. The membership of Federal Union grew apace, Curry's book attracted much attention and sold 100,000 copies within a year, and prominent persons made public statements recommending federation. In Britain, the idea was publicly advocated by many government figures, who had been conducting the war effort in coalition.

Sir William (later Lord) Beveridge, Director of the London School of Economics and technical adviser to the Ministry of Labour, maintained that "Federalism carried beyond national boundaries presents itself each day more clearly as the means by which international order can be combined with the preservation of national cultures and individualities."

The Secretary of State for Air, Sir Archibald Sinclair, declared: "An essential principle of modern social policy is that we are all members of one another, and the same principle must be applied in the life of nations if we are to succeed in outlawing war. The federation principle supplies an obvious line of approach."

The Minister of Information at the time, the Rt. Hon. Alfred Duff Cooper, said: "We hope to see in Europe a unity based on the free will and consent of the various nations who will pool their resources, share their responsibilities and combine their armed forces while retaining their own liberty."

Arthur Greenwood, War Minister without Portfolio, asserted: "In our view a lasting peace is obtainable by the establishment of a commonwealth of states, whose collective authority shall transcend, in its proper sphere, the sovereign rights of individual nations."

Similar views were expressed by other Cabinet Ministers, including Lieut.-Col. Moore-Brabazon (who stated in a broadcast that individual states should never again be permitted exclusive ownership or control of air forces), Herbert Morrison, R. A. Butler, and Harold Nicholson.

In the United States in December 1941, following the attack on Pearl Harbor by the Japanese, advocates of federation of the democracies advertised in the *New York Times*, urging the President to submit a program to Congress for constitutional union with the other democratic nations. Among them were Justice Owen Roberts of the Supreme Court and Mr. Harold Ickes, Secretary of the Interior. At that time, a survey of public opinion in the USA, conducted by the magazine *Fortune*, showed that 30 million Americans were in favor of a union of the democracies which would keep the peace after the war.

Federal Union, prompted by Henry Usborne, MP, and Harold S. Bidmead, set out to establish a Federation of Federal Union Movements, which became the World Movement for World Federal Government which, as mentioned above, held its first Congress in Montreux, Switzerland, in 1947. In the same year, a Parliamentary Committee of the House of Commons in England, chaired by Henry Usborne, produced a report entitled "The Plan in Outline," proposing a Crusade for World Government. The report was endorsed by 78 members of the United Kingdom Parliament (besides the 16 members of the committee). This marked the inception of the movement calling itself Parliamentarians for World Federation. The plan was sponsored by Sir William Beveridge and Sir John Boyd-Orr, while Winston Churchill gave his tacit approval.

The first and main item of the Plan was to organize a World Constituent Assembly consisting of delegates elected from as many countries as possible, each representing a constituency of a million voters. To ensure high quality representatives, it was proposed to pay the delegates from funds voluntarily donated, on the same scale as Members of Parliament. Once drafted, the Constitution was to be ratified by national governments and would come into effect if ratified by legislatures representing at least half of the world's population. The departments of government to be allotted to the federal body were to be Defense, Foreign Relations, and Atomic Energy, with power to raise money (from federal taxation) for its own operation. Everything else was to be reserved to the national administrations.

In the spring of the following year (1948), Henry Usborne visited the United States, where he became confident that at least 10 delegates would be elected to the Constituent Assembly by some 30 million voters. On his return he predicted that permanent peace would be assured by 1955. Usborne had addressed meetings in all the major cities in the United States, and he reported that "the idea had caught on," and had captured the imagination of the audiences in all of these cities. The emergency Committee of American Atomic Scientists, headed by Albert Einstein, who remained insistent that world federal government was essential if a calamitous nuclear conflict was to be prevented, supported the plan with a large financial donation, and there was an encouraging response from a number of other countries, apart from Britain where support was estimated at 80% of the electorate. Similar enthusiasm was displayed in Belgium, Germany,

Australia, New Zealand, and (although somewhat less) Denmark. In the British general election, Henry Usborne stood as a candidate advocating world government, and won with a majority of 24,000 in a constituency casting 44,000 votes. Twelve Scottish MPs expressed themselves in favor of the World Constituent Assembly, and six of the twelve candidates standing in London boroughs, who had given their support to the idea, were elected.

In the United States, Fyke Farmer led a movement in the state of Tennessee, and secured a resolution passed by both houses of the Tennessee state legislature (with only one dissenting vote in the Senate) to send delegates to the World Constituent Assembly. Action of the same kind was taken in twenty-six other American states, as well as in France, West Germany, Holland, Belgium and Italy. Referenda in four American states showed large majorities in favor of world government, and six passed resolutions directing the US Congress to consider amending the Constitution to enable the United States to join a world federation. At the same time, a movement to transform the United Nations into a World Federation was gaining ground in America, with the approval of 111 Congressmen. The United World Federalists organization came into being, and commenced drafting a World Federal Constitution to be ratified by the United Nations.

A number of societies supporting the peace movement joined with the World Unity Movement in London to set up an International Liaison Committee for World Government under the direction of Gerry Krause (a Jewish refugee from Nazism), who started the international newsletter *Across Frontiers* to propagate the idea of a People's World Assembly to draft a World Constitution.

In the summer of 1948, at the instigation of the United World Federalists, a Steering Committee was set up to organize preparations for a People's World Convention at Geneva in 1950. The United World Federalists held a Congress at Stockholm, under the presidency of Boyd-Orr, in 1949, but by that time, the Steering Committee had not yet met. It was decided that a meeting should be held and that its organization should be in the hands of Fyke Farmer. Farmer then toured a number of European countries trying to recruit support for the Convention, while Krause pressed on with his efforts to propagate the idea through the pages of *Across Frontiers*. Attempts to enlist the support of the Soviet Union proved abortive, and difficulties were encountered in finding a venue for the Steering Committee. Eventually Krause found support in Belgium, and the meeting was held in Ghent, at the Hotel de la Poste, with 150 delegates (including a number of eminent international personalities) representing over 20 countries. At this meeting an Executive Committee and sub-committees were elected to organize elections and propaganda, and arrangements for the Geneva Convention got under way. Twenty-five thousand copies of a report on the Ghent Conference were printed in English, French, German and Italian, and were widely distributed. Detailed press releases were published by the Belgian newspapers, and there was considerable international press coverage.

Krause collected a number of influential people to form a new International Liaison Committee, including Sir John Boyd-Orr, Lord Beveridge, Hamai Shinto (the mayor of Hiroshima), the American physical chemist Harold Urey, Chancellor Robert Hutchins of the University of Chicago, Dr. Nnamdi Azikiwe of Nigeria, G. Chiostergi (Vice-President of the Italian Parliament), and many others recruited from some fifty or more countries. Meanwhile, Farmer had been trying to persuade the other states of the United States to elect delegates, and Usborne attempted to introduce a Private Bill for an analogous purpose into the House of Commons. Neither was successful, and in the end, besides the Tennessee delegates, only one other was elected to the Convention, Professor Eyo Ita from Eastern Nigeria.

The People's World Convention eventually met in the Palais Electoral in Geneva on December 30, 1950. Although there were only four elected delegates, the meeting was attended by more than 500 representatives from 47 countries. Groups of parliamentarians came from the United Kingdom, France, Italy, Belgium, Holland, Denmark, Sweden, and Finland. There were even participants from Yugoslavia and from two countries behind the Iron Curtain (Poland and Hungary). Congratulatory messages were read from Einstein, Boyd-Orr (who was not himself in attendance), Pandit Nehru, and the Partisans of Peace in Soviet Russia, as well as encouraging messages from trade union leaders in Haiti, Vietnam, and Brazil.

Clearly, at this time there was keen worldwide interest in the Federalist movement, but it was not long before a significant change occurred, as will presently be noted, and the whole idea faded into the background of political thinking. Even the Geneva Convention had little impact, and the direction of effort was soon to be diverted.

The Convention proceedings continued for seven days, during which a large number of resolutions were debated, some of them of substantial importance, but others little more than frivolous. Proposals were made for the election of delegates to future Conventions, but no clear agreement was reached. Attempts to draft a Constitution met with difficulties and disagreements, and nothing definite emerged there as well. The participants were eager and expectant, but the final result was sadly minimal. A Committee of Continuation was elected, to organize another meeting in Paris to be held in November of the following year.

The whole objective of the Paris meeting was altered by Krause, even before it came to pass. He decided that a change of tactics was necessary and that the movement should now advocate a popularly elected Second Chamber for the United Nations. This was a diversion which was subsequently to debilitate the whole enterprise toward world government. The new proposal was labeled UN+P, and the Paris Convention deteriorated into a public demonstration outside the Palais Chaillot (where a United Nations meeting was in progress) to protest against the failure of the Secretary-General, Trygve Lie, to respond to an invitation to address the Convention, and to display the new banner, UN+P. The demonstration was dispersed by the Paris police, and subsequent attempts to affix the UN+P banner to the statue of Marshal Foch (the hero of Verdun) resulted in arrests and prosecutions—although the ringleading German student involved was let off with a caution. In the end, all that was achieved was the distribution of leaflets and a certain amount of press publicity. The whole series of events excited dismay, distaste, and opposition among the various Federalist movements in the United States, France, and Britain, and led to a permanent rift between Farmer and Krause. The Paris Convention went ahead with reduced attendance, but achieved little besides condemnation of the methods used by Gerry Krause.

Krause, after some speaking engagements at rallies in Germany, resigned from the secretaryship of the World People's Convention, handed over *Across Frontiers* to Philip Isely, and went off to Nigeria to pursue various industrial projects. Although these projects were successful, he eventually abandoned them and retired to Thailand.

Public opinion meanwhile had become diverted by other considerations. European federalists turned their attention to European Union, while elsewhere, especially in America, the intensification of hostility between the Western countries and the Soviet Union, and the emergence of the Cold War, prompted doubts about the whole conception of world federation. The Governor of Tennessee repealed the law which had authorized the election of delegates, and similar laws that had been drafted elsewhere were never enacted.

How could it be possible, people asked, for the Western democracies to federate with communist dictatorships such as those of the Soviets and China? It is ironic that as the world situation became more desperate, and the threat of a universal nuclear holocaust ever more imminent, the one means of averting disaster, the abolition of national sovereignties and the establishment of world government, lost its appeal.

But the Federalist movement was by no means dead. The World Federalist Union continued in the United States, and the Association of World Federalists in Britain and on the Continent. The Campaign for World Government was active under its secretary, Georgia Lloyd (daughter of Lola Maverick), in collaboration with Students for Federal World Government, operating from Northwestern University under the direction of Professor Paul Schilpp. Perhaps more important than all the rest, the World Constitution and Parliament Association, led by its Secretary-General, Philip Isely, persisted, not simply in discussing and advocating world government, but in pressing on with the practical work of convening a Constituent Assembly and drafting a Constitution. We shall return to this development presently. First, something must be said about some other aspects of the Federalist movement.

In 1948, Garry Davis, an American by birth, interrupted the proceedings of the United Nations General Assembly by attempting to appeal for world government. He was removed by security guards before he could voice more than his opening formula. He had previously camped outside the Palais de Chaillot in an attempt to publicize his cause. In 1949, he addressed a mass meeting in the Vélodrome d'Hiver, followed by another in the Salle Playel in Paris, to both of which more than a thousand people came. Albert Einstein and Sir John (later Lord) Boyd-Orr sent messages of support, as well as several British Members of Parliament. Albert Camus and Andre Breton were with him on the platform. Declaring himself to be World Citizen No. 1, he tore up his US passport and issued himself with a World Citizen Identity Card, which he thereafter presented to customs authorities wherever he traveled. All and sundry were invited to register as World Citizens and to acquire similar identity cards. So began the World Citizen Movement which continues to this day.

Garry Davis, unfortunately, apart from the publication of *World Citizen News*, has virtually given up any attempt to organize his movement. He simply declares that world government already exists, presumably on the strength of the establishment of the so-called "World Service Authority," an office which registers World Citizens and issues World Citizen Identity Cards, World Passports, and World Birth Certificates to those who apply. Meanwhile, Davis himself sits more or less in splendid isolation, giving no support to the other world federalist movements which work in a more practical way to bring about their aim.

Meanwhile, Jean-Marie Breton, a French jurist and scientist, in conjunction with such individuals as Harold Bidmead, heads a mundialist movement that also registers World Citizens, and aims to convene a Constituent Assembly to draft a World Constitution which will be popularly elected by registered World Citizens. The first 100,000 registered World Citizens elected 20 delegates to what they called the "Peoples' Congress," to be augmented as more people register. It is this Peoples' Congress that is intended eventually to elect a World Constituent Assembly to draft a World Constitution. The idea of a Peoples' Congress was initiated in 1957 by Alfred Rodrigues-Brent, Jaques Savary, and Maurice Cosyn, and it has continued to grow. Eight elections have so far been held, each electing eight delegates. It is envisaged that the Constituent Assembly will be composed of constitutional and other jurists, social scientists, educators, and physical scientists drawn from a wide variety of countries.

This movement has adopted Esperanto as its official language, while it circulates its propaganda in as many of the major languages as it can. It is now spearheaded by a group that calls itself "4M": the name in Esperanto being Mondo Movado de Mondanistaj Militantoj (in English it is "W3M": World Movement of Mundialist Militants). It describes itself as a nonviolent, pacifist, cooperative acting group from many countries on all continents, and as open to any registered World Citizen.

One group of World Citizens has formed the World Citizen Diplomats, which has organized conferences to discuss and advance international peace and understanding, and has sent a group of "ambassadors" around the world in an "International Peace Caravan" to foster its ideas. These ambassadors are to organize meetings with the ordinary people in as many countries in the world as possible to discuss, in two-day seminars, the global problems confronting humanity and the means to their solution, with the overall aim of organizing a worldwide demonstration of unity on the first day of the second millennium, at which will be declared a new era of peace.

Under the inclusive banner of World Citizens, a number of minor organizations have come together, including the World Citizen Assembly started by Lucile Green. Some of these work for reform of the United Nations, either by adding to it a second assembly popularly elected as an advisory body to the General Assembly, or an assembly of parliamentarians from the member nations in a similar capacity, or both. Other organizations, having given up on United Nations reform, work more directly for federal world government. All these associations have more recently been represented in a coalition, presided over by Ross Smyth, a Canadian, which calls itself the World Government Organizations Coalition, which issues a periodical (*News and Views*), and which works towards cooperation and unity among the various Federalist societies.

Meanwhile, a considerable body of literature has grown up arguing for and advocating world government. Even before the writings of Clarence Streit and W. B. Curry, as early as 1915, A. O. Crozier produced *Nation of Nations: The Way to Permanent Peace: A Supreme Constitution for the Government of Governments*. O. Newfang produced *The Road to World Peace: A Federation of the Nations* in 1924, and *World Federation* in 1939, followed by *World Government* in 1942. Lord Lothian's book, *The Ending of Armageddon*, appeared in 1939. Lionel Curtis had published *Civitas Dei* in 1938, and three years later *The Way to Peace*, to be followed in 1945 by *World War: Its Cause and Cure*. In 1939, *The Federal Idea*, by H. N. Brailsford, appeared; and in 1941, Barbara Wooton's *Socialism and Federation. The World in Union*, by J. S. Hoyland, was published in 1940, and there followed a veritable spate of books on the same topic: G. A. Borgese, *Foundations of the World Republic*; Jean-Marie Breton, *l'Emergence du Droit Mundial*; B. B. Ferencz and K. Keyes, *Planethood*; J. E. Johnson, *Federal World Government*; E. Junger, *Der Weltstaat, Organismus und Organisation*; E. E. Harris, *The Survival of Political Man*, then 16 years later, *Annihilation and Utopia*, and more recently, *One World or None: A Prescription for Survival*; A. M. Lilienthal, *Which Way to World Government*; M. Lipsky, *Never Again War: The Case for World Government*; E. L. Millard, *Freedom in a Federal World*; R. B. Perry, *One World in the Making*; H. Pinheiro de V., *The World State, or the New Order of Common Sense*; E. Reves, *An Anatomy of Peace*; J. B. Selander, *World Union Now*; H. Wofford, *It's Up to Us: Federal World Government in Our Time*; E. Wynner, *World Federal Government: Why? What? How?*; R. J. Glossop, *World Federation? A Critical Analysis of World Government*, and J. A. Yunker, *World Union on the Horizon: The Case for Supernational Federation*. And these do not exhaust the list.

At the same time, numerous draft constitutions have been composed. M. Breton claims that there have been over a hundred and fifty, but mention need only be made of the more important: namely, R. M. Hutchins' *Preliminary Draft of a World Constitution*, Noble P. Bassett's *Constitution of the United*

Nations of the World, and T. C. Breitner's *World Constitution: A Study on the Legal Framework of a World Federation*. But the most significant, because of the way in which it came into being, is the Constitution for the Federation of Earth, the product of many years' consultative work in a World Constituent Assembly convened by the World Constitution and Parliament Association, the course of whose development must now be recounted.

The World Constitution and Parliament Association is an organization which owes its existence and progress almost entirely to the untiring efforts of Philip and Margaret Isely, who have spent considerable amounts of money, virtually all their time, and have begrudged no effort in organizing and forwarding its activities worldwide. Together with two others, in 1958, they decided to call a World Constitutional Convention, and circulated a call for delegates worldwide, requesting both the national governments and peoples in every country to send representatives. In the following two years, having set up a Committee for a World Constitutional Convention, organizers were sent around the world to garner support and circulate an agreement, which was signed by a great many prominent leaders, to further the project. In 1961, a definitive call to the World Constitutional Convention was adopted and issued. It was endorsed by many persons, including the heads of the governments of Costa Rica, Nigeria, Senegal, Sierra Leone, and Pakistan. A first Preparatory Congress was held in Denver, Colorado, two years later, with delegates from five continents, and another call to the Constitutional Convention was publicly issued and circulated for more signatures and more widespread response. In 1965, a second Preparatory Congress assembled in Milan, Italy, to formulate an outline, on the basis of alternative choices, for debate and drafting of a World Constitution. It was agreed that a Peoples' World Parliament should also be convened and should meet concurrently with the Convention. A third Preparatory Congress met in 1967, and decided to convene the Convention in the following year, whether or not any government delegates were sent to it. Three hundred Peoples' delegates were pledged, and in 1968, the first working sessions of the Peoples' World Convention and the World Constitutional Convention took place at Interlaken, Switzerland, and at Wolfach, Germany, with 200 delegates from 27 countries on five continents. The work of drafting a Constitution began at this stage.

An emergency Council of World Trustees having been elected, it met at Santa Barbara, California, to formulate a strategy for Reclaiming the Earth for Humanity, and issued the first Decree for the Protection of Life, outlawing nuclear weapons. It also drew up directions for a Commission drafting the World Constitution. This Commission, consisting of four persons, worked for two months in 1972, and produced an almost complete draft of a Constitution. During the following year the draft was finished and then printed and circulated worldwide for comment, together with a call for a second session in 1977 of what was now designated the World Constituent Assembly. In 1975, the comments on the first draft were collected and compiled, and the Drafting Commission met again in the following year. They completed a new draft and circulated it, then the second session of the Constituent Assembly took place as planned at Innsbruck, Austria, where the Constitution was debated, paragraph by paragraph, amended, and finally adopted and signed by 138 delegates from 25 countries on six continents. The Assembly issued a call for the ratification of the Constitution by all nations and peoples of the Earth, and copies were sent to the General Assembly of the United Nations and to all national governments. It was also circulated worldwide for consideration, debate and ratification before the third session of the World Constituent Assembly was held in January, 1979, in Colombo, Sri Lanka, where a declaration was drawn up defining the rights of all people to convene an Assembly, draft a Constitution, and obtain ratification. An appeal for ratification was made and issued to all national parliaments.

In 1981, the World Constitution and Parliament Association met at New Delhi in India and issued a call for the Provisional World Parliament to meet in the following year under the terms of Article 19 of the Constitution for the Federation of Earth (as it now came to be called). One hundred and fifty prominent persons were enrolled as honorary sponsors. The first session of the Provisional World Parliament duly met at Brighton, England, as planned, the delegates coming from 25 countries on six continents. The Parliament passed five Legislative Acts to establish a World Disarmament Agency, to organize World Economic Development, and to define the ownership of Oceans and Seabeds. It also set up a Graduate School of World Problems, and a system of World Courts. The First District Provisional World Court was organized in Los Angeles to take up the case of outlawing nuclear weapons.

Plans to hold further sessions of the Provisional World Parliament in the Sudan and Nigeria were thwarted by military coups, but a second session assembled in New Delhi in 1985, was opened by the President of India and presided over by the Speaker of Lok Sabha. Three more Legislative Acts were adopted for an Emergency Earth Rescue Administration, for World Government Funding, and for a Commission on Terrorism. Yet a third session of the Provisional Parliament was held in 1987 at Miami Beach, Florida, in which three more World Legislative Acts were passed, for a Global Finance System, for Environmental Protection, and for the promotion of Hydrogen Energy.

During the following year, a plan was launched for many other organizations to collaborate in preparation for the next session of the World Constituent Assembly, and 150 joined the Preparatory Committee. Two meetings of the WCPA were held in New York with United Nations ambassadors, to explain the work of the Association and to distribute copies of the Constitution. The list of honorary sponsors was reconfirmed and further expanded. A call for delegates to a fourth session of the Constituent Assembly was issued. The government of Egypt agreed to host the meeting, but the outbreak of the Gulf War prevented the invitation from being accepted, and the venue was changed, somewhat abruptly, to Troia, Portugal, where the Assembly met in May, 1991. The delegates adopted 59 amendments to the Constitution, and set afoot a campaign for ratification, appealing to all peoples and governments. Subsequently, the Global Ratification and Election Network was established, which as of 1997 had been joined by more than 1000 non-governmental organizations in 115 countries.

A call was issued to a fourth session of the Provisional World Parliament to be held in Innsbruck in 1996; but the Austrian government, chiefly by delaying tactics, made difficulties about issuing visas to most of the delegates. The meeting had to be postponed and the place was changed to Andorra, which requires no visas. Nevertheless, to reach Andorra, many delegates had to acquire French or Spanish visas, and these were not granted. A rump meeting was held in Barcelona of those who were able to enter the country, and a Manifesto was issued for ownership by the World Government of oceans, seabeds, Antarctica, and the Moon. It was decided to proceed with arrangements for a fifth session in 1997, and the Government of the Congo offered its Palace of Parliament as the venue for the meeting.

The World Constitution and Parliament Association is unique among Federalist organizations in that it is the only one that has, over the past 40 years, continuously taken practical steps to attempt to construct machinery for the establishment of an operative world government. That is why its activities have been of particular significance, even though they have been, thus far, routinely disparaged and/or ignored by the great majority of the world's population. The World Constituent Assembly has not been popularly elected, but until a Constitution has been approved, defining the method of election, it cannot have been. On the other hand, its delegates have responded to a universal invitation and have been drawn from a wide variety of peoples, not only from those of the developed world but equally from those of the so-called Third World. The Assembly has thus been truly international and representative of many peoples in all the inhabited continents. Among its delegates, there have been some very distinguished lawyers, constitutional and other, as well as highly qualified professional political theorists and parliamentarians. The Constitution is a comprehensive document, carefully thought out, and it has been thoroughly discussed and debated. It is based on fundamental democratic principles and establishes democratic procedures. It provides for special sessions of the World Parliament, immediately on becoming operative, and at regular intervals thereafter, to consider constitutional amendments, if and as thought necessary by a sufficient majority. It is offered for adoption and ratification by the free choice of all individuals and organizations. If so ratified, it would be thoroughly democratic.

The World Federalist movement, however, has not concerted its efforts in a single direction. Apart from the World Citizens Assembly, 4M, and WCPA, other groups have developed. One advocates Federation of the Democracies (FEDEM), insisting that democracy is the paramount condition for world federation and seeking, therefore, to exclude (at least temporarily, until they have been reformed) any undemocratic regimes. Another, supported by some members of the World Citizens Assembly, agitates for a popularly elected Second Assembly to be added to the United Nations in an advisory capacity to the General Assembly. This is led by Harry Lerner and Jeffrey Segall, who have launched a series of meetings designated Conferences for a More Democratic United Nations (CAMDUN). The World Federalist Movement advocates a UN Parliamentary Assembly elected by national legislatures; and yet another splinter group calls itself the Action Coalition for Global Change (ACGC). Such moves are held to be intermediate steps toward world federation, some certainly involving amendment of the United Nations Charter, and others thought to be possible under its existing provisions. More radical Federalists, however, assert that nothing short of the replacement of the United Nations Charter by a World Federal Constitution can ensure either world peace or effective implementation of measures to preserve the planetary environment.

This dissipation of effort, not to mention finances, can hardly advance the cause of world government in the immediate future. Disunity among World Federalists plays into the hands of those who have a vested interest (or believe they do) in maintaining the status quo. Although it is obvious that the World Federalist movement has far to go before it will be within sight of success, the large volume of thought and effort in the cause of world government throughout the 20th century clearly manifest a fundamental human aspiration toward worldwide political unity—an aspiration which hopefully will finally be realized in the dawning years of the 21st century.

For Further Reading

Agar, Herbert, and the Committee of Fifteen. *The City of Man: A Declaration on World Democracy*. New York: Viking Press, 1941.

Allott, Philip. *Eunomia: New Order for a New World*. New York: Oxford University Press, 1990.

Alting von Geusau, Frans A. M. *European Perspectives on World Order*. Leyden: A. W. Sijthoff, 1975.

Armstrong, James D., and Lorna Lloyd. *From Versailles to Maastricht: International Organization in the Twentieth Century*. New York: St. Martin's Press, 1996.

Arnold, Guy. *World Government by Stealth: The Future of the United Nations*. London: Macmillan, 1997.

Banks, Michael, and John W. Burton, eds. *Conflict in World Society: A New Perspective on International Relations*. New York: St. Martin's Press, 1984.

Baratta, Joseph P. *Strengthening the United Nations: A Bibliography on U.N. Reform and World Federalism*. Westport, CT: Greenwood Press, 1987.

Barker, Ernest. *Principles of Social and Political Theory*. Oxford: Clarendon Press, 1951.

Bassett, Noble P. *Constitution of the United Nations of the World*. Boston: Christopher, 1944.

Bennett, Alvin LeRoy. *International Organizations: Principles and Issues*, 6th ed. Englewood Cliffs, NJ: Prentice-Hall, 1995.

Beres, Louis Rene. *Apocalypse: Nuclear Catastrophe in World Politics*. Chicago: University of Chicago Press, 1982.

Beres, Louis Rene, and Harry R. Targ, eds. *Planning Alternative World Futures: Values, Methods and Models*. New York: Praeger, 1975.

Bidmead, Harold S. *The Parliament of Man: The Federation of the World*. Barnstaple: Patton, 1992.

Borgese, Giuseppe A. *Foundations of the World Republic*. Chicago: University of Chicago Press, 1953.

Brailsford, Henry N. *The Federal Idea*. London: Federal Union, 1941.

Breitner, Thomas C. *World Constitution: A Study on the Legal Framework of a World Federation*. Berkeley, CA: Author, 1963.

Breton, Jean-Marie. *l'Emergence du Droit Mondial.* Paris: Club Humaniste, 1993.

Brown, Lester R., et al. *The State of the World: The Worldwatch Institute Report on Progress toward a Sustainable Society.* New York: W. W. Norton, annual since 1984.

Brown, Seyom. *International Relations in a Changing Global System: Toward a Theory of the World Polity.* Boulder, CO: Westview Press, 1992.

Bull, Hedley. *The Anarchical Society: A Study of Order in World Politics,* 2nd ed. New York: Columbia University Press, 1995.

Childers, Erskine, and Brian Urquhart. *A World in Need of Leadership: Tomorrow's United Nations.* Uppsala, Sweden: Dag Hammerskjold Foundation, 1990.

Clark, Grenville, and Louis B. Sohn. *World Peace through World Law,* 2nd rev. ed. Cambridge: Harvard University Press, 1960.

Claude, Inis L. *States and the Global System: Politics, Law and Organization.* New York: St. Martin's Press, 1988.

————. *Swords into Plowshares: The Problems and Progress of International Organizations.* New York: Random House, 1964.

Cleveland, Harlan. *Birth of a New World: An Open Moment for International Leadership.* San Francisco: Jossey-Bass, 1993.

————. *The Third Try at World Order: U.S. Policy for an Interdependent World.* Philadelphia: World Affairs Council, 1976.

Collingwood, Robin George. *The New Leviathan, or, Man, Society, Civilization and Barbarism.* Oxford: Clarendon Press, 1942.

Corbett, Percy E. *World Government Proposals before Congress.* New Haven: Yale Institute of International Studies, 1950.

Cousins, Norman. *In Place of Folly.* New York: Harper, 1962.

Cox, Robert W. *Approaches to World Order.* New York: Cambridge University Press, 1996.

Crozier, Alfred Owen. *League of Nations: Shall It Be an Alliance or a Nation of Nations? (It Must Be One or the Other!)* New York: Lecauver Press, 1919.

————. *Nation of Nations: A Supreme Constitution for the Government of Governments.* Cincinnati, OH: Stewart and Kidd, 1915.

Curry, William B. *The Case for Federal Union.* Harmondsworth, England: Penguin, 1939.

Curtis, Lionel. *Civitas Dei (World Order),* 2nd rev. ed. London: George Allen and Unwin, 1950.

————. *World War: Its Cause and Cure.* London: Oxford University Press, 1946.

————. *The Way to Peace.* London: Oxford University Press, 1944.

Davis, Garry. *World Government, Ready or Not!* Sorrento, ME: Juniper Ledge, 1984.

————. *The World Is My Country.* New York: Putnam, 1961.

Desai, Meghnad, and Paul Redfern, eds. *Global Governance: Ethics and Economics of the World Order.* New York: Pinter, 1995.

Dewitt, David, David Haglund, and John Kirton, eds. *Building a New Global Order: Emerging Trends in International Security.* New York: Oxford University Press, 1993.

Diehl, Paul F., ed. *The Politics of Global Governance: International Organizations in an Interdependent World.* Boulder, CO: Lynne Rienner, 1997.

————, ed. *The Politics of International Organization: Patterns and Insights.* Chicago: Dorsey Press, 1989.

Dilloway, James. *Is World Order Evolving? An Adventure into Human Potential.* New York: Pergamon Press, 1986.

Duguit, Leon. *Traité de Droit Constitutionnel,* 2nd ed. Paris: Boccard, 1921.

Dunn, John M. *Contemporary Crisis of the Nation-State?* Washington DC: U.S. Institute of Peace Press, 1994.

Eaton, Howard O., et al. *The Coming Structure of World Government.* Norman: University of Oklahoma Press, 1944.

Ekins, Paul. *A New World Order: Grassroots Movements for Global Change.* New York: Routledge, 1992.

Fahey, Joseph, and Richard Armstrong, eds. *A Peace Reader: Essential Readings on War, Justice, Non-Violence and World Order.* New York: Paulist Press, 1992.

Falk, Richard A. *On Humane Governance: Toward a New Global Politics.* University Park: Pennsylvania State University Press, 1995.

———. *Explorations at the Edge of Time: The Prospects for World Order.* Philadelphia: Temple University Press, 1992.

———. *A Study of Future Worlds.* New York: Free Press, 1975.

Falk, Richard A., and Robert C. Johansen, eds. *The Constitutional Framework of World Peace.* Albany: State University of New York Press, 1993.

Ferencz, Benjamin B. *A Common Sense Guide to World Peace.* Dobbs Ferry, NY: Oceana Publications, 1985.

Ferencz, Benjamin B., and Ken Keyes, Jr. *Planethood: The Key to Your Survival and Prosperity*, rev. ed. Coos Bay, OR: Vision Books, 1991.

Gibson, John S. *International Organization, Constitutional Law, and Human Rights.* New York: Praeger, 1991.

Glossop, Ronald J. *Confronting War: An Examination of Humanity's Most Pressing Problem*, 3rd ed. Jefferson, NC: McFarland, 1994.

———. *World Federation? A Critical Analysis of Federal World Government.* Jefferson, NC: McFarland, 1993.

Gore, Al. *Earth in the Balance: Ecology and the Human Spirit.* Boston: Houghton Mifflin, 1992.

Granotier, Bernard. *Pour le gouvernnement mondial.* Paris: Flammarian, 1984.

Guehenno, Jean-Marie. *The End of the Nation-State.* Minneapolis: University of Minnesota Press, 1995.

Hamilton, Alexander, John Jay, and James Madison. *The Federalist Papers.* First published 1787-1789.

Harris, Errol E. *One World or None: A Prescription for Survival.* Atlantic Highlands, NJ: Humanities Press, 1993.

———. *Annihilation and Utopia: The Principles of International Politics.* London: George Allen and Unwin, 1966.

———. *The Survival of Political Man: A Study in the Principles of International Order.* Johannesburg: Witwatersrand University Press, 1950.

Heater, Derek B. *World Citizenship and Government: Cosmopolitan Ideas in the History of Western Political Thought.* New York: St. Martin's Press, 1996.

Hemleben, Sylvester J. *Plans for World Peace through Six Centuries.* Chicago: University of Chicago Press, 1943.

Henrikson, Alan K., ed. *Negotiating World Order: The Artisanship and Architecture of Global Diplomacy.* Wilmington, DE: Scholarly Resources, 1986.

Hoyland, John S. *The World in Union.* London: Peace Book, 1940.

Hula, Erich. *Nationalism and Internationalism: European and American Perspectives.* Lanham, MD: University Press of America, 1984.

Hutchins, Robert M., et al. *Preliminary Draft of a World Constitution*, Chicago: University of Chicago Press, 1948.

Jablonsky, David. *Paradigm Lost? Transitions and the Search for a New World Order*. Westport, CT: Praeger, 1995.

Jessup, Philip C. *A Modern Law of Nations*. New York: Macmillan, 1952.

Johnson, Julia E., comp. *Federal World Government*. New York: H. W. Wilson, 1948.

Junger, Ernst. *Der Weltstaat: Organismus und Organisation*. Stuttgart: E. Klett, 1960.

Keeton, George W., and Georg Schwartzenberger. *Making International Law Work*. London: Peace Book, 1939.

Keijser, Johan M. L. F., and Samba Faal. *Political World Union 1962-1981: A Documentary Appraisal*. The Hague: Working Group World Union, 1982.

Kelsen, Hans. *General Theory of Law and the State*. New York: Russell and Russell, 1961.

———. *Law and Peace in International Relations*. Cambridge, MA: Harvard University Press, 1942.

Keys, Donald. *Earth at Omega: Passage to Planetization*. Boston: Branden, 1985.

Kiang, John C. K. *One World: The Approach to Permanent Peace on Earth and General Happiness of Mankind*. Notre Dame, IN: One World, 1992.

Kim, Samuel S. *The Quest for a Just World Order*. Boulder, CO: Westview Press, 1984.

Kothari, Rajni. *Transformation and Survival: In Search of a Humane World Order*. Delhi: Ajanta, 1988.

———. *Footsteps into the Future: Diagnosis of the Present World and a Design for an Alternative*. New York: Free Press, 1975.

Krabbe, Hugo. *The Modern Idea of the State*. New York: Appleton, 1922.

Lanza, Robert, ed. *One World: The Health and Survival of the Human Species in the 21st Century*. Santa Fe, NM: Health Press, 1996.

Laski, Harold J. *A Grammar of Politics*, 4th ed. London: George Allen and Unwin, 1950.

Laursen, Finn. *Unity with Diversity: Federalist Essays (1972-1986)*. Amsterdam: Institute for Global Policy Studies, 1993.

———. *Federalism and World Order: What Makes Wars and How to Organize Peace*. Garden City, New York: Doubleday, Doran & Co., 1973.

Lauterpacht, Hersh. *The Function of Law in the International Community*. Oxford: Clarendon Press, 1933.

Lilienthal, Alfred M. *Which Way to World Government?* New York: Foreign Policy Association, 1950.

Lipsky, Mortimer. *Never Again War: The Case for World Government*. South Brunswick, NJ: A. S. Barnes, 1971.

Lothian, Lord (Philip Kerr). *Pacifism Is Not Enough: Collected Lectures and Speeches*. London: Lothian Foundation Press, 1990.

———. *The Ending of Armageddon*. Oxford: Aldon Press, 1939.

Luard, Evan. *Types of International Society*. New York: Free Press, 1976.

Macleod, Wayne. *Foundations of the World State*. Vancouver: Author, 1986.

Mangone, Gerard J. *The Idea and Practice of World Government*. New York: Columbia University Press, 1951.

Mayne, Richard, and John Pinder. *Federal Union: The Pioneers (A History of Federal Union)*. London: Macmillan, 1990.

McGhee, George C. *International Community: A Goal for a New World Order*. Lanham, MD: University Press of America, 1992.

McKinlay, Robert D. *Global Problems and World Order*. London: Pinter, 1986.

McTavish, Hugh. *Ending War in Our Lifetime: A Concrete, Realistic Plan*. Dixon, KY: West Fork Press, 1994.

Mendlovitz, Saul H., ed. *On the Creation of a Just World Order: Preferred Worlds for the 1990s*. New York: Free Press, 1975.

Millard, Everett L. *Freedom in a Federal World*. Dobbs Ferry, NY: Oceana Publications, 1961.

Mitrany, David. *A Working Peace System*. Chicago: Quadrangle Books, 1966.

Moynihan, Daniel Patrick. *On the Law of Nations*. Cambridge: Harvard University Press, 1990.

Newcombe, Hanna. *Design for a Better World*. Lanham, MD: University Press of America, 1983.

Newcombe, Hanna, and Alan C. Newcombe. *Alternative Paths to World Government*. Dundas, Ontario: Peace Research Institute, 1974.

Newfang, Oscar. *World Government*. New York: Barnes and Noble, 1942.

———. *World Federation*. New York: Barnes and Noble, 1939.

———. *The Road to World Peace: A Federation of Nations*. New York: G. P. Putnam, 1924.

North, Robert Carver. *War, Peace, Survival: Global Politics and Conceptual Synthesis*. Boulder, CO: Westview Press, 1990.

Patterson, Ernest M., ed. *World Government*. Philadelphia: Annals of the American Academy of Political and Social Science, 1949.

Perillier, Louis, and Jean Jacques Tur. *Le Mondialisme*. Paris: PUF, 1977.

Perry, Ralph B. *One World in the Making*. New York: Current Books, 1945.

Pimentel, A. Fonseca. *Democratic World Government and the United Nations*, 2nd ed. Brasilia: Escopo Editions, 1980.

Pinheiro de Vasconcellos, Henrique. *The World State, or, The New Order of Common Sense*. Rio de Janeiro: Grafica Olimpia, 1944.

Publius II (Owen J. Roberts, John F. Schmidt, and Clarence K. Streit). *The New Federalist*. New York: Harper, 1950.

Reves, Emery. *The Anatomy of Peace*, 2nd. ed. New York: Harper, 1945.

Rider, Fremont. *The Great Dilemma of World Organization*. New York: Reynal and Hitchcock, 1946.

Riggs, Robert E., and Jack C. Plano. *The United Nations: International Organization and World Politics*, 2nd ed. Belmont, CA: Wadsworth, 1994.

Righter, Rosemary. *Utopia Lost: The United Nations and World Order*. New York: Twentieth Century Fund Press, 1995.

Robbins, Lionel. *Economic Aspects of Federation*. London: Macmillan, 1941.

Roberts, John. *List of Works on World Federalism*. London: Association of World Federalists, 1990.

Roche, Douglas. *A Bargain for Humanity: Global Security by 2000*. Edmonton: University of Alberta Press, 1993.

Rosenau, James N., and Ernst-Otto Czempiel, eds. *Governance without Government: Order and Change in World Politics*. New York: Cambridge University Press, 1992.

Rotblat, Joseph, ed. *World Citizenship: Allegiance to Humanity*. New York: St. Martin's Press, 1997.

Russell, Bertrand. *Has Man a Future?* New York: Simon and Schuster, 1962.

Scelle, Georges. *Précis de Droit des Gens: Principes et Systématique*. Paris: Centre National de la Recherche Scientifique, 1984.

Schell, Jonathan. *The Fate of the Earth*. New York: Knopf, 1982.

Schiffer, Walter. *The Legal Community of Mankind: Critical Analysis of the Modern Concept of World Organization*. New York: Columbia University Press, 1954.

Scott, George. *The Rise and Fall of the League of Nations*. New York: Macmillan, 1973.

Seitz, John L. *Global Issues: An Introduction*. Oxford: Blackwell, 1995.

Selander, J. B. *World Union Now*. Berkeley, CA: Gazette Press, 1944.

Simai, Mihály. *The Future of Global Governance: Managing Risk and Change in the International System*. Washington DC: U.S. Institute of Peace Press, 1994.

Simon, Geoffrey L. *UN Malaise: Power, Problems and Realpolitik*. New York: St. Martin's Press, 1995.

Sprading, Charles T. *The World State Craze*. Los Angeles: Wetzel, 1954.

Stonier, Tom. *Nuclear Disaster*. Harmondsworth, England: Penguin, 1964.

Strange, Susan. *The Retreat of the State: The Diffusion of Power in the World Economy*. New York: Cambridge University Press, 1996.

Streit, Clarence K. *Union Now: A Proposal for an Atlantic Federal Union of the Free*. New York: Harper, 1949.

———. *World Government or Anarchy? Our Urgent Need for World Order*. Chicago: World Citizens Association, 1939.

Suganami, Hidemi. *The Domestic Analogy and World Order Proposals*. New York: Cambridge University Press, 1989.

Wagar, Warren. *The City of Man: Prophecies of a World Civilization in Twentieth Century Thought*. Boston: Houghton Mifflin, 1963.

Walker, Barbara, compiler. *Uniting the Peoples and the Nations: Readings in World Federalism*. Washington DC: World Federalist Association, 1993.

Walker, R. B. J. *One World, Many Worlds: Struggles for a Just World Peace*. Boulder, CO: Lynne Rienner, 1988.

Weatherford, Roy. *World Peace and the Human Family*. New York: Routledge, 1993.

Weiss, Thomas G., and Leon Gordenker, eds. *NGOs, the UN, and Global Governance*. Boulder, CO: Lynne Rienner, 1996.

Wheare, Kenneth C. *Federal Government*, 4th ed. London: Oxford University Press, 1964.

Wilkie, Wendell. *One World*. New York: Simon and Schuster, 1943.

Williamson, Hugh. *World Government*. London: Chancery Books, 1963.

Wofford, Harris, Jr. *Road to the World Republic: Policy and Strategy for Federalists*. Chicago: Federalist Press, 1948.

———. *It's Up to Us: Federal World Government in Our Time*. New York: Harcourt, Brace, 1946.

Wootton, Barbara. *Socialism and Federation*. London: Macmillan, 1941.

Wynner, Edith. *World Federal Government: Why? What? How?* Afton, NY: Fedonat Press, 1954.

Wynner, Edith, and G. Lloyd. *Searchlight on Peace Plans: Choose Your Road to World Government*. New York: Dutton, 1949.

Yunker, James A. *World Union on the Horizon: The Case for Supernational Federation*. Lanham, MD: University Press of America, 1993.

Zuckerman, Edward. *The Day after World War III*. New York: Viking Press, 1979.

Index

About the Contributors

JEAN-MARIE BRETON, a Judiciary Expert recorded by the Paris Court of Appeals, is Professor in the Institute of Mundialist Studies. He is an Engineer of Arts and Manufactures, Master of Electrical Engineering, and Master of Public Law. He is Secretary-General of the International Registry of Citizens of the World; former Head of the EDP Department, Ministry of Justice of Morocco; and UNESCO Expert in Information Science. He is the author of *l'Emergence du Droit Mondial*.

RICHARD FALK is Albert G. Milbank Professor of International Law and Practice in the Center of International Studies of Princeton University, where he has been on the faculty since 1961. He has been associated with the World Order Project since its founding in the mid-1960s. His most recent books are *Explorations at the Edge of Time: The Prospects for World Order* and *On Humane Governance: Toward a New Global Politics*.

RONALD J. GLOSSOP is Professor of Philosophical Studies and Coordinator of Peace Studies at Southern Illinois University at Edwardsville. He has published over 40 articles in scholarly journals and presented numerous papers at professional meetings. He is the author of *Philosophy: An Introduction to Its Problems and Vocabulary*; *Confronting War: An Examination of Humanity's Most Pressing Problem*; and *World Federation? A Critical Analysis of Federal World Government*.

DAVID RAY GRIFFIN is Professor of Philosophy and Religion at the Claremont School of Theology and Claremont Graduate School (Claremont, California). He is the author and editor of several books, including *Evil Revisited*, *Spirituality and Society: Postmodern Visions*, and *Unsnarling the World-Knot: Consciousness, Freedom, and the Mind-Body Problem*. He is currently working on a multi-volume project tentatively entitled *The Divine Cry of Our Time:*

Theology for a Peaceable and Sustainable Human Existence, a theological-political argument for the possibility and necessity of a global democratic government.

ERROL E. HARRIS was John Evans Professor of Moral and Intellectual Philosophy at Northwestern University (now Emeritus); formerly Professor of Philosophy at the University of the Witwatersrand (Johannesburg); Roy Roberts Distinguished Professor of Philosophy at the University of Kansas; Cowling Professor at Carlton College; and Distinguished Visiting Professor of Christian Philosophy at Villanova University. In 1978 he was a research fellow in the Institute for Advanced Studies in the Humanities at Edinburgh University. He is the author of over 70 articles and book chapters, and of 24 books on philosophy and political theory, of which the three most relevant to the present volume are: *The Survival of Political Man: A Study in the Principles of International Order*; *Annihilation or Utopia: The Principles of International Politics*; and *One World or None: A Prescription for Survival*.

PHILIP ISELY is Professor of World Problems and World Government in the Graduate School of World Problems. He is Secretary-General of the World Constitution and Parliament Association, and for many years has been foremost in organizing meetings of the World Constituent Assembly and the Provisional World Parliament.

GLEN T. MARTIN is Associate Professor of Philosophy and Religious Studies at Radford University in Virginia. He is founder of the program in Peace and World Security Studies at Radford University, an active member of the World Constitution and Parliament Association, and currently President of International Philosophers for Peace, the Prevention of Nuclear Omnicide, and Other Threats to Global Existence. He is author of *From Nietzsche to Wittgenstein: The Problem of Truth and Nihilism in the Modern World*, as well as many articles and reviews on a variety of topics in comparative philosophy, the spirituality of human liberation, and global social issues.

JOHN C. de V. ROBERTS, by training a historian, is Emeritus Professor of International Studies, and French-Canadian university professor. He has been sometime Magistrate in Middlesex. For 17 years he was editor of *World Federalist*, the UK bulletin; formerly chairing the World Federalist Movement. He is ex-secretary to the *Edition of Works of Sir Walter Raleigh*, and author of *Devon and the Armada*, *World Citizenship and Mundialism*, and a dozen current affairs pamphlets, including "Twenty-five Years to a Governed World." He is coauthor of *The Pioneer*, a history of the British World Federalist Movement.

JAMES A. YUNKER is Professor of Economics at Western Illinois University in Macomb, where he teaches economic theory, econometrics and comparative systems. For the last 20 years his primary research interest has been market socialism, and, in addition to many articles on the subject, in 1992 he published the book *Socialism Revised and Modernized: The Case for Pragmatic Market Socialism*. This was followed in 1993 by *World Union on the Horizon: The Case for Supernational Federation*.

ISBN 0-275-96417-5

HARDCOVER BAR CODE